DRIVING STANDARDS AGENCY

D0539442

2.∞

THE OFFICIAL

THEORY TEST
for Car Drivers
and Motorcyclists

**Including the questions and answers
valid for tests taken from 6 July 1998**

London: The Stationery Office

Written and compiled by the Publications Unit of the Driving Standards Agency

Questions and answers compiled by the National Foundation for Educational Research

Illustrations by Vicky Squires

Published by The Stationery Office.

© Crown Copyright 1998

Reprinted with amendments 1998

Published with the permission of the Driving Standards Agency on behalf of the Controller of Her Majesty's Stationery Office Applications for reproduction should be made in writing to The Copyright Unit, Her Majesty's Stationery Office, St Clements House, 2–16 Colegate, Norwich NR3 1BQ

First edition Crown copyright 1996

ISBN 0 11 552017 1

A CIP catalogue record for this book is available from the British Library

Acknowledgements

The Driving Standards Agency would like to thank the following for their assistance:

National Foundation for Educational Research

Transport Research Laboratory

Department of Environment, Transport and the Regions

Driver and Vehicle Testing Agency, Northern Ireland

The staff of the Driving Standards Agency

The Driving Standards Agency (DSA) is an executive agency of the Department of Environment, Transport and the Regions (DETR). You'll see its logo at test centres.

DRIVING
STANDARDS
AGENCY

"Safe driving for life"

The aim of DSA is to promote road safety through the advancement of driving standards.

DSA

- conducts practical driving tests for drivers or riders of cars, motorcycles, lorries, buses and other vehicles

- plans, maintains and supervises the theory test for drivers or riders of cars, motorcycles, lorries and buses

- controls the register of Approved Driving Instructors (ADIs)

- controls the voluntary register of Large Goods Vehicle (LGV) trainers

- supervises Compulsory Basic Training (CBT) courses for motorcyclists

- aims to provide a high-quality service to its customers.

DVTA

The Driver and Vehicle Testing Agency (DVTA) is an Executive Agency within the Department of the Environment for Northern Ireland. Its primary aim is to promote and improve road safety through the advancement of driving standards and implementation of the Government's policies for improving the mechanical standards of vehicles.

With the ever-increasing volume of traffic on today's roads, it's important to make sure that new drivers have a broad spread of driving knowledge. Since July 1996 new car drivers and motorcycle riders have been required to pass a separate theory test before obtaining a full driving licence. This is a major step towards improving road safety in the UK.

This book is intended to help new drivers prepare for the theory test. An extensive knowledge of driving theory will help towards a better understanding of practical driving skills. This is necessary to become a safe and confident driver.

The performance of all aspects of the theory test is continually monitored and as a result the question bank has been updated. This book contains the theory test question bank, set out in an easy-to-read style with plenty of illustrations. To assist preparation for the test it explains why the answers are correct and identifies good driving practice.

There are other books in the Driving Skills series that will help you to develop your skills:

The Driving Manual
The Motorcycling Manual
The Driving Test

All are published by The Stationery Office.

The Stationery Office also publishes a range of videos, which are designed to explain what to expect during the tests and to dispel some of the myths associated with it. A fully interactive CD-ROM, *Driving Skills: The Theory Test and Beyond* (version ii) is also available to help you to develop your knowledge using this modern approach to learning.

Robin Cummins

The Chief Driving Examiner
Driving Standards Agency

This book will help you to

▶ study for your theory test
▶ prepare and help you to pass

Part One gives you information on how to get started.

Part Two tells you about the question paper and how to answer it.

Part Three shows you the questions that may be used on your test. Don't worry, you won't have to answer all of them. Your paper will have 35 questions.

The questions are in the left-hand column with a choice of answers beneath. On the right of the page you'll find the correct answers and a brief explanation of why the answers are correct.

Books for study

Although this book helps to explain the answers, you should study other publications that cover the subjects in more detail. Buy and study a copy of *The Highway Code* (The Stationery Office). Don't borrow one, buy your own copy then you can be sure it is up to date. DSA's *The Driving Manual* explains driving skills in more detail, and *Know Your Traffic Signs* is highly recommended (both published by The Stationery Office). Practice papers are also available.

These books will help you to answer the questions correctly and will also guide you when studying for your practical test. Keep them so that you can refer to them throughout your driving life. You can find them in any good bookshop, together with relevant books from other publishers.

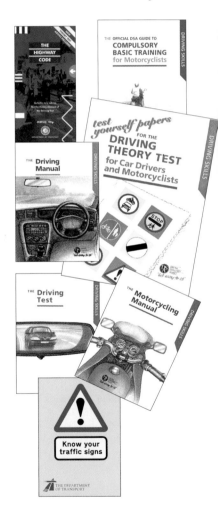

DSA THEORY TEST for car drivers and motorcyclists

It's important that you study – not just to pass the test but to become a safe driver.

To ensure that all candidates are tested fairly, questions used in the theory test are under continuous review. Some of the questions used will be changed periodically to reflect changes in legislation, or as a result of customer feedback. If you take the theory test you may find questions that don't appear in this book. The information needed to answer them is readily available in the series of Driving Skills products and The Highway Code.

Driving is a life skill.

Your tests are just the beginning.

When you pass your test you will be given a certificate. This has a life of 2 years from the date of your test. You will have to take and pass your practical test within this 2 years. If you don't, you will have to take and pass the theory test again before a booking for a practical test can be accepted.

Some of the questions in this book give 'correct answers' that don't apply to Northern Ireland.

 These are marked with NI and an explanation is given in the text.

If you're a motorcycle rider there will be some specific questions on motorcycling. In this book those questions are marked with a motorcycle symbol.

If you want to drive a car

DSA approves instructors to teach learner drivers for payment. These instructors have their standards checked regularly.

Approved Driving Instructors (ADIs) must

- pass a series of difficult examinations

- reach a high standard of instruction

- be registered with DSA or DVTA

- display an Approved Driving Instructor's certificate (except in Northern Ireland).

These professional instructors will give you guidance on

- what books to read

- your practical skills

- how to study and practise

- when you're ready for your tests

- further training after passing your practical test.

DSA and the main bodies representing ADIs place great emphasis on professional standards and business ethics. A code of practice has been created setting a framework within which all instructors should operate. Details of this can be obtained from DSA headquarters Tel: 0115 901 2500

It isn't necessary for someone to be on the ADI register to give training for the theory test alone. You may find a training course to help you to prepare for the test. Look in your local paper or visit your local library for information.

There are also videos and CD-ROMs available to help you to study. The CD-ROM *Driving Skills: The Theory Test and Beyond* helps you to learn interactively and goes beyond the theory test, teaching you driving skills for life. There are also practice theory test papers that have been produced by various companies. Visit your local bookshop or ask your driving instructor about relevant material.

If you want to ride a motorcycle

Before you take your practical motorcycle test you must attend and successfully complete a Compulsory Basic Training (CBT) course (except in Northern Ireland). CBT courses can only be given by training bodies approved by DSA. Frequent checks are made to ensure a high standard of instruction.

The course will include

- classroom training

- practical skills training.

You can find out about CBT courses from

- your local Road Safety Officer

- your motorcycle dealer

- DSA Tel: 0115 901 2595.

DSA also publish *The Official DSA Guide to Compulsory Basic Training for Motorcyclists* (The Stationery Office) which will give you details about the course.

You'll have to answer specific questions on motorcycling in the theory test. DSA's *The Motorcycling Manual* (The Stationery Office) tells you about motorcycling skills in more detail. Books from other publishers are also available. In addition, buy

and read a copy of *The Highway Code.* Keep it and refer to it after you've passed your tests. Make sure that you have the latest copy as it's updated periodically.

Applying for your licence

You'll need to apply for a provisional driving licence as you must produce it at the theory test centre. An application form (D1) can be obtained from any post office.

When you receive your provisional licence sign it immediately. Don't drive until you've done so.

Residency requirements

You can't take a test or obtain a full licence unless you are normally resident in this country. Normal residence means the place where you reside because of personal or occupational ties. However, if you moved to the United Kingdom (UK) having recently been permanently resident in another state of the EC/EEA (European Economic Area), you must have been normally resident in the UK for 185 days in the 12 months prior to your application for a full driving licence.

About the theory test

The actual delivery of the test is undertaken by DriveSafe Services Ltd, although DSA has overall responsibility for managing the theory test operation.

The theory test is straightforward and you'll pass if you're well prepared. You need to have a knowledge of *The Highway Code* and understand the principles of road safety.

Does everyone have to take the theory test?

If you don't hold a full UK or full EEA licence you'll have to take a theory test. If you hold a full licence for another category of vehicle you may not have to take the test. Holders of a full car licence who wish to obtain a motorcycle licence don't have to take the theory test. Nor will holders of a full motorcycle licence who require a full car licence. If you passed a theory test and then a practical moped test then you won't have to take the theory test again in order to upgrade to a car or motorcycle licence.

Can I take my practical test first?

No. You have to take and pass your theory test before a booking for the practical test is accepted.

Will I be asked to do lots of writing?

No. The question paper is designed so that you only have to put a cross against the answers you think are correct.

How many questions are there?

There are 35 questions in the paper. You should try to answer all of them.

How long do I have to complete the test?

Each test session lasts for 40 minutes. You can take all this time if you need to, and there will be a clock in the room to remind you of the time. The invigilator will also tell you when there are five minutes left.

Where do I have to go to take the test?

There are over 150 test centres throughout England, Scotland, Wales and Northern Ireland. Most people have a test centre within 20 miles of their home, but this will vary depending on the density of the population. You can find a list of test centres at the back of this book or telephone the information line 0870 01 01 372.

When are the test centres open?

Sessions are provided on weekdays, evenings and on Saturdays. However, where demand is less than 100 tests per year test sessions may be less frequent.

Will I know the result straight away?

Not straight away, but you'll be informed in about seven to ten days.

Some centres provide a facility for results while you wait, at a premium fee. You can ask about this service when you book your test.

If I don't pass when can I take the test again?

You will have to wait a minimum of three days before you take the test again. If you fail your test you've shown that you aren't fully prepared. Good preparation will save you time and money.

Is the test only available in English?

No. The paper is available in the following languages

English	Chinese
Gujarati	Welsh
Hindi	Bengali
Punjabi	Urdu

If you can speak English but can't read in the languages provided a member of staff will be available to read through the test on a one-to-one basis. State this on your application form or ask the operator when you call to book your test.

Can I bring a translator with me?

Yes. If you can't read or write any of the languages available you're allowed to bring a translator with you when you take your test. You can only bring a translator who's approved by DSA. You should tell the booking office that you intend to bring a translator with you.

Are there any provisions for special needs?

Every effort has been made to ensure that the theory test can be taken by all candidates. It's important that you state your needs when booking so that the necessary arrangements can be made.

If you're dyslexic or have difficulty with reading, don't worry. You may be allowed double the normal time to take the test or have the paper read to you if it's necessary. In order that DSA can provide you with these additional services, we will require a letter from a teacher or educationalist, a psychologist or doctor (if appropriate) which confirms your special needs. If it isn't possible to get this confirmation from a relevant professional, DSA will consider a statement from an independent person who knows something about your reading ability. This could be your employer, but if you're unsure about who to ask

A DriveSafe booking operator

telephone the theory test information line 0870 01 01 372 and ask for the special needs department

Post or fax your documentation as soon as possible, along with your booking reference number or driving licence number to the following address

Special Needs
DSA
PO Box 445
Coventry
CV1 2ZZ

Fax: 0870 0104 372

DSA are unable to take responsibility for the safe return of any original documentation sent, so it is advisable to send copies only.

If you're deaf and also have difficulty reading, a British Sign Language signer or lip-speaker can be provided. If you have any physical disability that could prevent you marking the boxes on the test paper help will be available for you.

If you require wheelchair access and your nearest test centre doesn't provide this DSA will arrange for you to take the test at a suitable location, such as a library or job centre or take you to another test centre where the facilities are provided. Telephone the theory test information line for more details.

How do I book a test?

Application forms are available from

- theory test centres

- driving test centres

- your Approved Driving Instructor.

The easiest way to book a test is by telephone, using your credit or debit card. If you book by this method you'll be given the date and time of your test immediately. You can do this by calling 0870 01 01 372 at any time between 8 am and 6 pm Monday to Friday. When you phone you should have ready your

- DVLA driving licence number

- credit or debit card details.

If you're deaf and need a minicom machine ring 0870 01 06 372.

Welsh speakers can ring 0870 01 00 372.

You'll be given a booking number. Take this, together with your signed driving licence and photo identity, when you attend your theory test.

For information about cancelling a test please refer to page 411.

At the test centre

Make sure that you have all the necessary documents with you. You'll need

- your signed driving licence
- your appointment card or booking number
- photo identity **if your licence does not show your photograph.**

The form of photographic identification acceptable at both theory and practical tests are as follows

- **your passport**, which doesn't have to be a British passport
- **cheque guarantee card or credit card** with your signature and photograph
- **an employer's identity or workplace pass** with your photograph and name or signature or both
- **Trade Union Card** with your photograph and signature
- **Student Union Card** with reference to either the NUS or an education establishment/course reference number. The card must display your photograph or signature or both
- **School Bus Pass** with the name of the issuing authority and your photograph and signature

I _____ (name of certifier), certify that this is a true likeness of _____, who has been known to me for (number) months / years in my capacity as _____

Signed

Dated

- **card issued in connection with sale and purchase of reduced price railway tickets** with the name of the issuing authority. This is a card issued by a Railway Authority or other authorised body to purchase a reduced price railway ticket (e.g. a Young Persons Railcard).
- **Gun Licence**, including a Firearm or Shotgun Certificate which bears your photograph and signature
- **Proof of Age Card** issued by the Portman Group with your photograph and signature
- **a Standard Acknowledgement Letter (SAL)** issued by the Home Office with your photograph and signature.

No photo
No licence
No test

If you don't have any of these you can bring a photograph, together with a statement that it's a true likeness of you. This can be signed by any of the following

- Approved Driving Instructor

- DSA-certified motorcycle instructor

- Member of Parliament

- medical practitioner

- local authority councillor

- teacher (qualified)

- Justice of the Peace

- civil servant (established)

- police officer

- bank official

- minister of religion

- barrister or solicitor

- Commissioned Officer in Her Majesty's Forces.

- LGV Trainers on the DSA Voluntary Register of LGV Instructors

If you don't bring these documents on the day you won't be able to take your test and you'll lose your fee. If you have any queries about what photographic evidence we will accept, contact the enquiry line.

Arrive in plenty of time so that you aren't rushed. The test centre staff will check your documents and ensure that you have the right category test paper to complete. If you arrive after the session has started you will not be allowed to sit the test.

Information by fax

DSA provide information by fax. If you have a fax machine dial the information number you require.

0336 800 PLUS:

Practical test appointment availability	-150
Booking a theory test	-151
Booking a practical test for a car or motorcycle	-152
A mock theory test	-153
Hints and tips on how to pass the practical test	-154
Take a practice test by phone	-155

THEORY TEST FOR DRIVERS

PRACTICE QUESTIONS

Surname

First Names

Booking Ref.   88

Pro. Licence No.

                              ENGLISH M.V.
Centre No.

Date   D D M M Y Y Y Y

Time   H H M M

GENERAL INSTRUCTIONS
1. For each question you must find the right answer(s) and mark an X in the box next to it.
2. Do not write any comments on your test paper.
3. Two examples have been done to show you how to mark your answers.
4. If you make a mistake cross out your original choice completely and mark your other choice as shown.

EXAMPLES

E1 You are invited to a pub lunch. You know that you will have to drive in the evening. You are advised to

Mark one answer
a avoid mixing your alcoholic drinks
b not drink any alcohol at all
c have some milk before drinking alcohol
d eat a hot meal with your alcoholic drinks

E2 You are approaching a roundabout. There are horses just ahead of you. You should

Mark two answers
a treat them like any other vehicle
b be prepared to stop
c give them plenty of room
d accelerate past them as quickly as possible
e sound your horn as a warning

P1 The pictured vehicle is 'Environmentally Friendly' because it

Mark three answers
a reduces noise pollution
b use diesel fuel
c uses electricity
d uses unleaded fuel
e reduces parking spaces
f reduces town traffic

P2 You see an elderly pedestrian about to cross the road ahead. You should

Mark one answer
a expect them to wait for you to pass
b speed up to get past them quickly
c stop and wave them across the road
d be careful, they may misjudge your speed

P3 Motorcyclists are more at risk from other road users because they

Mark one answer
a are less experienced then other drivers
b are more likely to break down than other motorists
c are always faster than other drivers
d are more difficult to see than other vehicles

P4 You are approaching this cyclist. You should

Mark one answer
a overtake before the cyclist gets to the junction
b flash your headlights at the cyclist
c slow down and allow the cyclist to turn
d overtake the cyclist on the left hand side

11 A vehicle has a flashing green light. What does this mean?

Mark one answer

a ☒ A doctor is answering an emergency call

b ☒ The vehicle is slow moving

c ☒ It is a motorway police patrol vehicle

d ☒ A vehicle is carrying hazardous chemicals

12 You MUST obey signs giving orders. These signs are mostly in

Mark one answer

a ☒ blue rectangles

b ☒ green rectangles

c ☒ red triangles

d ☒ red circles

13 Another driver does something that upsets you. You should

Mark one answer

a ☒ try not to react

b ☒ let them know how you feel

c ☒ flash your headlamps several times

d ☒ sound your horn

14 You are driving behind a cyclist. You wish to turn left just ahead. You should

Mark one answer

a ☒ overtake the cyclist before the junction

b ☒ pull alongside the cyclist and stay level until after the junction

c ☒ hold back until the cyclist has passed the junction

d ☒ go around the cyclist on the junction

15 Which TWO of the following are correct? When overtaking at night you should

Mark two answers

a ☒ wait until a bend so you can see the oncoming headlights

b ☒ sound your horn twice before moving out

c ☒ be careful because you can see less

d ☒ beware of bends in the road ahead

e ☒ put headlights on full beam

I

1 Which sign means no overtaking?

Mark one answer

a ☒

b ☒

c ☒

d ☒

2 You are turning left into a side road. Pedestrians are crossing the road near the junction. You must

Mark one answer

a ☒ wave them on

b ☒ sound your horn

c ☒ wait for them to cross

d ☒ switch on your hazard lights

3 As a car driver, which THREE lanes must you NOT use?

Mark three answers

a ☒ Crawler lane

b ☒ Bus lane at the times shown

c ☒ Overtaking lane

d ☒ Acceleration lane

e ☒ Cycle lane

f ☒ Tram lane

4 You are driving at night and are dazzled by the headlights of an oncoming car. You should

Mark one answer

a ☒ slow down or stop

b ☒ close your eyes

c ☒ flash your headlights

d ☒ pull down the sun visor

5 What does this sign mean?

Mark one answer

a ☒ Through traffic use left lane

b ☒ Right-hand lane T junction only

c ☒ Right-hand lane closed ahead

d ☒ 11 ton weight limit

On the front of the paper you'll find some practice questions. You'll be given time to look at and attempt these before the test begins.

There will be different types of questions in the paper. Most of them will ask you to mark ONE correct answer from four. Other questions will ask for TWO or more correct answers from a selection. Some of the questions will show you a picture. This is to test your knowledge of traffic signs or your ability to spot a hazard. Look at the question carefully.

The questions will cover a variety of topics relating to road safety. Mark the box alongside the answers you think are correct.

Some questions will take longer to answer than others. The questions won't try to trick you. If you're well prepared you won't find them difficult. Take your time and read the questions carefully. You're given plenty of time, so relax and don't rush. Try to answer all 35 questions.

If you have learning difficulties, don't worry – you may be given extra time to complete your question paper.

When you think you've finished look at the paper again and check your answers before you hand the paper in.

If you're taking a motorcycle theory test

As well as questions that apply to all road users, you'll be asked some specific questions on motorcycling matters.

The topics covered in the question paper

ALERTNESS

The need to be alert and attentive when driving or riding. You must consider

- **Observation**   looking all around for other road users and pedestrians.

- **Anticipation**   looking ahead and giving yourself enough time to react to hazards.

- **Concentration**   being alert at all times when driving or riding.

- **Awareness**   understanding the actions of other road users.

- **Distraction**   not becoming distracted whilst driving or riding. Your attention must be on the road.

ATTITUDE

Your attitude will affect your driving. Attitude consists of

- **Consideration** considering other road users. Be positive but treat them as you would wish to be treated.

- **Positioning** not following too closely. As well as being dangerous, it can feel threatening to the driver in front.

- **Courtesy** treating other road users as colleagues or team members. They too are trying to complete their journey safely.

- **Priority** being aware that all rules on priority won't always be followed by other road users. Try to be calm and tolerant if other drivers or riders break the rules.

SAFETY AND YOUR VEHICLE

To prevent your vehicle endangering lives you must ensure that it's in good condition. You should be aware of

- **Fault detection** being able to detect minor faults on your vehicle.

- **Defects** an unroadworthy vehicle which might endanger your passengers or other road users.

- **Safety equipment** if you need to use safety equipment you should know the correct way to use it.

- **Emissions** your vehicle must comply with correct emissions regulations.

- **Noise** vehicles are noisy. Prevent excessive noise, especially at night.

SAFETY MARGINS

You must be aware of the safety margins when driving in all conditions. You should consider

- **Stopping distances**   leaving enough room to stop in all conditions.

- **Road surfaces**   being aware of uneven or slippery surfaces.

- **Skidding**   preventing a skid is most important, but you should also be aware of how to react in the event of you losing control of your vehicle.

- **Weather conditions**   realising that weather conditions will have an effect on how your vehicle behaves.

HAZARD AWARENESS

Your good judgement and perception of the road ahead will lessen the risk of an accident. You should keep in mind

- **Anticipation**   planning ahead to prevent last-second reactions.

- **Hazard awareness**   recognising a hazard ahead and preparing yourself for it.

- **Attention**   looking out for problems ahead when you're driving or riding.

- **Speed and distance**   travelling at the correct speed for the situation. Leave enough distance to react if a problem arises.

- **Reaction time**   being aware that you need time to react.

- **Alcohol and drugs**   these will affect your reaction time.

- **Tiredness**   don't drive or ride if you're tired. You need to be alert at all times.

VULNERABLE ROAD USERS

Others on the road may need more time or room. Potential hazards to consider are

- **Pedestrians**   be aware of their actions as they cross the road.

- **Children**   particularly unpredictable on and around roads.

- **People with disabilities**   might not be able to react to danger as quickly or easily as the able-bodied.

- **Motorcyclists**   be aware of their presence on the road.

- **Cyclists**   may need to swerve to avoid obstructions or poor road surfaces, and are often affected by weather conditions.

- **Horse riders**   animals can be unpredictable and may move rather slowly.

OTHER TYPES OF VEHICLE

Other vehicles might behave differently on the road. You should consider

- **Motorcycles**   need as much room as a car.

- **Lorries**   are larger and need more room on the road.

- **Buses**   are usually large and might make frequent stops.

VEHICLE HANDLING

You need to adapt your driving or riding to the different conditions on the road. You should be aware of

- **Weather conditions**   wet or icy roads will affect the handling of your vehicle.

- **Road conditions**   the road surface may affect your vehicle.

- **Time of day**   hazards when driving or riding at night.

- **Speed**   it's more difficult to control your vehicle at high speeds.

- **Traffic calming**   measures to slow down traffic where there are pedestrians.

MOTORWAY RULES

You must know the rules that apply to you and your vehicle on the motorway. Factors to consider are

- **Speed limits**   being aware of the speed restrictions on the motorway.

- **Lane discipline** keeping to the left unless overtaking.

- **Stopping**   knowing when and where you can stop on the motorway.

- **Lighting**   being aware of the importance of being seen.

- **Parking**   not parking on the motorway unless in an emergency.

RULES OF THE ROAD

You should know the rules of the road. Aspects include

- **Speed limits**   being aware of the speed limits for different types of vehicle.

- **Parking**   choosing a sensible place to park.

- **Lighting**   not letting your vehicle become a hazard.

ROAD AND TRAFFIC SIGNS

Traffic signs are a means of giving messages to road users. You should know what they mean. You should consider

- **Road signs**   they tell you about the road ahead.

- **Speed limits**   recognise signs showing speed limits.

- **Road markings** directions might be painted on the road surface.

- **Regulations**   these can be shown to you by means of a road sign.

DOCUMENTS

You and your vehicle must be licenced to be on the road. The documents you'll need include

- **Licence**   you must know what the law requires.

- **Insurance**   you must have the cover you need to drive or ride.

- **MOT**   you should be aware of the safety checks your vehicle must
  certificate   undergo to gain an MOT certificate.

ACCIDENTS

You should know what to do if you arrive at or are involved in an accident. You should be aware of

- **First Aid**   if you're qualified and fit, your fast, effective action
                       might save a life.

- **Warning**   knowing how to warn other road users of an accident.
  devices

- **Reporting**   knowing where and when to report an accident.
  procedures

- **Safety**   knowing what to do if a vehicle carrying hazardous
  regulations   loads is involved in an accident.

VEHICLE LOADING

You should be aware of the the importance of secure loads. You should consider

- **Stability**   making sure that your load doesn't affect the stability of
                       your vehicle.

- **Towing**   being aware of the effects of towing a trailer and the rules
                       that apply.

About Part Three

In this part of the book you'll find questions that might be used in your theory test. The answers have been provided to help you to study.

For easy reference and to help you to study, the questions have been divided into topics and put into sections. Although this isn't how you'll find them on your question paper it's helpful if you want to refer to particular subjects.

The questions are in the left-hand column with a choice of answers beneath. On the right-hand side of the page you'll find the correct answers and a brief explanation of why the answers are correct. There will also be some advice on correct driving procedures.

DON'T JUST LEARN THE ANSWERS. It's important that you know **why** the answers are correct. This will help you with your practical skills and prepare you to become a safe and confident driver.

Taking exams or tests is rarely a pleasant experience but you can make it easier by being confident that you have the knowledge to answer the questions correctly.

Make studying more fun by involving friends and relations. Take part in a question-and-answer game. Test those 'experienced' drivers who've had their licence a while: they might learn something too!

If you're taking a motorcycle theory test

In this part of the book the specific
 questions for motorcyclists are marked with a motorcycle symbol.

Most of the other questions refer to all road users, so you should study these too. Some will appear on your paper with slight changes, for example 'rider' instead of 'driver' or 'headlight' instead of 'headlights'.

This section looks at alertness and attention when you're driving.

The questions will ask you about

- observation
- anticipation
- concentration
- awareness
- distraction
- boredom.

Question 1.1

When turning your car in the road you should

Mark one answer

- ☒ overhang the kerb
- ☒ use a driveway if possible
- ☒ check all around for other road users
- ☒ keep your hand on the handbrake throughout.

Answer

✖ check all around for other road users

There might be an occasion when you need to turn your car around to face the opposite way. Ensure that you're fully aware of other road users by practising good observation. The road you intend to turn around in shouldn't be busy. If it is, find a quiet side road to turn in.

Question 1.2

Before you make a U-turn in the road you should

Mark one answer

- ☒ look over your shoulder for a final check
- ☒ signal so that other drivers can slow down for you
- ☒ give arm signals as well as use your indicators
- ☒ select a higher gear than normal.

Answer

✖ look over your shoulder for a final check

If you want to make a U-turn, slow down and ensure that the road is clear in both directions. Make sure that the road is wide enough to carry out the manoeuvre safely.

Question 1.3

To move off safely from a parked position you should

Mark one answer

- ☒ signal if other drivers will need to slow down
- ☒ NOT look round if there is a parked vehicle close in front of you
- ☒ give a hand signal as well as using your indicators
- ☒ use your mirrors and look round for a final check.

Answer

✖ use your mirrors and look round for a final check

When moving off from the side of the road you should always use your mirrors. Look all around for a final check. There may be a road user you haven't seen in your mirrors.

Question 1.4

To move off safely from a parked position you should

Mark one answer

☒ signal if other drivers will need to slow down

☒ NOT look round if there is a parked vehicle close in front of you

☒ give a hand signal as well as using your indicators

☒ look over your shoulder for a final check.

Answer

✖ **look over your shoulder for a final check**

If you're intending to move off from the side of the road on a motorcycle you must take a final look around over your shoulder. There may be another road user not visible in your mirrors.

Question 1.5

You are parked on the left. Before you move off you should

Mark one answer

☒ signal right before looking behind and selecting a gear

☒ check mirrors and look round for a final check

☒ rely only on mirrors when looking behind for other traffic

☒ always wait for oncoming traffic to be out of sight.

Answer

✖ **check mirrors and look round for a final check**

Always make your safety checks as a routine. Look over your shoulder as well as looking in your mirrors. There could be a blind spot hiding an unseen hazard.

Wait for a safe gap in the traffic before you move off and look over your shoulder again just before doing so.

Question 1.6

As a driver what does the term 'Blind Spot' mean?

Mark one answer

☒ An area covered by your right hand mirror.

☒ An area not covered by your headlamps.

☒ An area covered by your left hand mirror.

☒ An area not seen in your mirrors.

Answer

✖ **An area not seen in your mirrors.**

Modern vehicles today provide the driver with well positioned mirrors which are essential to driving safely. However, they cannot see every angle of the scene behind. It is essential you are aware of this and check over your shoulder to eliminate any dangers not reflected in your mirrors.

Question 1.7

Objects hanging from your interior mirror may

Mark two answers

- [ ] restrict your view
- [ ] improve your driving
- [ ] distract your attention
- [ ] help your concentration

Answers

- ☒ **restrict your view**
- ☒ **distract your attention**

Ensure that you can see clearly through the windscreen of your vehicle. Stickers or hanging objects could affect your field of vision or draw you eyes away from the road .

Question 1.8

The interior mirror of your car should be adjusted so that you can see

Mark one answer

- [ ] through the rear window especially to the nearside
- [ ] straight through the rear side window
- [ ] the rear window and what is happening on the rear seat
- [ ] through the rear window especially to the offside.

Answer

- ☒ **through the rear window especially to the offside**

Before you move off make sure that your mirrors are clean and adjusted to give you the best possible view of the road behind. You should be able to get a good view without having to move your head. Do this as a matter of routine.

Question 1.9

When riding, you find your shoulders obstruct your mirrors. To overcome this you should

Mark one answer

- [ ] extend the mirror arms
- [ ] fit smaller mirrors
- [ ] use your indicators earlier than normal
- [ ] not use the mirrors.

Answer

- ☒ **extend the mirror arms**

It's essential that you have a clear view all around. Check the position of the mirrors before you move off.

Question 1.10

You want to change lanes in busy, moving traffic. Why could looking over your shoulder help?

Mark two answers

- [ ] Mirrors may not cover blind spots.
- [ ] To avoid having to give a signal.
- [ ] So traffic ahead will make room for you.
- [ ] So your balance will not be affected.
- [ ] Following motorists would be warned.

Answers

- [X] **Mirrors may not cover blind spots.**
- [X] **Following motorists would be warned.**

Before you change lanes you need to know that there's a safe gap to move into. Looking over your shoulder

- allows you to see into the area not covered by the mirrors and which could hide another vehicle
- warns following motorists that you want to change lanes.

Question 1.11

You are about to turn right. What should you do just before you turn?

Mark one answer

- [ ] Give the correct signal.
- [ ] Take a 'lifesaver' glance over your shoulder.
- [ ] Select the correct gear.
- [ ] Get in position ready for the turn.

Answer

- [X] **Take a 'lifesaver' glance over your shoulder.**

When you're turning right plan your approach to the junction. Signal and select the correct gear in good time. Just before you turn give a 'lifesaver' glance to the rear for a final check behind and alongside.

Question 1.12

What, according to *The Highway Code*, do the letters MSM mean?

Mark one answer

- [ ] Mirror, signal, manoeuvre.
- [ ] Manoeuvre, signal, mirror.
- [ ] Mirror, speed, manoeuvre.
- [ ] Manoeuvre, speed, mirror.

Answer

- [X] **Mirror, signal, manoeuvre.**

Always use the MSM routine when you're approaching a hazard.

Use your mirrors to check the position of traffic around you. Signal your intention to change course or slow down. Do this in good time. A 'manoeuvre' is any change of speed or position, from slowing or stopping the car to turning off a busy main road.

Question 1.13

What is the 'lifesaver' when riding a motorcycle?

Mark one answer

☒ A certificate every motorcyclist must have.

☒ A final, rearward glance before changing direction.

☒ A part of the motorcycle tool kit.

☒ A mirror fitted to check blind spots.

Answer

✖ **A final, rearward glance before changing direction.**

This action makes you aware of what's happening behind and alongside. This glance should be timed so that you still have time to react if it isn't safe to perform the manoeuvre.

Question 1.14

What is the safest way to brake?

Mark one answer

☒ Brake lightly, then harder as you begin to stop, then ease off just before stopping.

☒ Brake hard, put your gear lever into neutral and pull your handbrake on just before stopping.

☒ Brake lightly, push your clutch pedal down and pull your handbrake on just before stopping.

☒ Put your gear lever into neutral, brake hard, then ease off just before stopping.

Answer

✖ **Brake lightly, then harder as you begin to stop, then ease off just before stopping.**

Try to plan ahead so you don't need to brake harshly. Brake lightly, then harder as you begin to stop, then ease off just before stopping. Don't put your gear lever into neutral until you come to a complete stop, as this might cause a loss of control.

Question 1.15

You are driving on a wet road. You have to stop your vehicle in an emergency. You should

Mark one answer

☒ apply the handbrake and footbrake together

☒ keep both hands on the wheel

☒ select reverse gear

☒ give an arm signal.

Answer

✖ **keep both hands on the wheel**

As you drive look well ahead and all around so that you're ready for any hazards that might occur. There may be occasions when you have to stop in an emergency. React as soon as you can whilst keeping control of the vehicle.

You see road signs showing a sharp bend ahead. What should you do?

Mark one answer

- ☒ Continue at the same speed.
- ☒ Slow down as you go around the bend.
- ☒ Slow down as you come out of the bend.
- ☒ Slow down before the bend.

Answer

☒ Slow down before the bend.

Road signs might give you warning of a hazard ahead. Always look and plan well ahead. This will avoid the need for late, harsh braking. Your vehicle should be moving in a straight line when you brake. This will ensure maximum control when dealing with the hazard.

As you approach this bridge you should

Mark three answers

- ☒ move into the middle of the road to get a better view
- ☒ slow down
- ☒ get over the bridge as quickly as possible
- ☒ consider using your horn
- ☒ find another route
- ☒ beware of pedestrians.

Answers

☒ slow down

☒ consider using your horn

☒ beware of pedestrians

This sign gives you a warning. You can't see over the bridge for oncoming traffic so you must be cautious; slow right down. Consider the hidden hazards and be ready to react if necessary.

When following a large vehicle you should keep well back because

Mark one answer

- ☒ it allows the driver to see you in his mirrors
- ☒ it helps the large vehicle to stop more easily
- ☒ it allows you to corner more quickly
- ☒ it helps you keep out of the wind.

Answer

☒ it allows the driver to see you in his mirrors

You also need to keep well back so that you get the best view of the road ahead.

Question 1.19

You wish to overtake a long, slow-moving vehicle on a busy road. You should

Mark one answer

☒ wait behind until the driver waves you past

☒ flash your headlights for the oncoming traffic to give way

☒ follow it closely and keep moving out to see the road ahead

☒ keep well back until you can see that it is clear.

Answer

☒ **keep well back until you can see that it is clear**

If you're following another vehicle that's travelling very slowly try to be patient. Keeping well back will increase your view of the road ahead. Wait until there's a safe place to overtake before you do so.

Question 1.20

In which of these situations should you avoid overtaking?

Mark one answer

☒ Just after a bend.

☒ In a one-way street.

☒ On a 30 mph road.

☒ Approaching a dip in the road.

Answer

☒ **Approaching a dip in the road.**

As you begin to think about overtaking ask yourself if it's really necessary. If you can't see well down the road stay back and wait for a safer place to pull out.

Question 1.21

Which of the following may cause loss of concentration on a long journey?

Mark four answers

☒ Loud music.

☒ Arguing with a passenger.

☒ Using a mobile phone.

☒ Putting in a cassette tape.

☒ Stopping regularly to rest.

☒ Pulling up to tune the radio.

Answers

☒ **Loud music.**

☒ **Arguing with a passenger.**

☒ **Using a mobile phone.**

☒ **Putting in a cassette tape.**

You should not allow other factors to distract you from driving. You need to concentrate fully to ensure you are safe on the road. Loud music could mask other sounds, such as the audible warning of an emergency vehicle.

Any distraction which causes you to take your hands off the steering wheel unnecessarily is dangerous.

The white arrow means that you should not plan to

Answer

 overtake

Look out for road signs and markings as you drive. The arrow on the road surface means that it not safe to pull out to overtake.

Mark one answer

- ☒ slow down
- ☒ turn right
- ☒ overtake
- ☒ turn left.

This road marking warns

Answer

 overtaking drivers to move back to the left

You should plan your overtaking to take into consideration any hazards ahead. In this picture the marking indicates that you are approaching a junction. You will not have time to overtake and move back into the left safely.

Mark one answer

- ☒ drivers to use the hard shoulder
- ☒ overtaking drivers there is a bend to the left
- ☒ overtaking drivers to move back to the left
- ☒ drivers that it is safe to overtake.

Question 1.24

You are driving along this narrow country road. When passing the cyclist you should drive

Mark one answer

- [ ] slowly, sounding the horn as you pass
- [ ] quickly, leaving plenty of room
- [ ] slowly, leaving plenty of room
- [ ] quickly, sounding the horn as you pass.

Answer

X slowly, leaving plenty of room

Look well ahead and only pull out if it is safe. You will need to use all of the road to pass the cyclist so be extra cautious.

Look out for entrances to fields where there could be tractors or equipment pulling out.

Question 1.25

You should only use a hand-held telephone when

Mark one answer

- [ ] your vehicle has an automatic gear change
- [ ] driving at low speeds
- [ ] you have stopped at a safe place
- [ ] travelling on minor roads.

Answer

X you have stopped at a safe place

A mobile telephone is a useful means of communication whilst away from home or the office. It can also be invaluable for use in an emergency or when you've broken down.

If you have an in-car telephone always stop in a safe place before using it. Don't use it while moving.

You are driving a vehicle fitted with a hand-held telephone. To answer the telephone you MUST

Mark one answer

- [ ] find a safe place to stop ✗
- [ ] reduce your speed
- [ ] steer the car with one hand
- [ ] be particularly careful at junctions.

On a motorcycle you should only use a mobile telephone when

Mark two answers

- [ ] you have parked in a safe place ✗
- [ ] you have a hands-free system fitted to your helmet ✗
- [ ] you have a pillion passenger to help
- [ ] you have an automatic motorcycle
- [ ] you are travelling on a quiet side road.

Answer

✗ find a safe place to stop

Your attention should be on your driving at all times. Never attempt to dial or reach out for your phone while on the move. This could mean taking your eyes off the road. In only a second your vehicle will travel about 27 metres if you are travelling at 60 mph.

Answers

✗ you have parked in a safe place

✗ you have a hands-free system fitted to your helmet

It's important that you're in full control of your machine at all times. If you need to use a hand-held phone you must stop at a safe place before you do so.

Stop in a safe place before you use the phone.

Question 1.28

On a long motorway journey boredom can cause you to feel sleepy. You should

Mark two answers

- [ ] leave the motorway and find a safe place to stop ✗
- [ ] keep looking around at the surrounding landscape
- [ ] drive faster to complete your journey sooner
- [ ] ensure a supply of fresh air into your vehicle ✗
- [ ] increase the volume of the car sound system
- [ ] stop on the hard shoulder for a rest.

Answers

- ☒ **leave the motorway and find a safe place to stop**
- ☒ **ensure a supply of fresh air into your vehicle**

Plan your journey to include suitable rest stops. You should take all precautions against feeling sleepy whilst driving. Any lack of concentration could have dire consequences.

Question 1.29

You are driving at night and are dazzled by the headlights of an oncoming car. You should

Mark one answer

- [ ] slow down or stop ✗
- [ ] close your eyes
- [ ] flash your headlights
- [ ] pull down the sun visor.

Answer

- ☒ **slow down or stop**

If you're driving at night there will be extra hazards. Speeds and distances can be more difficult to judge. If the darkness makes you feel drowsy then take a rest. The lights of oncoming vehicles can often distract. If you're dazzled by them don't

- close your eyes

- flash your headlights. This will only distract the oncoming driver too.

Question 1.30

You are riding at night and are dazzled by the headlights of an oncoming car. You should

Mark one answer

- [ ] slow down or stop ✗
- [ ] close your eyes
- [ ] flash your headlight
- [ ] turn your head away.

Answer

- ☒ **slow down or stop**

If you're riding a motorcycle, taking a hand off the handlebars to adjust your visor might lead to loss of control. A dirty or scratched visor could cause dazzle and impair vision further.

Whether riding or driving, slow down or stop until your eyes have adjusted.

Question 1.31

You are driving at dusk. You should switch your lights on

Mark two answers

- [ ] even when street lights are not lit ✗
- [ ] so others can see you ✗
- [ ] only when others have done so
- [ ] only when street lights are lit.

Question 1.32

Why are these yellow lines painted across the road?

Mark one answer

- [ ] To help you choose the correct lane.
- [ ] To help you keep the correct separation distance.
- [ ] To make you aware of your speed. ✗
- [ ] To tell you the distance to the roundabout.

Question 1.33

To overtake safely, which of the following applies?

Mark one answer

- [ ] Check the speed and position of following traffic. ✗
- [ ] Cut back in sharply when you have passed the vehicle.
- [ ] Get in close behind before signalling to move out.
- [ ] Steer round the vehicle sharply.

Answers

✗ even when street lights are not lit

✗ so others can see you

Your lights are there to help others on the road see you. It can be necessary to turn on your lights during the day due to bad light or heavy rain. In these conditions the light might fade before the street lights are timed to switch on. Be seen to be safe.

Answer

✗ To make you aware of your speed.

These lines are often found on an approach to a roundabout or a dangerous junction. They give you extra warning to adjust your speed. Look well ahead and do this in good time.

Answer

✗ Check the speed and position of following traffic.

You should do this as part of your MSM routine. There might be a vehicle about to overtake you, so assess the situation before you commit yourself to changing speed or direction.

Question 1.34

You are riding at night. You have your headlight on. Another vehicle overtakes you. When should you dip your headlight?

Mark one answer

- [ ] When the other vehicle signals to overtake.
- [ ] As soon as the other vehicle moves out to overtake.
- [ ] As soon as the other vehicle passes you. ✗
- [ ] When the other vehicle pulls in front of you.

Answer

✗ As soon as the other vehicle passes you.

At night you should dip your headlamp to avoid dazzling

- oncoming drivers
- drivers in front.

If you're being overtaken, dip your headlamp as the other vehicle comes past. When you dip you'll see less of the road so look ahead for hazards on your side of the road before dipping.

Question 1.35

You see an accident on the other side of the road. Your lane is clear. You should

Mark one answer

- [ ] assist the emergency services
- [ ] stop, and cross the road to help
- [ ] concentrate on what is happening ahead ✗
- [ ] place a warning triangle in the road.

Answer

✗ concentrate on what is happening ahead

Always concentrate on the road ahead. If you become distracted you may not see a hazard ahead until it's too late to avoid it.

Question 1.36

You leave a brightly lit building at night. Before riding off, you should

Mark one answer

- [ ] put on tinted glasses
- [ ] wait until your eyes adjust to darkness ✗
- [ ] use your sidelights only
- [ ] use a tinted visor.

Answer

✗ wait until your eyes adjust to darkness

Your eyes take a minute or two to adjust to sudden changes in lighting conditions. While your eyes are adjusting you could clean your lights, mirrors and visor.

SECTION 2 ATTITUDE

This section looks at your attitude to other
road users.

The questions will ask you about

- consideration
- close following
- courtesy
- priority.

Question 2.1

A pelican crossing that crosses the road in a STRAIGHT line and has a central island MUST be treated as

Mark one answer

☒ one crossing in daylight only

☒ one complete crossing

☒ two separate crossings

☒ two crossings during darkness.

Answer

☒ one complete crossing

The lights that control the crossing show to both directions of traffic. If a pedestrian from either side is still crossing when the amber light is flashing, you must wait.

Question 2.2

At a pelican crossing the flashing amber light means you should

Mark one answer

☒ stop, if you can do so safely

☒ give way to pedestrians already on the crossing

☒ stop and wait for the green light

☒ give way to pedestrians waiting to cross.

Answer

☒ give way to pedestrians already on the crossing

Pelican crossings are light-controlled crossings where pedestrians use push-button controls to change the signals. Pelican crossings have no red-and-amber stage before green. Instead, they have a flashing amber light, which means you must give way to pedestrians on the crossing.

If it's clear you may go on.

Question 2.3

You are approaching a pelican crossing. The amber light is flashing. You must

Mark one answer

☒ give way to pedestrians who are crossing

☒ encourage pedestrians to cross

☒ not move until the green light appears

☒ stop even if the crossing is clear.

Answer

☒ give way to pedestrians who are crossing

While the pedestrians are crossing don't

- encourage people to cross by waving or flashing your headlights – others may misunderstand your signal

- rev your engine impatiently.

You are driving towards a zebra crossing. Pedestrians are waiting to cross. You should

Mark one answer

⊠ give way to the elderly and infirm only

⊠ slow down and prepare to stop

⊠ use your headlamps to indicate they can ˉ cross

⊠ wave at them to cross the road.

Answer

❌ **slow down and prepare to stop**

Zebra crossings have

- flashing amber beacons on both sides of the road
- black and white stripes on the crossing
- white zigzag markings on both sides of the crossing.

Where pedestrians are waiting to cross, slow down and prepare to stop.

You have stopped at a pedestrian crossing to allow pedestrians to cross. You should

Mark one answer

⊠ wait until they have crossed

⊠ edge your vehicle forward slowly

⊠ wait, revving your engine

⊠ signal to pedestrians to cross.

Answer

❌ **wait until they have crossed**

Be patient, especially if they are elderly or disabled. Don't rev your engine or sound your horn.

You are riding towards a zebra crossing. Pedestrians are waiting to cross. You should

Mark one answer

⊠ give way to the elderly and infirm only

⊠ slow down and prepare to stop

⊠ use your headlamp to indicate they can cross

⊠ wave at them to cross the road.

Answer

❌ **slow down and prepare to stop**

It's courteous to stop if you can do so safely, especially if

- anyone is waiting on the pavement with a pram or pushchair
- children or the elderly are hesitating to cross because of heavy traffic.

Question 2.7

Why should you give an arm signal on approach to a zebra crossing?

Mark three answers

- ☒ To warn following traffic.
- ☒ To let pedestrians know you are not stopping.
- ☒ To let pedestrians know you are slowing down.
- ☒ To warn oncoming traffic.
- ☒ To warn traffic you intend to turn.

Answers

- ✖ To warn following traffic.
- ✖ To let pedestrians know you are slowing down.
- ✖ To warn oncoming traffic.

By giving clear correct signals you will alert all other road users to your intentions. Be aware that a pedestrian may step out onto the crossing before you have stopped.

Question 2.8

At zebra crossings you should

Mark one answer

- ☒ rev your engine to encourage pedestrians to cross quickly
- ☒ park only on the zig zag lines on the left
- ☒ always leave it clear in traffic queues
- ☒ wave pedestrians to cross if you intend to wait for them.

Answer

- ✖ always leave it clear in traffic queues

Look well down the line of traffic ahead so that you don't stop over the crossing. This should be left clear so that pedestrians are able to cross.

Question 2.9

In fast traffic a 2-second gap may be enough only when conditions are

Mark one answer

- ☒ dry
- ☒ wet
- ☒ damp
- ☒ foggy.

Answer

- ✖ dry

You must be aware that when the weather is bad, you will have to keep a greater distance from the vehicle in front. It will take you further to stop. In wet weather it will take twice as far, in icy weather it could increase to ten times.

At puffin crossings which light will not show to a driver?

Mark one answer

☒ Flashing amber.

☒ Red.

☒ Steady amber.

☒ Green.

You are approaching a red light at a puffin crossing. Pedestrians are on the crossing. The red light will stay on until

Mark one answer

☒ you start to edge forward on to the crossing

☒ the pedestrians have reached a safe position

☒ the pedestrians are clear of the front of your vehicle

☒ a driver from the opposite direction reaches the crossing.

You could use the 'Two-Second Rule'

Mark one answer

☒ before restarting the engine after it has stalled

☒ to keep a safe gap from the vehicle in front

☒ before using the 'Mirror–Signal–Manoeuvre' routine

☒ when emerging on wet roads.

Answer

✗ Flashing amber.

A flashing amber light is shown at pelican crossings, but puffin crossings are different. They are controlled electronically and automatically detect when pedestrians are on the crossing.

The phase is shortened or lengthened according to the position of the pedestrians.

Answer

✗ the pedestrians have reached a safe position

The electronic device will automatically detect that the pedestrians have reached a safe position. Don't proceed until it is safe to do so.

Answer

✗ to keep a safe gap from the vehicle in front

To measure this, choose a reference point such as a bridge, sign or tree. When the vehicle ahead passes the object say to yourself 'Only a fool breaks the Two-Second Rule.' If you reach the object before you finish saying this you're TOO CLOSE.

Question 2.13

A two-second gap between yourself and the car in front is sufficient when conditions are

Mark one answer

☒ wet

☒ good

☒ damp

☒ foggy.

Answer

☒ **good**

In good, dry conditions an alert driver who's driving a vehicle with tyres and brakes in good condition needs a distance of at least two seconds from the car in front.

Question 2.14

'Tailgating' means

Mark one answer

☒ using the rear door of a hatchback car

☒ reversing into a parking space

☒ following another vehicle too closely

☒ driving with rear fog lights on.

Answer

☒ **following another vehicle too closely**

'Tailgating' is used to describe this dangerous practice, often seen in fast-moving traffic and on motorways. Following the vehicle in front too closely will

• restrict your view of the road ahead

• leave you no safety margin if the vehicle in front stops suddenly.

Question 2.15

You are driving on a clear night. There is a steady stream of oncoming traffic. The national speed limit applies. Which lights should you use?

Mark one answer

☒ Full beam headlights.

☒ Sidelights.

☒ Dipped headlights.

☒ Fog lights.

Answer

☒ **Dipped headlights.**

You should always be sure that you can be seen by other traffic. Use the main beam of your headlights only when you can be sure that you won't dazzle other traffic.

Following a large goods vehicle too closely is dangerous because

Mark one answer

☒ your field of vision is seriously reduced

☒ slipstreaming will reduce wind effect

☒ your engine will overheat

☒ your brakes need a constant cooling effect.

Answer

✖ your field of vision is seriously reduced

Staying back will increase your view of the road ahead. This will help you to see any hazards that might occur and allow you more time to react.

You are following this lorry. You should keep well back from it to

Mark one answer

☒ give you a good view of the road ahead

☒ stop following traffic from rushing through the junction

☒ prevent traffic behind you from overtaking

☒ allow you to hurry through the traffic lights if they change.

Answer

✖ give you a good view of the road ahead

By keeping well back you will increase your width of vision around the rear of the lorry. This will allow you to see further down the road and be prepared for any hazards.

Question 2.18

You are driving behind a large goods vehicle. It signals left but steers to the right. You should

Mark one answer

- [×] slow down and let the vehicle turn
- [×] drive on, keeping to the left
- [×] overtake on the right of it
- [×] hold your speed and sound your horn.

Answer

 slow down and let the vehicle turn

Large long vehicles need extra room when making turns at junctions. They may move out to the right in order to make a left turn. Keep well back and in this case don't attempt to pass on the left.

Question 2.19

What is meant by 'defensive' driving?

Mark one answer

- [×] Being alert and thinking ahead.
- [×] Always driving slowly and gently.
- [×] Always letting others go first.
- [×] Pulling over for faster traffic.

Answer

 Being alert and thinking ahead.

Defensive driving is based on planning well ahead, practising effective observation and being in control. Try to be ready for any hidden hazards.

You are following a vehicle on a wet road. You should leave a time gap of at least

Mark one answer

☒ one second

☒ two seconds

☒ three seconds

☒ four seconds.

Answer

☒ **four seconds**

Wet roads will increase the time it will take you to stop. The 'Two-Second Rule' will double to AT LEAST FOUR SECONDS.

You are driving along this road. The red van cuts in close in front of you. What should you do?

Mark one answer

☒ Accelerate to get closer to the red van.

☒ Give a long blast on the horn.

☒ Drop back to leave the correct separation distance.

☒ Flash your headlights several times.

Answer

☒ **Drop back to leave the correct separation distance.**

There are times when other drivers make incorrect or ill judged decisions.

Be tolerant and try not to react aggressively or retaliate. Always consider the safety of other road users, your passengers and yourself.

Question 2.22

While driving you approach a large puddle that is close to the left-hand kerb. Pedestrians are close to the water. You should

Mark two answers

- ☒ ignore the puddle
- ☒ brake suddenly and sound your horn
- ☒ slow down before the puddle
- ☒ try to avoid splashing the pedestrians
- ☒ wave at the pedestrians to keep back.

Answers

- ☒ **slow down before the puddle**
- ☒ **try to avoid splashing the pedestrians**

The effect of your vehicle driving through a puddle will be to throw water onto the pavement. If there are pedestrians close by they could be splashed by the water. Be considerate. If necessary, and it's safe to do so, avoid driving through it.

Question 2.23

When driving in towns you should always

Mark one answer

- ☒ stay well away from the kerb in busy shopping streets
- ☒ remain stopped at a flashing amber light at pelican crossings
- ☒ weave in and out when passing parked vehicles
- ☒ wave pedestrians across at zebra crossings.

Answer

- ☒ **stay well away from the kerb in busy shopping streets**

Be alert and expect that shoppers could step off the pavement into the road. They may only be concerned about making progress through the crowd of shoppers, choosing the road to pass others.

Question 2.24

You are in a line of traffic. The driver behind you is following very closely. What action should you take?

Mark one answer

- ☒ Slow down, gradually increasing the gap between you and the vehicle in front.
- ☒ Ignore the following driver and continue to drive within the speed limit.
- ☒ Signal left and wave the following driver past.
- ☒ Move out wider to a position just left of the road's centre line.

Answer

- ☒ **Slow down, gradually increasing the gap between you and the vehicle in front.**

It can be worrying to see that the car behind is following you too closely. If you ease back from the vehicle in front you'll give yourself a greater safety margin.

Question 2.25

You are driving at the legal speed limit. A vehicle comes up quickly behind, flashing its headlamps. You should

Mark one answer

☒ accelerate to maintain a gap behind you

☒ touch the brakes to show your brake lights

☒ maintain your speed and prevent the vehicle from overtaking

☒ allow the vehicle to overtake.

Answer

✗ allow the vehicle to overtake

Don't enforce the speed limit by blocking another vehicle's progress. This will only lead to the other driver becoming more frustrated. Slow down and allow the other vehicle to pass.

Question 2.26

You are waiting in a traffic queue at night. To avoid dazzling following drivers you should

Mark one answer

☒ apply the handbrake only

☒ apply the footbrake only

☒ switch off your headlights

☒ use both the handbrake and footbrake.

Answer

✗ apply the handbrake only

You should consider the driver behind; brake lights can dazzle.

However, if you are driving in fog it's safer to keep your foot on the footbrake. In this case it will give the following vehicle extra warning of your presence.

Question 2.27

When are you allowed to exceed the maximum speed limit?

Mark one answer

☒ Between midnight and 6 am.

☒ Never.

☒ When overtaking.

☒ When the road is clear.

Answer

✗ Never.

Speed limits are set for a reason. There are many aspects taken into consideration when the limit is set. It may depend on

• junctions

• schools

• pedestrians

• bends

• narrow roads.

Travelling at the correct speed will allow you more time to deal with potential hazards.

Question 2.28

You are driving at the legal speed limit.
A vehicle behind wants to overtake. Should
you try to prevent the driver overtaking?

Mark one answer

☒ No, unless it is safe to do so.

☒ Yes, because the other driver is acting
dangerously.

☒ No, not at any time.

☒ Yes, because the other driver is breaking
the law.

Answer

✗ **No, not at any time.**

Don't enforce the speed limit by blocking
their progress. If they wish to overtake and it
means they break the law, it's their risk.

Question 2.29

You are driving in traffic at the speed limit for
the road. The driver behind is trying to
overtake. You should

Mark one answer

☒ move closer to the car ahead, so the
driver behind has no room to overtake

☒ wave the driver behind to overtake when
it is safe

☒ keep a steady course and allow the
driver behind to overtake

☒ accelerate to get away from the driver
behind.

Answer

✗ **keep a steady course and allow the
driver behind to overtake**

Keep a steady course to give the driver
behind an opportunity to overtake safely. If
necessary, slow down. Reacting incorrectly to
another's impatience will only lead to danger.

Question 2.30

The driver behind is travelling too close to
you. You should

Mark one answer

☒ take no action and drive on

☒ slowly accelerate away from the car
behind

☒ position your car in the middle of the
road

☒ slow down to increase the gap in front.

Answer

✗ **slow down to increase the gap
in front**

Don't let the car behind worry you into
increasing your speed. If you gradually slow
down and leave a greater gap from the
vehicle in front you will have more time to
react if the driver ahead should slow down or
stop suddenly.

Question 2.31

You are driving at night on an unlit road
following a slower moving vehicle. You should

Mark one answer

- [ ] flash your headlights
- [ ] use dipped beam headlights
- [ ] switch off your headlights
- [ ] use full beam headlights

Answer

X use dipped beam headlights

If you follow another vehicle with your
headlights on full beam it could dazzle the
driver by reflecting on the interior mirror.
Leave a safe distance. Your dipped light beam
should fall short of the vehicle in front.

Question 2.32

A long, heavily-loaded lorry is taking a long
time to overtake you. What should you do?

Mark one answer

- [ ] Speed up.
- [ ] Slow down.
- [ ] Hold your speed.
- [ ] Change direction.

Answer

X Slow down.

A long lorry with a heavy load will need
more time to pass you than a car. It won't be
able to accelerate to pass you quickly,
especially on an uphill stretch of road. Ease
off the accelerator and allow the lorry to
pass.

Question 2.33

You are driving a slow-moving vehicle on a
narrow winding road. You should

Mark one answer

- [ ] keep well out to stop vehicles overtaking
  dangerously
- [ ] wave following vehicles past you if you
  think they can overtake quickly
- [ ] pull in safely when you can, to let
  following vehicles overtake
- [ ] give a left signal when it is safe for
  vehicles to overtake you.

Answer

**X pull in safely when you can, to let
following vehicles overtake**

Don't

- wave the other traffic on – they may not
  have seen your signal
- show discourtesy by not pulling in at a
  safe place.

Try to be courteous and considerate to other
road users. Imagine how you would feel if
you were the following driver or rider.

Question 2.34

You are driving a slow-moving vehicle on a narrow road. When traffic wishes to overtake you should

Mark one answer

☒ take no action

☒ put your hazard warning lights on

☒ stop immediately and wave them on

☒ pull in safely as soon as you can do so ✗

Answer

☒ **pull in safely as soon as you can do so**

Try not to hold up a queue of traffic. This might lead to other road users becoming impatient. If you're driving a slow-moving vehicle and the road is narrow look out for a safe place to pull in.

Question 2.35

You are driving a slow-moving vehicle on a narrow winding road. In order to let other vehicles overtake you should

Mark one answer

☒ wave to them to pass

☒ pull in when you can do ✗

☒ show a left turn signal

☒ keep left and hold your speed.

Answer

☒ **pull in when you can do**

Don't frustrate other road users by driving for long distances with a queue of traffic behind you. This could lead them into losing concentration or making ill-judged decisions.

Question 2.36

You are riding a motorcycle and following a large vehicle at 40 mph. You should position yourself

Mark one answer

☒ close behind to make it easier to overtake the vehicle

☒ to the left of the road to make it easier to be seen

☒ close behind the vehicle to keep out of the wind

☒ well back so that you can see past the vehicle. ✗

Answer

☒ **well back so that you can see past the vehicle**

You need to be able to see well down the road and be ready for any hazards that occur. Staying too close to the vehicle will leave you insufficient separation distance and also reduce your view of the road ahead.

Which THREE of the following emergency vehicles will use blue flashing beacons?

Mark three answers

- [ ] Motorway maintenance.
- [ ] Bomb disposal team.
- [ ] Blood transfusion.
- [ ] Police vehicle.
- [ ] Breakdown recovery vehicle.

Answers

- ☒ **Bomb disposal team.**
- ☒ **Blood transfusion.**
- ☒ **Police vehicle.**

Try to move out of the way of emergency vehicles with blue flashing beacons. Do so safely and without delay.

Which THREE of these emergency services might have blue flashing beacons?

Mark three answers

- [ ] Coastguard.
- [ ] Bomb disposal team.
- [ ] Gritting lorries.
- [ ] Animal ambulances.
- [ ] Mountain rescue.
- [ ] Doctors' cars.

Answers

- ☒ **Coastguard.**
- ☒ **Bomb disposal team.**
- ☒ **Mountain rescue.**

These vehicles will be travelling at speed. You should help their progress by pulling over and allowing them to pass. Do so safely. Don't stop suddenly or in a dangerous position.

When being followed by an ambulance showing a flashing blue beacon you should

Mark one answer

- [ ] pull over as soon as safely possible to let it pass
- [ ] accelerate hard to get away from it
- [ ] ignore it if possible, let it pass if forced to
- [ ] brake harshly and immediately stop in the road.

Answer

- ☒ **pull over as soon as safely possible to let it pass**

Pull over where the ambulance can pass safely. Check that there are no bollards or obstructions in the road that will prevent it doing so.

Question 2.40

You see a car showing a flashing green beacon. Should you give way to it?

Mark one answer

- ☒ Yes, it is a doctor going to an emergency.
- ☒ Yes, it is a fire crew support vehicle.
- ☒ No, it is a slow moving vehicle.
- ☒ No, it is a breakdown vehicle.

Answer

✘ **Yes, it is a doctor going to an emergency.**

Give way by pulling over and letting the vehicle pass. Think about this: don't just stop suddenly. Choose a place as soon as you can where you allow the doctor's vehicle to pass safely.

Question 2.41

What type of emergency vehicle is fitted with a green flashing beacon?

Mark one answer

- ☒ Fire engine.
- ☒ Road gritter.
- ☒ Ambulance.
- ☒ Doctor's car.

Answer

✘ **Doctor's car.**

A green flashing beacon on a vehicle means the driver or passenger is a doctor on an emergency call. Give way to them if it's safe to do so. Be aware that the vehicle may be travelling quickly or may stop in a hurry.

Question 2.42

A flashing green beacon on a vehicle means

Mark one answer

- ☒ police on non-urgent duties
- ☒ doctor on an emergency call
- ☒ road safety patrol operating
- ☒ gritting in progress.

Answer

✘ **doctor on emergency call**

If you see such a vehicle in your mirrors allow it to pass if you can. Be aware that someone's life could depend on the driver making good progress through traffic.

Question 2.43

A vehicle has a flashing green beacon. What does this mean?

Mark one answer

☒ A doctor is answering an emergency call.

☒ The vehicle is slow-moving.

☒ It is a motorway police patrol vehicle.

☒ A vehicle is carrying hazardous chemicals.

Answer

 A doctor is answering an emergency call.

A doctor attending an emergency might show a green flashing beacon on his or her vehicle. Give way to them as they will need to reach their destination quickly. Be aware that they might pull over suddenly.

Question 2.44

Diamond-shaped signs give instructions to

Mark one answer

☒ tram drivers

☒ bus drivers

☒ lorry drivers

☒ taxi drivers.

Answer

 tram drivers

These signs apply to trams only. They are directed at tram drivers but you should know their meaning so that you're aware of the priorities and are able to anticipate the actions of the driver.

Question 2.45

Scooter riders should be especially careful when crossing tram lines because scooters have

Mark one answer

☒ small engines

☒ wide panniers

☒ automatic gear boxes

☒ narrow tyres.

Answer

☒ **narrow tyres**

Tram rails can affect steering and braking, especially when wet. If you ride a small motorcycle with narrow tyres you can be affected more than riders on larger machines which have wider tyres.

Question 2.46

On a road where trams operate, which of these vehicles will be most at risk from the tram rails?

Mark one answer

☒ Cars.

☒ Cycles.

☒ Buses.

☒ Lorries.

Answer

 Cycles.

The narrow tyres of a cycle can become stuck in the tram rails. This could cause the cyclist to wobble or even lose balance altogether. The tram lines are also slippery and this could cause a cyclist to slide or fall off.

Question 2.47

At unmarked junctions where tram lines cross over roads, who has priority?

Mark one answer

☒ Cars.

☒ Motorcycles.

☒ Trams.

☒ Buses.

Answer

 Trams.

Be on the lookout and cross the junction with caution. Trams can often approach silently giving you no audible warning of approach.

Question 2.48

A bus is stopped at a bus stop ahead of you. Its right-hand indicator is flashing. You should

Mark one answer

☒ flash your headlights and slow down

☒ slow down and give way if it is safe to do so

☒ sound your horn and keep going

☒ slow down and then sound your horn.

Answer

✖ **slow down and give way if it is safe to do so**

Give way to buses whenever you can do so safely, especially when they signal to pull away from bus stops. Look out for people leaving the bus and crossing the road. Don't

- flash your headlights
- sound your horn
- give any other misleading signal.

A bus lane on your left shows no times of operation. This means it is

Mark one answer

- [ ] not in operation at all
- [ ] only in operation at peak times
- [ ] in operation 24 hours a day
- [ ] only in operation in daylight hours.

Answer

✗ **in operation 24 hours a day**

Don't drive or park in a bus lane when it's in operation. This can cause disruption and spoil the efficiency of public transport.

You should ONLY flash your headlamps to other road users

Mark one answer

- [ ] to show that you are giving way
- [ ] to show that you are about to reverse
- [ ] to tell them that you have right of way
- [ ] to let them know that you are there.

Answer

✗ **to let them know that you are there**

You should only flash your headlamps to warn others of your presence. Don't use them to

- greet others
- show impatience
- give up your priority.

What should you use your horn for?

Mark one answer

- [ ] To alert others to your presence.
- [ ] To allow you right of way.
- [ ] To greet other road users.
- [ ] To signal your annoyance.

Answer

✗ **To alert others to your presence.**

Don't use it to

- greet others
- show impatience
- give priority.

Your horn shouldn't be used between 11.30 pm and 7 am in a built-up area or when your vehicle's stationary – unless a moving vehicle poses a danger.

Question 2.52

A vehicle pulls out in front of you at a junction. What should you do?

Mark one answer

☒ Swerve past it and blow your horn.

☒ Flash your headlights and drive up close behind.

☒ Slow down and be ready to stop.

☒ Accelerate past it immediately.

Answer

✗ **Slow down and be ready to stop.**

Try to be ready for the unexpected. Plan ahead and learn to anticipate hazards. You'll then give yourself more time to react to any problems that might occur.

Be tolerant of the behaviour of other road users who don't behave correctly.

Question 2.53

When riding a motorcycle your normal road position should allow you to

Mark two answers

☒ be seen by traffic ahead emerging from junctions

☒ be seen in the mirrors of the vehicle in front

☒ hold back vehicles wishing to overtake

☒ let other vehicles overtake on the left

☒ remain within ½ metre (1.5 feet) from the kerb

Answers

✗ **be seen by traffic ahead emerging from junctions**

✗ **be seen in the mirrors of the vehicle in front**

Keep clear of the centre of the road. You might

• obstruct overtaking traffic

• put yourself in danger from oncoming traffic

• encourage other traffic to overtake you on the left.

Question 2.54

You are driving in a busy one-way street. What should you be **most** aware of?

Mark one answer

☒ Empty parking spaces.

☒ Local bus stops.

☒ Vehicles overtaking on either side.

☒ Pedestrians on the pavement.

Answer

✗ **Vehicles overtaking on either side.**

If you intend to change lanes or direction you will need to check for traffic behind. Be aware that if you intend to move into the left hand lane there might be traffic passing you on that side.

Question 2.55

You are in a one-way street and want to turn right. You should position yourself

Mark one answer

☒ in the right-hand lane

☒ in the left-hand lane

☒ in either lane, depending on the traffic

☒ just left of the centre line.

Answer

✖ **in the right-hand lane**

If you're travelling in a one-way street and wish to turn right you should take up a position in the right-hand lane. This will enable other road users not wishing to turn to proceed on the left. Indicate your intention and take up your position in good time.

Question 2.56

You wish to turn right ahead. Why should you take up the correct position in good time?

Mark one answer

☒ To allow other drivers to pull out in front of you.

☒ To give a better view into the road that you're joining.

☒ To help other road users know what you intend to do.

☒ To allow drivers to pass you on the right.

Answer

✖ **To help other road users know what you intend to do.**

If you wish to turn right into a side road take up your position in good time. Move to the centre of the road when it's safe to do so. This will allow vehicles to pass you on the left. Early planning will show other traffic what you intend to do.

Question 2.57

You are driving along a country road. A horse and rider are approaching. What should you do?

Mark two answers

☒ Increase your speed.

☒ Sound your horn.

☒ Flash your headlights.

☒ Drive slowly past.

☒ Give plenty of room.

☒ Rev your engine.

Answers

✖ **Drive slowly past.**

✖ **Give plenty of room.**

It's important that you reduce your speed. Passing too closely, at speed could startle the horse and unseat the rider.

Question 2.58

A person herding sheep asks you to stop. You should

Mark one answer

☒ ignore them as they have no authority

☒ stop and switch off your engine

☒ continue on but drive slowly

☒ try and get past quickly.

Answer

☒ **stop and switch off your engine**

Allow the animals to clear the road before you proceed. Animals are unpredictable and startle easily; they could turn and run into your path.

Question 2.59

When overtaking a horse and rider you should

Mark one answer

☒ sound your horn as a warning

☒ go past as quickly as possible

☒ flash your headlamps as a warning

☒ go past slowly and carefully.

Answer

☒ **go past slowly and carefully**

Horses can become startled by the sound of a car engine or the rush of air caused by passing too closely. Keep well back, and only pass when it is safe; leave them plenty of room. Consider that you may have to use the other side of the road to pass.

Question 2.60

At a puffin crossing what colour follows the green signal?

Mark one answer

☒ Steady red.

☒ Flashing amber.

☒ Steady amber.

☒ Flashing green.

Answer

☒ **Steady amber**

Puffin crossings have infra-red sensors which detect when pedestrians are crossing and hold the red traffic signal until the crossing is clear. The use of a sensor means there is no flashing amber phase as there is with a pelican crossing.

Question 2.61

You are waiting at a crossing controlled by a policeman. A pedestrian is crossing. You are signalled to move on. You should

Mark one answer

☒ drive on immediately.

☒ sound your horn.

☒ rev your engine and begin to move forward.

☒ wait until the pedestrian has crossed.

Answer

☒ **wait until the pedestrian has crossed**

You should never endanger the life of another road user. Use your judgement in these situations and take the safe option, which is to wait.

Question 2.62

You stop for pedestrians waiting to cross at a zebra crossing. They do not start to cross. What should you do?

Mark one answer

☒ Be patient and wait.

☒ Sound your horn.

☒ Drive on.

☒ Wave them to cross.

Answer

❌ **Be patient and wait.**

If you stop for pedestrians and they don't start to cross don't

- wave them across
- sound your horn.

This could be dangerous if another vehicle's approaching and hasn't seen or heard your signal.

Question 2.63

When should you beckon pedestrians to cross the road?

Mark one answer

☒ At pedestrian crossings.

☒ At no time.

☒ At junctions.

☒ At school crossings.

Answer

❌ **At no time.**

Beckoning pedestrians to cross can be dangerous. Other road users may not have seen your signal and you might lead the pedestrians into danger.

Question 2.64

Which of the following are at greatest risk from other road users?

Mark one answer

☒ Motorcyclists.

☒ Lorry drivers.

☒ Learner car drivers.

☒ Busy bus drivers.

Answer

❌ **Motorcyclists.**

Motorcycles tend to

- be small and more difficult to see than most other vehicles
- have little or no protective bodywork.

These factors make motorcyclists one of the most vulnerable of all road users.

Question 2.65

You are riding on a country road. Two horses with riders are in the distance. You should

Mark one answer

- [ ] continue at your normal speed
- [ ] change down the gears quickly
- [ ] slow down and be ready to stop
- [ ] flash your headlight to warn them.

Answer

✗ slow down and be ready to stop

Animals are easily frightened by moving motor vehicles. If you're approaching horses keep your speed down and watch to see if the rider has any difficulty keeping control. Always be ready to stop if necessary.

Question 2.66

You should never wave people across at pedestrian crossings because

Mark one answer

- [ ] there may be another vehicle coming
- [ ] they may not be looking
- [ ] it is safer for you to carry on
- [ ] they may not be ready to cross.

Answer

✗ there may be another vehicle coming

If it's safe you should always stop for pedestrians waiting at pedestrian crossings. Don't wave them to cross the road since another driver may not

- have seen them
- have seen your signal
- be able to stop safely.

Question 2.67

Puffin crossings are for use by

Mark one answer

- [ ] cyclists only
- [ ] pedestrians and cyclists
- [ ] horse riders
- [ ] pedestrians only.

Answer

✗ pedestrians only

Puffin crossings are designed only for use by pedestrians, while toucan crossings are shared by pedestrians and cyclists.

This section looks at safety and your vehicle.

The questions will ask you about

- fault detection

- defects and their effect on safety

- use of safety equipment

- emissions

- noise.

Question 3.1

When riding a different motorcycle you should

Mark one answer

☒ ask someone to ride with you for the first time

☒ ride as soon as possible as all controls and switches are the same

☒ leave your gloves behind so switches can be operated easier at first

☒ be sure you know where all controls and switches are.

Answer

✖ **be sure you know where all controls and switches are**

Before you ride any motorcycle make sure you're familiar with the layout of all the controls and switches. While control layouts are generally similar, there may be differences in their feel and method of operation.

Question 3.2

What would you use to check the engine oil level?

Mark one answer

☒ Con-rod.

☒ Dial gauge.

☒ Dipstick.

☒ Timing light.

Answer

✖ **Dipstick.**

You should be able to carry out routine safety checks and identify defects on your vehicle. Use the vehicle manual to find the location of oil and water fillers.

Question 3.3

When must you especially check the engine oil level?

Mark one answer

☒ Before a long journey.

☒ When the engine is hot.

☒ Early in the morning.

☒ Every 6000 miles.

Answer

✖ **Before a long journey.**

Also make checks on

- fuel
- water
- tyres.

Question 3.4

Your vehicle pulls to one side when you brake. What is the most likely fault?

Mark one answer

- [ ] Low brake fluid level
- [ ] Your handbrake is on
- [ ] Poorly adjusted brakes
- [ ] Incorrect tyre pressures

Answer

✖ **Poorly adjusted brakes**

Having your vehicle serviced regularly will allow for safety checks. You should be aware of the dangers caused by a badly serviced vehicle.

Question 3.5

Which of these, if allowed to get low, could cause an accident?

Mark one answer

- [ ] Antifreeze level.
- [ ] Brake fluid level.
- [ ] Battery water level.
- [ ] Radiator coolant level.

Answer

✖ **Brake fluid level.**

In order to keep your vehicle in good working order you should carry out frequent checks. As a driver or rider you must ensure that you're using a safe vehicle or machine that won't endanger other road users.

Question 3.6

Which FOUR of these **must** be in good working order for your car to be roadworthy?

Mark four answers

- [ ] Temperature gauge.
- [ ] Speedometer.
- [ ] Windscreen washers.
- [ ] Windscreen wipers.
- [ ] Oil warning light.
- [ ] Horn.

Answers

✖ **Speedometer.**
✖ **Windscreen washers.**
✖ **Windscreen wipers.**
✖ **Horn.**

Also check the

- lights – get someone to help you check the brake lights
- indicators
- battery – this may be maintenance-free and not need topping up
- steering – check for 'play' in the steering
- oil
- water
- suspension.

Question 3.7

A loose drive chain on a motorcycle could cause

Mark one answer

☒ the front wheel to wobble

☒ the ignition to cut out

☒ the brakes to fail

☒ the rear wheel to lock.

Answer

☒ **the rear wheel to lock**

Drive chains are subject to wear and require frequent adjustment and lubrication. If the chain is worn or slack it can jump off the sprocket and lock the rear wheel.

Question 3.8

A wrongly adjusted drive chain can

Mark three answers

☒ cause an accident

☒ make wheels wobble

☒ create a noisy rattle

☒ affect gear changing

☒ cause a suspension fault.

Answers

☒ **cause an accident**

☒ **create a noisy rattle**

☒ **affect gear changing**

A motorcycle drive chain will stretch as it wears and needs adjusting to keep the tension correct. If the chain is wrongly adjusted it can

- jump off the sprocket and lock the rear wheel causing loss of control
- rattle as it flaps loosely
- cause problems selecting gears.

Question 3.9

Which THREE does the law require you to keep in good condition?

Mark three answers

☒ Gears.

☒ Clutch.

☒ Headlights.

☒ Windscreen.

☒ Seat belts.

Answers

☒ **Headlights.**

☒ **Windscreen.**

☒ **Seat belts.**

Also check the

- lights – get someone to help you check the brake lights
- indicators
- battery – this may be maintenance-free and not need topping up
- steering – check for 'play' in the steering
- oil
- water
- suspension.

Whether driving or riding, check that the speedometer is working once you've moved off.

New petrol-engined cars must be fitted with catalytic converters. The reason for this is to

Mark one answer

☒ control exhaust noise levels

☒ prolong the life of the exhaust system

☒ allow the exhaust system to be recycled

☒ reduce harmful exhaust emissions.

Answer

☒ **reduce harmful exhaust emissions**

We should all be concerned by the effect traffic has on our environment. Fumes from vehicles are causing damage to the air around us. Catalytic converters act like a filter, removing some of the toxic waste.

Which TWO are badly affected if the tyres are under-inflated?

Mark two answers

☒ Braking.

☒ Steering.

☒ Changing gear.

☒ Parking.

Answers

☒ **Braking.**

☒ **Steering.**

Your tyres are your only contact with the road and therefore very important to your safety.

Incorrect tyre pressures will affect steering and braking, so it's very important that you take the time to attend to them. Correct tyre pressures can reduce the risk of skidding and will provide a more comfortable ride.

What can cause heavy steering?

Mark one answer

☒ Driving on ice.

☒ Badly worn brakes.

☒ Over-inflated tyres.

☒ Under-inflated tyres.

Answer

☒ **Under-inflated tyres.**

If your tyres don't have enough air in them they'll drag against the surface of the road. This makes the steering feel heavy.

Your car is fitted with power assisted steering. This will make the steering seem

Mark one answer

☒ lighter

☒ heavier

☒ quieter

☒ noisier.

Answer

☒ **lighter**

Some modern vehicles are fitted with power steering to help manoeuvring at low speeds. It lightens the steering enabling the driver to steer with less effort. This is especially useful when parking or steering into tight corners.

Question 3.14

What is the most important reason why you should keep your motorcycle regularly maintained?

Mark one answer

☒ To accelerate faster than other traffic.

☒ So the motorcycle can carry panniers.

☒ To keep the machine roadworthy.

☒ So the motorcycle can carry a passenger.

Answer

☒ **To keep the machine roadworthy.**

Whenever you use any vehicle on the road it must be in a roadworthy condition. Regular maintenance will help to identify any faults at an early stage and help avoid more serious problems.

Question 3.15

It is essential that tyre pressures are checked regularly. When should this be done?

Mark one answer

☒ After any lengthy journey.

☒ After driving at high speed.

☒ When tyres are hot.

☒ When tyres are cold.

Answer

☒ **When tyres are cold.**

When you check the tyre pressures do so when the tyres are cold. This will give you a more accurate reading. The heat generated from a long journey will raise the pressure inside the tyre.

Question 3.16

It is important that tyre pressures are correct. They should be checked at least

Mark one answer

☒ once a week

☒ every time the vehicle is serviced

☒ every four weeks

☒ every time the vehicle has an MOT test.

Answer

☒ **once a week**

Regular checks of the pressure should also highlight any tyre wear or damage.

Question 3.17

How often should motorcycle tyre pressures be checked?

Mark one answer

☒ Only during each regular service.

☒ After each long journey.

☒ At least monthly.

☒ At least weekly.

Answer

☒ **At least weekly.**

As a motorcyclist your tyres are vital to your safety. Make sure that you check the pressure in your tyres at least once a week. Don't ride your machine if the tyres are incorrectly inflated.

Question 3.18

Why should tyres be kept to the pressure the manufacturer tells you?

Mark one answer

☒ To keep the car the right height off the road.

☒ To save wear on the engine.

☒ To stop the car from sloping to one side.

☒ To help prevent the car from skidding.

Answer

☒ **To help prevent the car from skidding.**

If you aren't sure of the correct tyre pressures, check the vehicle handbook. If you don't have a handbook, go to a garage where a chart showing the correct pressures is displayed. Incorrect tyre pressures will affect steering and braking so it's very important to take the time to ensure that they're correct.

Question 3.19

Driving with under-inflated tyres can affect

Mark two answers

☒ engine temperature

☒ fuel consumption

☒ braking

☒ oil pressure.

Answers

☒ **fuel consumption**

☒ **braking**

Regular checks of tyre pressures can prevent these effects.

Question 3.20

The legal minimum depth of tread for motorcycle tyres is

Mark one answer

☒ 2.5 mm

☒ 4 mm

☒ 1 mm

☒ 1.6 mm.

Answer

☒ **1 mm**

The entire original tread should be continuous. Don't ride a machine with worn tyres.

Your tyres are your only contact with the road so it's very important that you ensure they're in good condition.

Question 3.21

A policeman orders your car to stop. He finds you have a faulty tyre. Who is responsible?

Mark one answer

☒ You, the driver.

☒ Whoever services the car.

☒ The previous owner.

☒ Whoever issued the current MOT.

Answer

❌ **You, the driver.**

You should check the condition of your tyres as a matter of routine. A worn or damaged tyre can have an affect on the handling of your vehicle. It can also have extremely dangerous results if the tyre bursts while you are driving.

Question 3.22

Your motorcycle has tubed tyres fitted as standard. When replacing a tyre you should

Mark one answer

☒ replace the tube if it is 6 months old

☒ replace the tube if it has covered 6,000 miles

☒ replace the tube only if replacing the rear tyre

☒ replace the tube with each change of tyre.

Answer

❌ **replace the tube with each change of tyre**

It isn't worth taking risks to save money. Your life could depend on the condition of your machine.

Question 3.23

You are riding a machine of more than 50cc. Which FOUR would make a tyre illegal?

Mark four answers

☒ Tread less than 1.6 mm deep.

☒ Tread less than 1 mm deep.

☒ A large bulge in the wall.

☒ A recut tread.

☒ Exposed ply or cord.

☒ A stone wedged in the tread.

Answers

❌ **Tread less than 1 mm deep.**

❌ **A large bulge in the wall.**

❌ **A recut tread.**

❌ **Exposed ply or cord.**

When checking tyres make sure there are no bulges or cuts in the side walls. Always buy your tyres from a reputable dealer to ensure quality and value for money.

Question 3.24

It is illegal to drive with tyres that

Mark one answer

- ☒ have a large deep cut in the side wall
- ☒ have been bought second-hand
- ☒ are of different makes
- ☒ have painted walls.

Answer

☒ **have a large deep cut in the side wall**

When checking your tyres for cuts and bulges in the side walls don't forget the inner walls (i.e., those facing each other under the vehicle).

Question 3.25

The legal minimum depth of tread for car tyres over three-quarters of the breadth is

Mark one answer

- ☒ 2.5 mm
- ☒ 4 mm
- ☒ 1 mm
- ☒ 1.6 mm.

Answer

☒ **1.6 mm**

Tyres must have a good depth of tread. The legal limit for cars is a minimum of 1.6 mm. This depth should be throughout the central three-quarters of the breadth of the tyre and around the entire circumference.

Question 3.26

How should you ride a motorcycle when **new** tyres have just been fitted?

Mark one answer

- ☒ Carefully, until the shiny surface is worn off.
- ☒ By braking hard especially into bends.
- ☒ Through normal riding with higher air pressures.
- ☒ By riding at faster than normal speeds.

Answer

☒ **Carefully, until the shiny surface is worn off.**

New tyres have a shiny finish which needs to be worn off before the tyre will give the best grip, especially if the roads are wet.

Question 3.27

Excessive or uneven tyre wear can be caused by faults in the

Mark two answers

- ☒ gearbox
- ☒ braking system
- ☒ suspension
- ☒ exhaust system.

Answers

☒ **braking system**

☒ **suspension**

Uneven wear on your tyres can be caused by the condition of your vehicle. Have it serviced regularly so that the brakes, steering and wheel alignment are checked.

Question 3.28

There is vibration on your steering wheel as you drive. You should check that the

Mark one answer

 doors are closed

☒ wheels are balanced

☒ exhaust is not loose

☒ engine oil level is correct.

Answer

☒ **wheels are balanced**

It could also mean that you have a badly worn or damaged tyre. Have the vehicle checked as soon as possible.

Question 3.29

New tyres should be run in at reasonable speeds for the first

Mark one answer

☒ 500 miles

☒ 100 miles

☒ 10 miles

☒ 1000 miles.

Answer

☒ **100 miles**

You should **always** drive at a reasonable speed. Be aware that the handling of the vehicle might feel different when you have had the tyres replaced.

Question 3.30

Your vehicle pulls to one side when braking. You should

Mark one answer

☒ change the tyres around

☒ consult your garage as soon as possible

☒ pump the pedal when braking

☒ use your handbrake at the same time.

Answer

☒ **consult your garage as soon as possible**

The brakes on your vehicle or machine must be effective and properly adjusted. If your vehicle pulls to one side when braking take it to be checked by a qualified mechanic. Don't take risks.

Question 3.31

The main cause of brake fade is

Mark one answer

☒ the brakes overheating

☒ air in the brake fluid

☒ oil on the brakes

☒ the brakes out of adjustment.

Answer

☒ **the brakes overheating**

If your vehicle is fitted with drum brakes they can get hot and may lose a lot of their effect. This happens when they're continually used, such as on a long, steep downhill stretch of road. Using a lower gear will assist the braking and prevent the vehicle gaining momentum.

Your anti-lock brakes warning light stays on.
You should

Mark one answer

☒ check the brake fluid level

☒ check the footbrake freeplay

☒ check that the handbrake is released

☒ have the brakes checked immediately. ⚹

Answer

☒ **have the brakes checked immediately**

Only drive the vehicle to a garage if it safe to
do so.

You should maintain cable operated brakes

Mark two answers

☒ by regular adjustment when necessary

☒ at normal service times only

☒ yearly, before taking the machine for
its MoT

☒ by oiling cables and pivots regularly.

Answers

☒ **by regular adjustment when
neccesary**

☒ **by oiling cables and pivots regularly**

Keeping your brakes in good working order
is vital for road safety. With cable operated
brakes the cables need

• adjustment because they will stretch with
  use

• lubrication to prevent friction and wear
  of the cables and pivots.

If you notice a strong smell of petrol as you
drive along you should

Mark one answer

☒ not worry, as it is only exhaust fumes

☒ carry on at a reduced speed

☒ expect it to stop in a few miles

☒ stop and investigate the problem.

Answer

☒ **stop and investigate the problem**

Don't smoke or put naked lights anywhere
near the leakage. Have it checked by a
qualified mechanic as soon as possible.
Your vehicle could be a fire hazard.

What does this instrument panel light mean
when lit ?

Mark one answer

☒ Gear lever in park.

☒ Gear lever in neutral.

☒ Handbrake on.

☒ Handbrake off.

Answer

☒ **Handbrake on.**

If you are not sure about any lights or
switches, check the vehicle manual. You
should be aware that a light on the
instrument panel could be a warning about
the condition of your vehicle.

Question 3.36

When must you use dipped headlights during the day?

Mark one answer

 All the time

 Along narrow streets

In poor visibility

When parking

Answer

 In poor visibility

This will allow other road users to see you. You should use them in heavy rain, mist, or in foggy conditions.

Question 3.37

Which instrument panel warning light would show that headlamps are on full beam ?

Mark one answer

Answer

You should be aware of where all the warning lights and visual aids are on the vehicle you are driving. If you are driving a vehicle for the first time you should take time to check all the controls.

Question 3.38

While driving, this warning light on your dashboard comes on. It means

Mark one answer

a fault in the braking system

the engine oil is low

a rear light has failed

your seat belt is not fastened.

Answer

 a fault in the braking system

Don't ignore this warning light. It could have dangerous consequences.

Question 3.39

When are you allowed to drive if your brake lights DO NOT work?

Mark one answer

☒ During the daytime.

☒ When going for an MOT test.

☒ At no time.

☒ In an emergency.

Answer

☒ At no time.

Before you drive or ride you must ensure that all your lights are in good working order. All lights on your vehicle must be capable of working whether it's day or night. Get someone to help you check the brake lights. Don't drive if they aren't working.

Question 3.40

You are driving on a motorway. The traffic ahead is braking sharply because of an accident. How could you warn following traffic?

Mark one answer

☒ Briefly use the hazard warning lights.

☒ Switch on the hazard warning lights continuously.

☒ Briefly use the rear fog lights.

☒ Switch on the headlamps continuously.

Answer

☒ Briefly use the hazard warning lights.

This situation (and on dual carriageways) is the only time you are permitted to use your hazard warning lights on the move. Only use them just long enough to ensure that your warning has been observed.

Question 3.41

When may you use hazard warning lights?

Mark one answer

☒ To park alongside another car.

☒ To park on double yellow lines.

☒ When you are being towed.

☒ When you have broken down.

Answer

☒ When you have broken down.

Hazard warning lights may be used to warn other road users when you

- have broken down and are causing an obstruction
- are on a motorway and want to warn the traffic behind you of a hazard ahead.

Don't use them when being towed.

Question 3.42

Hazard warning lights should be used when vehicles are

Mark one answer

☒ broken down and causing an obstruction

☒ faulty and moving slowly

☒ being towed along a road

☒ reversing into a side road.

Answer

☒ broken down and causing an obstruction

Don't use hazard lights as an excuse for illegal parking. If you do use them don't forget to switch them off when you move away. There must be a warning light on the control panel to show when the hazard lights are in operation.

Question 3.43

It is important to wear suitable shoes when you are driving. Why is this?

Mark one answer

☒ To prevent wear on the pedals.

☒ To maintain control of the pedals.

☒ To enable you to adjust your seat.

☒ To enable you to walk for assistance if you break down.

Answer

☒ **To maintain control of the pedals.**

When you're driving or riding ensure that you're wearing comfortable clothing. Comfortable shoes will ensure that you have proper control of the foot pedals.

Question 3.44

A properly adjusted head restraint will

Mark one answer

☒ make you more comfortable

☒ help you to avoid neck injury

☒ help you to relax

☒ help you to maintain your driving position.

Answer

☒ **help you to avoid neck injury**

The restraint should be adjusted so that it gives maximum protection to the head. This will help in the event of a rear-end collision.

Question 3.45

What will reduce the risk of neck injury resulting from a collision?

Mark one answer

☒ An air-sprung seat.

☒ Anti-lock brakes.

☒ A collapsible steering wheel.

☒ A properly adjusted head restraint.

Answer

☒ **A properly adjusted head restraint.**

Head restraints will reduce the risk of neck injury if you're involved in a collision. They must be properly adjusted. Make sure they aren't positioned too low, as in an accident they could cause damage to the neck.

Question 3.46

Which of the following WOULD NOT make you more visible in daylight?

Mark one answer

- [ ] A black helmet.
- [ ] A white helmet.
- [ ] Switching on your dipped headlamp.
- [ ] Wearing a fluorescent jacket.

Answer

☒ **A black helmet.**

Wearing bright or fluorescent clothes will help other road users to see you. Wearing a white helmet can also make you more visible.

Reflective

Reflective

Question 3.47

When riding and wearing brightly coloured clothing you will

Mark one answer

- [ ] dazzle other motorists on the road
- [ ] be seen more easily by other motorists
- [ ] create a hazard by distracting other drivers
- [ ] be able to ride on unlit roads at night with sidelights.

Answer

☒ **be seen more easily by other motorists**

For safety you want other road users to see you easily. One way of achieving this is to wear brightly coloured or fluorescent clothing during daylight. At night reflective clothing is the best material to help others to see you.

Question 3.48

You are riding a motorcycle in very hot weather. You should

Mark one answer

- [ ] ride with your visor fully open
- [ ] continue to wear protective clothing
- [ ] wear trainers instead of boots
- [ ] slacken your helmet strap.

Answer

☒ **continue to wear protective clothing**

In very hot weather it's tempting to ride in light summer clothes. Don't do this. If you fall from your machine you'll have no protection from the hard road surface. Always wear your protective clothing, whatever the weather.

Question 3.49

Why should you wear fluorescent clothing when riding in daylight?

Mark one answer

☒ It reduces wind resistance.

☒ It prevents injury if you come off the machine.

☒ It helps other road users to see you.

☒ It keeps you cool in hot weather.

Answer

☒ **It helps other road users to see you.**

When riding a motorcycle it's very important that other road users are able to see you clearly. Fluorescent clothing will help towards this, reducing the risk of an accident. You must be visible from all sides.

Question 3.50

Why should riders wear reflective clothing?

Mark one answer

☒ To protect from the cold.

☒ To protect from direct sunlight.

☒ To be seen better in daylight.

☒ To be seen better at night.

Answer

☒ **To be seen better at night.**

Fluorescent clothing will help others to see you during the day. At night, however, you should wear clothing that reflects the light. This allows other road users to see you with their headlights. Ask your local motorcycle dealer about the correct clothing.

Question 3.51

Which of the following makes it easier for motorcyclists to be seen?

Mark three answers

☒ Using dipped headlights.

☒ A fluorescent jacket.

☒ A white helmet.

☒ A grey helmet.

☒ Black leathers.

☒ A tinted visor.

Answers

☒ **Using dipped headlights.**

☒ **A fluorescent jacket.**

☒ **A white helmet.**

Many road accidents involving motorcyclists occur because another road user didn't see them. Using some form of visibility aid will help others to see you. Be aware that you're vulnerable and ride defensively.

Question 3.52

You are carrying two children and their parents in your car. Who is responsible for seeing that the children wear seat belts?

Mark one answer

☒ The children's parents.

☒ You.

☒ The front-seat passenger.

☒ The children.

Answer

 You.

Seat belts save lives and reduce the risk of injury. You MUST wear a seat belt unless you're exempt. There are also legal requirements for your passengers. Make sure that you know the rules for wearing seat belts. Check the chart below.

Question 3.53

You are driving a friend's children home from school. They are both under 14 years old. Who is responsible for making sure they wear a seat belt?

Mark one answer

☒ An adult passenger.

☒ The children.

☒ You, the driver.

☒ Your friend.

Answer

☒ You, the driver.

Children should always be secured and safe. They should be encouraged to fasten their seat belts themselves from an early age so that it becomes a matter of routine. As the driver you must check that the seat belts are fastened securely, it's your responsibility.

	FRONT SEAT	REAR SEAT	RESPONSIBILITY
Driver	Seat belt must be worn if fitted		Driver
Child under 3 years	Appropriate child restraint must be worn	Appropriate child restraint must be worn if fitted	Driver
Child aged 3 to 11 and under 1.5 metres (about 5 feet)	Appropriate child restraint must be worn if available. If not, an adult seat belt must be worn if fitted.	Appropriate child restraint must be worn if available. If not, an adult seat belt must be worn if fitted.	Driver
Child aged 12 or 13 or a younger child 1.5 metres in height (about 5 feet) or more	Adult seat belt must be worn if fitted	Adult seat belt must be worn if fitted	Driver
Adult passengers	Seat belt must be worn if fitted	Seat belt must be worn if fitted	Passenger

Question 3.54

Car passengers MUST wear a seat belt if one is available, unless they are

Mark one answer

- under 14 years old
- under 1.5 metres (5 feet) in height
- sitting in the rear seat
- exempt for medical reasons.

Answer

- **exempt for medical reasons**

Although it's your adult passengers' responsibility for wearing a seat belt, remind them to put them on as they get in the car.

Question 3.55

Excessive or uneven tyre wear can be caused by faults in which THREE?

Mark three answers

- The gearbox.
- The braking system.
- The accelerator.
- The exhaust system.
- Wheel alignment
- The suspension.

Answers

- **The braking system.**
- **Wheel alignment**
- **The suspension.**

Regular servicing will help to detect faults at an early stage and help prevent minor faults becoming serious or even dangerous.

Question 3.56

A car driver MUST ensure that seat belts are worn by

Mark one answer

- all front-seat passengers
- all passengers
- all rear-seat passengers
- children under 14.

Answer

- **children under 14**

Study the chart regarding seat belts. You could be responsible for your passenger wearing the appropriate restraint.

You are alone on a motorway and your car has broken down. After telephoning for help you should

Mark one answer

☒ accept a lift from a passing motorist

☒ remain in a safe place with your vehicle

☒ beckon another motorist to stop

☒ walk along the motorway to the nearest services.

Answer

❌ **remain in a safe place with your vehicle**

Don't put yourself at risk by standing at the edge of the carriageway. Keep well back, as the traffic will be travelling at speed. Look out for the emergency services. When they arrive check that they have an identity card and that they are aware of the details you gave over the phone.

Which of the following fairings would give you the best weather protection?

Mark one answer

☒ Handlebar.

☒ Sports.

☒ Touring.

☒ Windscreen.

Answer

❌ **Touring.**

Fairings give protection to the hands, legs and feet. They also make riding more comfortable by keeping you out of the wind.

It would be illegal to ride **with** a helmet on when

Mark one answer

☒ the helmet is not fastened correctly

☒ the helmet is more than four years old

☒ you have borrowed someone else's helmet

☒ the helmet does not have chin protection.

Answer

❌ **the helmet is not fastened correctly**

In an accident a motorcycle helmet which is incorrectly fastened is liable to come off and provide little or no protection. The law requires that when you ride on the road your helmet must be correctly fastened.

Question 3.60

Your safety helmet has a small crack. You should

Mark one answer

- [x] get a new one before riding   ✗
- [x] ride at low speeds only
- [x] ask the police to inspect it
- [x] have it repaired by an expert.

Answer

✗ get a new one before riding

If you damage your motorcycle helmet, even slightly, buy a new one. The smallest damage can make a helmet unreliable. A little expense now may save your life later.

Buy a white helmet if possible. They're much more easily seen by other road users.

Question 3.61

Your visor becomes badly scratched. You should

Mark one answer

- [x] polish it with a fine abrasive
- [x] replace it   ✗
- [x] wash it in soapy water
- [x] clean it with petrol.

Answer

✗ replace it

Your visor protects your eyes from wind, rain, insects and road dirt. It's therefore important to keep it clean and in good repair. A badly scratched visor might

- obscure your view
- cause dazzle from lights of oncoming vehicles.

Question 3.62

When riding on public roads a motorcyclist's visor or goggles must display which Kite mark?

Mark one answer

- [x] ACU.
- [x] BMF.
- [x] MAG.
- [x] BSI.

Answer

✗ BSI.

A visor or goggles are vital to protect your eyes from wind, rain, insects and road dirt. Make sure that yours comply with the British Standard Institute and have the mark to show that they do.

Question 3.63

You want to ride your motorcycle in the dark. What could you wear to be seen more easily ?

Mark two answers

- ☒ Fluorescent clothing.
- ☒ Reflective clothing.
- ☒ A white helmet. ✗
- ☒ A red helmet.
- ☒ A black leather jacket.

Answers

- ☒ **Reflective clothing.**
- ☒ **A white helmet.**

When riding in the dark you will be more easy to see if you wear

- reflective clothing
- a white helmet.

At night a white helmet contrasts starkly with the surrounding darkness, while reflective clothing reflects the light from other vehicles and makes the rider much more visible.

Question 3.64

You are testing your suspension. You notice that your vehicle keeps bouncing when you press down on the front wing. What does this mean?

Mark one answer

- ☒ Worn tyres.
- ☒ Tyres under-inflated.
- ☒ Steering wheel not located centrally.
- ☒ Worn shock absorbers. ✗

Answer

- ☒ **Worn shock absorbers.**

If you find that your vehicle bounces as you drive around a corner or bend the shock absorbers might be worn. Press down on the front wing and if the vehicle continues to bounce take it to be checked by a qualified mechanic.

Question 3.65

In which of these containers may you carry petrol in a motor vehicle?

Mark one answer

- ☒ A.
- ☒ B.
- ☒ C.
- ☒ D.

Answer

- ☒ **A.**

Petrol may be carried in your vehicle but it must be carried in a container designed for that purpose. Don't use other types as these might leak or perish. Suitable containers are available in most motor shops and petrol stations.

Question 3.66

You must NOT sound your horn

Mark one answer

☒ between 10 pm and 6 am in a built-up area

☒ at any time in a built-up area

☒ between 11.30 pm and 7 am in a built-up area ✗

☒ between 11.30 pm and 6 am on any road.

Answer

✗ **between 11.30 pm and 7 am in a built-up area**

Vehicles can be noisy. Every effort must be made to prevent excessive noise, especially in built-up areas at night. Don't

- rev the engine

✗ • sound the horn between 11.30 pm and 7 am (unless it's necessary to warn a moving vehicle).

Question 3.67

When should you NOT use your horn in a built-up area?

Mark one answer

☒ Between 8 pm and 8 am.

☒ Between 9 pm and dawn.

☒ Between dusk and 8 am.

☒ Between 11.30 pm and 7 am. ✗

Answer

✗ **Between 11.30 pm and 7 am.**

Flash your headlights as an alternative. Only sound your horn to prevent an accident.

Question 3.68

Why are mirrors on the outside of vehicles often slightly curved (convex)?

Mark one answer

☒ They give a wider field of vision. ✗

☒ They totally cover blind spots.

☒ They make it easier to judge the speed of following traffic.

☒ They make following traffic look bigger.

Answer

✗ **They give a wider field of vision.**

Modern vehicles provide the driver with the equipment to help increase the field of vision. However, you should always be aware that even these mirrors might not reflect all that is around the vehicle. A check over the shoulder before you move off will be required.

Question 3.69

You cannot see clearly behind when reversing. What should you do?

Mark one answer

☒ Open your window to look behind.

☒ Open the door and look behind.

☒ Look in the nearside mirror.

☒ Ask someone to guide you. ✗

Answer

☒ **Ask someone to guide you.**

If you want to turn your car around try to find a place where you have good all-round vision. If this isn't possible and you're unable to see clearly, then get someone to guide you.

Question 3.70

Why can it be helpful to have mirrors fitted on each side of your motorcycle ?

Mark one answer

☒ To judge the gap when filtering in traffic.

☒ To give protection when riding in poor weather.

☒ To make your machine appear larger to other drivers.

☒ To give you the best view of the road ✗ behind.

Answer

☒ **To give you the best view of the road behind.**

When riding on the road you need to know as much about following traffic as you can. A mirror fitted on each side of your motorcycle will help give you the best view of the road behind.

Question 3.71

When must you use a dipped headlight during the day?

Mark one answer

☒ On country roads.

☒ Along narrow streets.

☒ In poor visibility. ✗

☒ When parking.

Answer

☒ **In poor visibility.**

It's important that other road users can see you clearly at all times. It will help other road users to see you if you use a dipped headlight during the day. If there's limited visibility you MUST use it.

Question 3.72

Your side stand is not raised fully when you start to ride. What could this do?

Mark one answer

☒ Alter the machine's centre of gravity.

☒ Catch on your feet.

☒ Dig into the ground when you are cornering.

☒ Cause the machine to steer badly

Answer

☒ **Dig into the ground when you are cornering.**

Make sure that your side stand's fully up before you move off. If it isn't up it could dig into the ground as you move away and might lead to an accident.

Question 3.73

What will cause high fuel consumption?

Mark one answer

☒ Poor steering control.

☒ Accelerating around bends.

☒ Driving in high gears.

☒ Harsh braking and accelerating. ✗

Answer

☒ **Harsh braking and accelerating.**

Look after your vehicle or machine. Have it regulary serviced and keep all the lights and windows (on a vehicle) clean. Driving or riding 'sympathetically' will help you to keep fuel consumption down. This practice is kinder to the environment and will also save you money.

Question 3.74

A properly serviced vehicle will give

Mark two answers

☒ lower insurance premiums

☒ you a refund on your road tax

☒ better fuel economy ✗

☒ cleaner exhaust emissions. ✗

Answers

☒ **better fuel economy**

☒ **cleaner exhaust emissions**

When you purchase your vehicle, check at what intervals you should have it serviced. This can vary depending on model or manufacturer. Use the service manual and keep it up to date. The cleaner, the engine the cleaner it's emissions.

Question 3.75

You are riding a machine of more than 50cc. Which FOUR would make a tyre illegal?

Mark four answers

- ☒ Tread less than 1.66 mm deep.
- ☒ Tread less than 1mm deep.
- ☒ A huge bulge in the wall.
- ☒ A recut tread.
- ☒ Exposed ply or cord.
- ☒ A stone wedged in the tread.

Answers

- ☒ **Tread less than 1mm deep.**
- ☒ **A huge bulge in the wall.**
- ☒ **A recut tread.**
- ☒ **Exposed ply or cord.**

Question 3.76

When driving a car fitted with automatic transmission what would you use 'kick down' for?

Mark one answer

- ☒ Cruise control.
- ☒ Quick acceleration.
- ☒ Slow braking.
- ☒ Fuel economy.

Answer

- ☒ **Quick acceleration.**

'Kick down' selects a lower gear, enabling the vehicle to accelerate faster.

Question 3.77

You should avoid driving a vehicle fitted with an empty roof-rack. Why is this?

Mark one answer

- ☒ It is illegal.
- ☒ It will waste fuel.
- ☒ It will affect your braking.
- ☒ It will affect the suspension.

Answer

- ☒ **It will waste fuel.**

We are all responsible for the environment we live in. By each driver taking individual responsibility for conserving fuel, together it will make a difference.

Question 3.78

A roof rack fitted to your car will

Mark one answer

☒ reduce fuel consumption

☒ improve the road handling

☒ make your car go faster

☒ increase fuel consumption.

Answer

☒ **increase fuel consumption**

Make sure that any cover is securely fitted and does not flap about in the wind when driving. There are roof boxes available which will reduce wind resistence and in turn fuel consumption.

Question 3.79

Your car will use more fuel if fitted with

Mark one answer

☒ a tow bar

☒ a roof rack

☒ an oil cooler

☒ a sunroof.

Answer

☒ **a roof rack**

You should be aware that even an empty roof rack will increase the fuel consumption of your vehicle. If you are not going to use it for a while, remove it.

Question 3.80

The pictured vehicle is 'environmentally friendly' because it

Mark three answers

☒ reduces noise pollution

☒ uses diesel fuel

☒ uses electricity

☒ uses unleaded fuel

☒ reduces parking spaces

☒ reduces town traffic.

Answers

☒ **reduces noise pollution**

☒ **uses electricity**

☒ **reduces town traffic**

The electric motors of trams don't emit dirty fumes which would add to those already emmitted by the other town traffic. These types of motor are also much quieter than petrol or diesel engines.

Question 3.81

Driving at 70 mph uses more fuel than driving at 50 mph by up to

Mark one answer

- ☒ 30%
- ☒ 100%
- ☒ 10%
- ☒ 75%.

Answer

☒ **30%**

Your vehicle will be cheaper to run if you avoid heavy acceleration. The higher the engine revs, the more fuel you will use.

Question 3.82

A motorcyclist may only carry a pillion passenger when

Mark three answers

- ☒ the rider has successfully completed CBT
- ☒ the rider holds a full licence for the category of machine
- ☒ the motorcycle is fitted with rear foot pegs
- ☒ the rider has a full car licence and is over 21
- ☒ there is a proper passenger seat fitted
- ☒ there is no sidecar fitted to the machine.

Answers

☒ **the rider holds a full licence for the category of machine**

☒ **the motorcycle is fitted with rear foot pegs**

☒ **there is a proper passenger seat fitted**

Before carrying a passenger on a motorcycle the rider must hold a full licence for the category being ridden and make sure that

- passenger footrests are fitted
- a proper passenger seat is fitted.

Question 3.83

On your vehicle, where would you find a catalytic converter ?

Mark one answer

- ☒ In the fuel tank.
- ☒ In the air filter.
- ☒ On the cooling system.
- ☒ On the exhaust system.

Answer

☒ **On the exhaust system.**

Although carbon dioxide is still produced, it reduces the toxic and polluting gases by up to 90%. Unleaded fuel must be used in vehicles fitted with a catalytic converter.

Question 3.84

For which TWO of these may you use hazard warning lights?

Mark two answers

☒ When driving on a motorway, to warn other drivers behind of a hazard ahead.

☒ When you are parked on a two-way road.

☒ When your direction indicators are not working.

☒ When warning oncoming traffic that you intend to stop.

☒ When your vehicle has broken down and is causing an obstruction.

Answers

✗ **When driving on a motorway, to warn other drivers behind of a hazard ahead.**

✗ **When your vehicle has broken down and is causing an obstruction.**

Don't use them as an excuse to park illegally, such as when using a cash machine or postbox. They are an important safety feature and should only be used to warn other road users of a hazard.

This section looks at safety margins and how
they can be affected by conditions.

The questions will ask you about

- stopping distances

- road surfaces

- skidding

- weather conditions.

Question 4.1

Stopping in good conditions at 30 mph takes at least

Mark one answer

☒ one car length

☒ two car lengths

☒ three car lengths

☒ six car lengths.

Answer

☒ **six car lengths**

It's very important that you know your overall stopping distance at all speeds. Stopping distances increase dramatically as road speed increases. Knowing your stopping distance will reduce the risk of an accident as you'll know how much room you need to leave between you and the vehicle in front.

Question 4.2

You are on a good, dry road surface and in a vehicle with good brakes and tyres. What is the shortest overall stopping distance at 40 mph?

Mark one answer

☒ 23 metres (75 feet).

☒ 96 metres (315 feet).

☒ 53 metres (175 feet).

☒ 36 metres (120 feet).

Answer

☒ **36 metres (120 feet).**

Factors that affect how long it takes you to stop include

- how fast you're going
- whether you're travelling on the level, uphill or downhill
- the weather and road conditions
- the condition of tyres, brakes and suspension
- your reaction times.

Question 4.3

What is the braking distance at 50 mph?

Mark one answer

☒ 55 metres (180 feet).

☒ 24 metres (79 feet).

☒ 14 metres (45 feet).

☒ 38 metres (125 feet).

Answer

☒ **38 metres (125 feet).**

The braking distance is how far you travel from the moment you first apply the brakes to the point where you stop.

Stopping distance can be divided into

- thinking distance
- braking distance.

The thinking distance is how far you travel from the moment you see the **need** to brake to the moment you **apply** the brakes.

Question 4.4

Your overall stopping distance will be longer when riding

Mark one answer

- [X] at night
- [X] in the fog
- [X] with a passenger
- [X] up a hill.

Answer

[X] **with a passenger**

When carrying a passenger on a motorcycle the overall weight will be much more than when riding alone. This additional weight will make it harder for you to stop in an emergency.

Question 4.5

When dealing with a bend you should brake

Mark one answer

- [X] hard before you enter the bend
- [X] gently before you enter the bend ✗
- [X] gently as you enter the bend
- [X] hard as you enter the bend.

Answer

[X] **gently before you enter the bend**

You should look well down the road and plan ahead. Don't go into a bend too fast. Reduce speed **before** you enter the bend, braking **on** the bend can make your vehicle unstable.

At 30 mph

Thinking distance 9m (30ft)
Braking distance 14m (45ft)
Overall stopping distance 23m (75ft)

At 50 mph

Thinking distance 15m (50ft)
Braking distance 38m (125ft)
Overall stopping distance 53m (175ft)

At 70 mph

Thinking distance 21m (70ft)
Braking distance 75m (245ft)
Overall stopping distance 96m (315ft)

Question 4.6

Braking hard at speed on a sharp bend can make your vehicle

Mark one answer

☒ more stable

☒ unstable   ✗

☒ stall

☒ corner safely.

Answer

✖ **unstable**

Adjust your speed in good time so that you are able to drive around the bend under gentle acceleration.

Question 4.7

You are riding a motorcycle in good road conditions. The most effective way to use the brakes is to

Mark one answer

☒ apply both brakes with greater pressure on the rear

☒ apply both brakes with equal pressure

☒ apply the rear brake first and the front just before you stop

☒ apply both brakes with greater pressure ✗ on the front.

Answer

✖ **apply both brakes with greater pressure on the front**

This technique gives the best stopping power in good conditions because

- the combined weight of the machine and rider is thrown forward
- the front tyre is pressed more firmly on the road, giving a better grip.

Question 4.8

What is the shortest stopping distance at 70 mph?

Mark one answer

☒ 53 metres (175 feet).

☒ 60 metres (200 feet).

☒ 73 metres (240 feet).

☒ 96 metres (315 feet).   ✗

Answer

✖ **96 metres (315 feet).**

Note that this is the shortest distance. It will take at least this distance to think, brake and stop.

You are driving at 50 mph in good conditions. What would be your shortest stopping distance?

Mark one answer

⊠ 23 metres (75 feet).

⊠ 36 metres (120 feet).

⊠ 53 metres (175 feet). ✗

⊠ 73 metres (240 feet).

Answer

✖ **53 metres (175 feet).**

Stopping distances can be difficult to visualise. Try thinking in terms that mean something to you. This could be

• car or motorcycle lengths

• the 100 metre sprint

• the length of a football pitch (which is about 100 metres/330 feet).

You are travelling at 50 mph on a good, dry road. What is your shortest overall stopping distance?

Mark one answer

⊠ 36 metres (120 feet).

⊠ 53 metres (175 feet). ✗

⊠ 75 metres (245 feet).

⊠ 96 metres (315 feet).

Answer

✖ **53 metres (175 feet).**

Even in good conditions it will take you further than you think for your car to stop. Don't just learn the figures – **understand** how far the distance is.

What is the shortest overall stopping distance on a dry road from 60 mph?

Mark one answer

⊠ 53 metres (175 feet).

⊠ 58 metres (190 feet).

⊠ 73 metres (240 feet). ✗

⊠ 96 metres (315 feet).

Answer

✖ **73 metres (240 feet).**

Pace out 73 metres and then look back. It's probably further than you think.

Question 4.12

When driving in fog, which of the following are correct?

Mark three answers

- [ ] Use dipped headlights.
- [ ] Use headlamps on full beam.
- [ ] Allow more time for your journey.
- [ ] Keep close to the car in front.
- [ ] Slow down.
- [ ] Use side lights only.

Answers

- [x] **Use dipped headlights.**
- [x] **Allow more time for your journey.**
- [x] **Slow down.**

If your journey is not necessary, don't venture out. You will be taking unecessary risks. If you have to travel and someone is expecting you the other end, let them know that you will be taking longer than usual for your journey. This will stop them worrying if you don't turn up on time and you from hurrying to get there.

Question 4.13

"Only a fool breaks the Two-Second Rule" refers to

Mark one answer

- [ ] the time recommended when using the choke
- [ ] a separation distance riding in good conditions
- [ ] restarting a stalled engine in busy traffic
- [ ] the time you should keep your foot down at a junction.

Answer

- [x] **a separation distance riding in good conditions.**

It is very important that you always leave a safe gap between yourself and any vehicle you're following. In good conditions you need to leave

- at least one metre for every mile per hour of your speed or
- a two-second time interval.

Question 4.14

You are on a fast, open road in good conditions. For safety, the distance between you and the vehicle in front should be

Mark one answer

- [ ] a two-second time gap
- [ ] one car length
- [ ] 2 metres (6 feet 6 inches)
- [ ] two car lengths.

Answer

- [x] **a two-second time gap**

One useful method of checking that you've allowed enough room between you and the vehicle in front is the 'Two-Second Rule'.

You should allow a two-second time gap as a safe separation distance. Begin by saying 'Only a fool breaks the Two-Second Rule' when the vehicle in front passes a fixed point. You shouldn't reach that point before you finish saying this. If you do, you're travelling too close and should drop back.

The 'Two-Second Rule' helps you to

Mark one answer

☒ keep a safe distance from the car in front ✗

☒ keep the correct distance from the kerb

☒ check your blind spot

☒ check your mirrors.

Answer

✗ **keep a safe distance from the car in front**

Some people find it difficult to judge distances in metres or feet. The 'Two-Second Rule' is an easy way to judge your separation distance.

Question 4.16

Your overall stopping distance will be much longer when driving

Mark one answer

☒ in the rain ✗

☒ in fog

☒ at night

☒ in strong winds.

Answer

✗ **in the rain**

Extra care should be taken in wet weather. Wet roads will affect the time it takes you to stop. Your stopping distance could be at least doubled.

Question 4.17

On a wet road what is the safest way to stop?

Mark one answer

☒ Change gear without braking.

☒ Use the back brake only.

☒ Use the front brake only.

☒ Use both brakes. ✗

Answer

✗ **Use both brakes.**

Motorcyclists need to take extra care when stopping on wet road surfaces. Plan well ahead so that you're able to brake in good time. You should

• ensure your machine is upright

• brake when travelling in a straight line.

Question 4.18

The road surface is very important to motorcyclists because

Mark one answer

- there can be many areas where road markings are poor

- some roads are tarmac and others concrete

- as traffic increases there is less room for riders

- only a small part of the tyre touches the road.

Answer

☒ **only a small part of the tyre touches the road.**

A motorcyclist needs to be aware of the affect road conditions have on stability, steering and braking. Only a small part of the tyre is in contact with the road at any time which means that any change to the road surface can affect the grip on the road.

Question 4.19

Road surface is very important to motorcyclists. Which FOUR of these are more likely to reduce the stability of your machine?

Mark four answers

- Pot-holes.

- Drain covers.

- Concrete.

- Oil patches.

- Tarmac.

- Loose gravel.

Answers

☒ **Pot-holes.**

☒ **Drain covers.**

☒ **Oil patches.**

☒ **Loose gravel.**

Apart from the weather conditions, the road surface and any changes in it can affect the stability of your motorcycle. Be on the lookout for poor road surfaces

Question 4.20

What is the main reason why your stopping distance is longer after heavy rain?

Mark one answer

☒ You may not be able to see large puddles.

☒ The brakes will be cold because they're wet.

☒ Your tyres will have less grip on the road. ✗

☒ Water on the windscreen will blur your view of the road ahead.

Answer

☒ Your tyres will have less grip on the road.

When the roads are wet the water will reduce your tyres' grip on the road. When the tyres lose their grip, you lose control.

You can cause the tyres to lose their grip by

- excessive acceleration (wheelspin)
- cornering too fast
- braking too hard
- harsh steering (swerving).

Question 4.21

You are riding in town. The roads are wet following rain. The reflections from wet surfaces will

Mark one answer

☒ make it easy to see unlit objects

☒ help you to make progress

☒ make it hard to see unlit objects ✗

☒ affect your stopping distance.

Answer

☒ make it hard to see unlit objects

If you can't see clearly, slow down and stop. Make sure that your visor or goggles are clean.

Be extra cautious in these conditions.

Bike skidding to the left

Direction of steering to correct skid

- **Ease off brake**
- **Steer to left**

Question 4.22

What is the most common cause of skidding?

Mark one answer

☒ Worn tyres.

☒ Driver error. ✗

☒ Other vehicles.

☒ Pedestrians.

Answer

☒ **Driver error.**

Skids don't just happen. They're caused by a driver asking too much of the vehicle for the amount of grip the tyres have on the road at the time.

Question 4.23

When braking hard in a straight line, the weight of the vehicle will shift onto the

Mark one answer

☒ front wheels ✗

☒ rear wheels

☒ left wheels

☒ right wheels.

Answer

☒ **front wheels**

This in turn will throw you and your passengers forward, then back again as the vehicle comes to a stop. This harsh braking could also lead to the wheels locking and skidding on the road surface.

Question 4.24

You are driving in heavy rain when your steering suddenly becomes very light. To get control again you must

Mark one answer

☒ brake firmly to reduce speed

☒ ease off the accelerator ✗

☒ use the accelerator gently

☒ steer towards a dry part of the road.

Answer

☒ **ease off the accelerator**

If you find that your steering becomes light your tyres are losing their grip on the road. To regain control ease off the accelerator. Don't suddenly steer sharply in any direction.

You are driving in heavy rain. Your steering suddenly becomes very light. You should

Mark one answer

☒ steer towards the side of the road

☒ apply gentle acceleration

☒ brake firmly to reduce speed

☒ ease off the accelerator. ✗

Answer

✗ **ease off the accelerator**

Braking harshly in this situation could cause the tyres to lift off the road surface and the wheels to lock, which will result in loss of control. If your vehicle's fitted with an anti-lock braking system (ABS) and it starts to slide on the wet road surface, apply and maintain maximum force to the brake pedal.

Rear of car skids to the right   **Driver steers to the right**

You are riding in heavy rain when your rear wheel skids as you accelerate. To get control again you must

Mark one answer

☒ change down to a lower gear

☒ ease off the throttle ✗

☒ brake to reduce speed

☒ put your feet down.

Answer

✗ **ease off the throttle**

If you feel your back wheel beginning to skid as you pull away, ease off the throttle. This will give your rear tyre the chance to grip the road and stop the skid.

You have driven through a flood. What is the first thing you should do?

Mark one answer

☒ Stop and check the tyres.

☒ Stop and dry the brakes.

☒ Switch on your windscreen wipers.

☒ Test your brakes. ✗

Answer

✗ **Test your brakes.**

After passing through a flood or ford test your brakes. Before you do so make sure that you check behind for following traffic. Don't brake sharply. The vehicle behind may not be able to stop quickly. If necessary, signal your intentions.

Question 4.28

You are driving along a country road. You see this sign. AFTER dealing safely with the hazard you should always

Mark one answer

- ☒ check your tyre pressures
- ☒ switch on your hazard warning lights
- ☒ switch on your rear fog lamps
- ☒ test your brakes. ✗

Answer

☒ **test your brakes**

Deep water can affect your brakes, so you should check that they're working properly before you build up speed again. Check your mirrors and consider what's behind you before you do this.

Question 4.29

Braking distances on ice can be

Mark one answer

- ☒ twice the normal distance
- ☒ five times the normal distance
- ☒ seven times the normal distance
- ☒ ten times the normal distance. ✗

Answer

☒ **ten times the normal distance**

Braking and stopping distances will also be affected by icy and snowy weather. You need to take extra care and expect your stopping distance to increase by up to ten times the normal distance.

Question 4.30

When cornering in freezing conditions you should

Mark one answer

- ☒ push the brake down firmly
- ☒ steer with short sharp movements
- ☒ treat the controls of the car gently ✗
- ☒ slow down by braking on the bend.

Answer

☒ **treat the controls of the car gently**

Harsh steering and braking could result in you losing control. All but the most gentle braking will lock your wheels on packed snow and ice.

Question 4.31

Freezing conditions will affect the distance it takes you to come to a stop. You should expect stopping distances to increase by up to

Mark one answer

- [ ] two times
- [ ] five times
- [ ] three times
- [x] ten times.

Answer

- [x] **ten times**

You must take the road and weather conditions into account when driving. It will take considerably longer to stop in bad weather.

Question 4.32

When driving in icy conditions, the steering becomes light because the tyres

Mark one answer

- [ ] have more grip on the road
- [ ] are too soft
- [ ] are too hard
- [x] have less grip on the road.

Answer

- [x] **have less grip on the road**

In icy conditions the tyres will lose much of their grip on the road. This could result in the steering becoming light. If you ease off the accelerator you should regain some steering control.

Question 4.33

You are driving on an icy road. How can you avoid wheelspin?

Mark one answer

- [x] Drive at a slow speed in as high a gear as possible.
- [ ] Use the handbrake if the wheels start to slip.
- [ ] Brake gently and repeatedly.
- [ ] Drive in a low gear at all times.

Answer

- [x] **Drive at a slow speed in as high a gear as possible.**

If you're travelling on an icy road extra caution will be required to avoid any loss of control. You can reduce wheelspin by driving

- at a slow speed
- in as high a gear as possible.

Question 4.34

Skidding is mainly caused by

Mark one answer

- [ ] the weather
- [x] the driver
- [ ] the vehicle
- [ ] the road.

Answer

- [x] **the driver**

You should always consider the conditions and drive accordingly.

Question 4.35

It is snowing. Before starting your journey you should

Mark one answer

- [x] think if you need to ride at all
- [x] try to avoid taking a passenger
- [x] plan a route avoiding towns
- [x] take a hot drink before setting out.

Answer

[x] **think if you need to ride at all.**

Snow is one weather condition when it's better not to ride at all. If you must go out try and keep to main roads which are the most likely to be clear and well gritted.

Question 4.36

How can you avoid wheelspin when driving in freezing conditions?

Mark one answer

- [x] Stay in first gear all the time.
- [x] Put on your handbrake if the wheels begin to slip.
- [x] Drive in as high a gear as possible.
- [x] Allow the vehicle to coast in neutral.

Answer

[x] **Drive in as high a gear as possible.**

A low gear will cause the wheels to skid and you'll lose control. A high gear with steady accelerator control will help you to maintain some control.

Question 4.37

You are driving in freezing conditions. Which TWO should you do when approaching a sharp bend?

Mark two answers

- [x] Accelerate into the bend.
- [x] Slow down before you reach the bend.
- [x] Gently apply your handbrake.
- [x] Avoid sudden steering movements.
- [x] Position towards the middle of the road.

Answers

[x] **Slow down before you reach the bend.**

[x] **Avoid sudden steering movements.**

When you're approaching a sharp bend and the road is likely to be icy don't

- accelerate into the bend
- apply your handbrake
- coast (hold the clutch down).

These actions could lead to loss of control.

Question 4.38

You are driving in freezing conditions. What should you do when approaching a sharp bend?

Mark two answers

- [ ] Slow down before you reach the bend. ✗
- [ ] Gently apply your handbrake.
- [ ] Firmly use your footbrake.
- [ ] Coast into the bend.
- [ ] Avoid sudden steering movements. ✗

Answers

- ✗ **Slow down before you reach the bend.**
- ✗ **Avoid sudden steering movements.**

Avoid steering and braking at the same time. In icy conditions it's very important that you constantly assess what's ahead.

Question 4.39

When riding in extremely cold conditions what can you do to keep warm?

Mark one answer

- [ ] Stay close in behind the vehicles in front.
- [ ] Wear suitable clothing. ✗
- [ ] Lie flat on the tank.
- [ ] Put your hands one at a time on the exhaust pipe.

Answer

- ✗ **Wear suitable clothing.**

Motorcyclists are exposed to the elements and can become very cold when riding in wintry conditions. It's important to keep warm or concentration could be affected. The only way to stay warm is to wear suitable clothing.

If you do find yourself getting cold then stop at a suitable place to warm up.

Question 4.40

You are turning left on a slippery road. The back of your vehicle slides to the right. You should

Mark one answer

- [ ] brake firmly and not turn the steering wheel
- [ ] steer carefully to the left
- [ ] steer carefully to the right ✗
- [ ] brake firmly and steer to the left.

Answer

- ✗ **steer carefully to the right**

This should stop the sliding and allow you to regain control. Don't

- use the accelerator
- use the brakes
- use the clutch.

Question 4.41

You are braking on a wet road. Your vehicle begins to skid. Your vehicle does not have anti-lock brakes. What is the FIRST thing you should do?

Mark one answer

☒ Quickly pull up the handbrake.

☒ Release the footbrake fully. ✗

☒ Push harder on the brake pedal.

☒ Gently use the accelerator.

Answer

✗ **Release the footbrake fully.**

If the skid has been caused by braking too hard for the conditions release the brake. This will allow the wheels to turn and so limit the skid.

Skids are much easier to get into than they are to get out of. Prevention is better than cure. Stay alert to the road and weather conditions. Never drive so fast that you can't stop within the distance that you can see to be clear.

Question 4.42

How can you tell when you are driving over black ice?

Mark one answer

☒ It is easier to brake.

☒ The noise from your tyres sounds louder.

☒ You see black ice on the road.

☒ Your steering feels light. ✗

Answer

✗ **Your steering feels light.**

Sometimes you may not be able to see that the road is icy. Black ice makes a road look damp. The signs that you're travelling on black ice can be

• the steering feels light

• the noise from your tyres suddenly goes quiet.

Question 4.43

Coasting the vehicle

Mark one answer

☒ improves the driver's control

☒ makes steering easier

☒ reduces the driver's control ✗

☒ uses more fuel.

Answer

✗ **reduces the driver's control**

'Coasting' is the term used when the clutch is held down and the vehicle is freewheeling. This reduces the driver's control of the vehicle. When you coast the engine can't drive the wheels or hold the car back.

Question 4.44

Before starting a journey in freezing weather you should clear ice and snow from your vehicle

Mark four answers

- [ ] aerial
- [ ] windows
- [ ] bumper
- [ ] lights
- [ ] mirrors
- [ ] number plates.

Answers

- ☒ **windows**
- ☒ **lights**
- ☒ **mirrors**
- ☒ **number plate**

Don't travel unless it you really have to. Making unnecessary journeys will increase the risk of an accident. It is important that any snow or ice is not covering lights, mirrors, number plates or windows.

Question 4.45

You are driving in falling snow. Your wipers are not clearing the windscreen. You should

Mark one answer

- [ ] set the windscreen demister to cool
- [ ] be prepared to clear the windscreen by hand
- [ ] use the windscreen washers
- [ ] increase the windscreen wiper speed.

Answer

- ☒ **be prepared to clear the windscreen by hand**

Before you set off you should ensure that you can see clearly through all the windows. Don't be lazy and rely on the wipers to clear the front and rear, this will leave dangerous blind spots.

Question 4.46

When driving on snow it is best to keep in as high a gear as possible. Why is this?

Mark one answer

- [ ] To help you slow down quickly when you brake.
- [ ] So that the wheelspin does not cause your engine to run too fast.
- [ ] To leave a lower gear available in case of wheelspin.
- [ ] To help to prevent wheelspin.

Answer

- ☒ **To help to prevent wheelspin.**

If the ground is covered in snow, move off in as high a gear as possible. Stay in the highest gear you can. This reduces power to the wheels and so lessons the chance of skidding.

Question 4.47
You are trying to move off on snow. You should use

Mark one answer
- ☒ the lowest gear you can
- ☒ the highest gear you can
- ☒ a high engine speed
- ☒ the handbrake and footbrake together.

Answer

☒ **the highest gear you can**

If you attempt to move in a low gear such as first (1) the engine will rev at a higher speed. This could cause the wheels to spin and dig into the snow further.

Question 4.48
When driving in falling snow you should

Mark one answer
- ☒ brake firmly and quickly
- ☒ be ready to steer sharply
- ☒ use sidelights only
- ☒ brake gently in plenty of time. ✕

Answer

☒ **brake gently in plenty of time**

Braking on snow can be extremely dangerous. Be gentle with both the accelerator and brake to prevent wheel spin.

Question 4.49
The **main** benefit of having four-wheel drive is to improve

Mark one answer
- ☒ road holding ✕
- ☒ fuel consumption
- ☒ stopping distances
- ☒ passenger comfort.

Answer

☒ **road holding**

This does not replace the skills you need to drive safely. The extra grip the drive on the wheels provide help when travelling in slippery or uneven roads.

Question 4.50
When driving in fog in daylight you should use

Mark one answer
- ☒ sidelights
- ☒ full beam headlights
- ☒ hazard lights
- ☒ dipped headlights.

Answer

☒ **dipped headlights**

Don't drive in fog unless you really have to. Use dipped headlights during daylight. If the visibility is below 100 metres (330 feet) use fog lights and high-intensity rear lights. Let other road users know that you're there.

Question 4.51

You are at a junction with limited visibility. You should

Mark one answer

☒ inch forward, looking to the right

☒ inch forward, looking to the left

☒ inch forward, looking both ways ✗

☒ be ready to move off quickly.

Answer

☒ **inch forward, looking both ways**

At some road junctions you might find that you can't see clearly into the road that you're joining. Before you commit yourself you have to inch foward, looking both ways. Only emerge when you can see that it's safe to do so. Don't

- speed out hoping the way will be clear
- look one way only.

Question 4.52

Why should you ride with a dipped headlamp on in the daytime?

Mark one answer

☒ It helps other road users to see you. ✗

☒ It means that you can ride faster.

☒ Other vehicles will get out of the way.

☒ So that it is already on when it gets dark.

Answer

☒ **It helps other road users to see you.**

Your life could depend on being seen clearly.

Question 4.53

Motorcyclists are only allowed to use high-intensity rear fog lights when

Mark one answer

☒ a pillion passenger is being carried

☒ they ride a large touring machine

☒ visibility is 100 metres (330 feet) or less ✗

☒ they are riding on the road for the first time.

Answer

☒ **visibility is 100 metres (330 feet.) or less**

If your motorcycle is fitted with high-intensity rear fog lamps you should only use them when visibility is 100 metres (330 feet) or less. This rule applies to all other motor vehicles using these lamps

Question 4.54

In very hot weather the road surface can get soft. Which TWO of the following will be affected most?

Mark two answers

☒ The suspension.

☒ The steering. ✗

☒ The braking. ✗

☒ The windscreen.

Answers

✗ **The steering.**

✗ **The braking.**

Take care when braking or cornering. Tyres don't grip well on soft tarmac.

Question 4.55

In very hot weather the road surface can get soft. Which TWO of the following will be affected most?

Mark two answers

☒ The suspension.

☒ The grip of the tyres. ✗

☒ The braking. ✗

☒ The exhaust.

Answers

✗ **The grip of the tyres.**

✗ **The braking.**

Only a small part of your motorcycle's tyres are in contact with the road. This is why you must consider and respect the surface you're on.

Question 4.56

You are riding in very hot weather. What are TWO effects that melting tar has on the control of your machine?

Mark two answers

☒ It can make the surface slippery. ✗

☒ It can reduce tyre grip.

☒ It can reduce stopping distances.

☒ It can improve braking efficiency.

Answers

✗ **It can make the surface slippery.**

✗ **It can reduce tyre grip.**

In hot weather never be tempted to ride without protective clothing. If you fall from your machine you'll have no protection from the road surface.

Where are you most likely to be affected by a crosswind?

Mark one answer

☒ On a narrow country lane.

☒ On an open stretch of road.

☒ On a busy stretch of road.

☒ On a long, straight road.

Answer

✗ **On an open stretch of road.**

In windy conditions care must be taken on exposed roads. A strong gust of wind can blow you off course. Watch out for other road users, who may be affected more than you, such as

• cyclists

• motorcyclists

• high-sided lorries

• vehicles towing trailers.

In windy conditions you need to take extra care when

Mark one answer

☒ using the brakes

☒ making a hill start

☒ turning into a narrow road

☒ passing pedal cyclists. ✗

Answer

✗ **passing pedal cyclists**

You should **always** give cyclists plenty of room when overtaking. When it's windy a sudden gust could blow them off course.

Your indicators may be difficult to see in bright sunlight. What should you do?

Mark one answer

☒ Put your indicator on earlier.

☒ Give an arm signal as well as using your indicator. ✗

☒ Touch the brake several times to show the stop lamp.

☒ Turn as quickly as you can.

Answer

✗ **Give an arm signal as well as using your indicator.**

You should always ensure that other road users are aware of your intentions. If you feel your indicator might not be seen then give an arm signal as well.

Question 4.60

What should you do to help you see at night?

Mark one answer

☒ Allow a gap beneath your visor or goggles.

☒ Keep your visor or goggles clean. ✗

☒ Wear a tinted visor or goggles.

☒ Don't use a visor or goggles at all.

Answer

✖ **Keep your visor or goggles clean.**

If you're riding a motorcycle at night it's important that you can see clearly. Keep your visor or goggles clean and without smears. Don't wear a tinted visor or goggles at night.

Question 4.61

You are riding at night. To be seen more easily you should

Mark two answers

☒ ride with your headlight on dipped beam ✗

☒ wear reflective clothing ✗

☒ keep the motorcycle clean

☒ stay well out to the right

☒ wear fluorescent clothing.

Answers

✖ **ride with your headlight on dipped beam**

✖ **wear reflective clothing**

Reflective clothing works by reflecting light from the headlights of the other vehicles. This will make it easier for you to be seen. Fluorescent clothing, although effective during the day, won't show up as well as reflective clothing at night.

Question 4.62

When riding at night you should

Mark two answers

☒ ride with your headlight on dipped beam ✗

☒ wear reflective clothing ✗

☒ wear a tinted visor

☒ ride in the centre of the road

☒ give arm signals.

Answers

✖ **ride with your headlight on dipped beam**

✖ **wear reflective clothing**

Fluorescent clothing shows up in daylight, but at night you should wear reflective clothing. This could be a tabard or reflective body strap.

Question 4.63

You **must** use your headlight

Mark three answers

- ☒ when riding in a group
- ☒ at night when street lighting is poor
- ☒ when carrying a passenger
- ☒ on motorways during darkness
- ☒ at times of poor visibility
- ☒ when parked on an unlit road.

Answers

- ☒ **at night when street lighting is poor**
- ☒ **on motorways during darkness**
- ☒ **at times of poor visibility**

Your headlight is to help you see in the dark and to help other road users to see you.

You must use your headlight at night

- on all roads where street lighting is more than 185 metres (600 feet) apart
- on all lit motorways

and at other times when visibility is seriously reduced.

Question 4.64

You are about to go down a steep hill. To control the speed of your vehicle you should

Mark one answer

- ☒ select a high gear and use the brakes carefully
- ☒ select a high gear and use the brakes firmly
- ☒ select a low gear and use the brakes carefully
- ☒ select a low gear and avoid using the brakes.

Answer

- ☒ **select a low gear and use the brakes carefully**

When travelling down a steep hill your vehicle will tend to increase speed. This will also make it more difficult for you to stop. To maintain control and prevent the vehicle running away

- select a lower gear – the engine will then help to control your speed
- use the brakes carefully.

Question 4.65

You are on a long, downhill slope. What should you do to help control the speed of your vehicle?

Mark one answer

- ☒ Grip the steering wheel tightly.
- ☒ Select neutral.
- ☒ Select a low gear.
- ☒ Put the clutch down.

Answer

- ☒ **Select a low gear.**

Selecting a low gear when travelling downhill will help you to control your speed. The engine will assist the brakes and prevent your vehicle gathering speed.

Question 4.66

How can you use the engine of your vehicle as a brake ?

Mark one answer

☒ By changing to a lower gear.

☒ By selecting reverse gear.

☒ By changing to a higher gear.

☒ By selecting neutral gear.

Answer

☒ **By changing to a lower gear.**

You should do this for downhill stretches of road. This will prevent excess use of the brakes which could lessen their effectiveness.

Question 4.67

You wish to park facing DOWNHILL. Which TWO of the following should you do?

Mark two answers

☒ Turn the steering wheel towards the kerb.

☒ Park close to the bumper of another car.

☒ Park with two wheels on the kerb.

☒ Put the handbrake on firmly.

☒ Turn the steering wheel away from the kerb.

Answers

☒ **Turn the steering wheel towards the kerb.**

☒ **Put the handbrake on firmly.**

The kerb will help stop any forward movement of the vehicle.

Question 4.68

You are driving in a built-up area. You approach a speed hump. You should

Answer

☒ **slow your vehicle right down**

Many towns have speed humps to slow down traffic. They're often where there are pedestrians, so

- slow right down when driving over them

- look out for pedestrians.

They might affect your steering and suspension if you drive too fast.

Mark one answer

☒ move across to the left-hand side of the road

☒ wait for any pedestrians to cross

☒ slow your vehicle right down

☒ stop and check both pavements.

When approaching a right-hand bend you should keep well to the left. Why is this?

Mark one answer

☒ To improve your view of the road.

☒ To overcome the effect of the road's slope.

☒ To let faster traffic from behind overtake.

☒ To be positioned safely if the vehicle skids.

Answer

☒ **To improve your view of the road.**

Don't

- move over to the right to try and straighten the bend. You could endanger yourself by getting too close to oncoming traffic.

- cross or straddle unbroken white lines along the centre of the road

- drive so fast that you can't stop within your range of vision.

You are coming up to a right-hand bend. You should

Mark one answer

☒ keep well to the left as it makes the bend faster

☒ keep well to the left for a better view around the bend

☒ keep well to the right to avoid anything in the gutter

☒ keep well to the right to make the bend less sharp.

Answer

☒ **keep well to the left for a better view around the bend**

There could be a hazard just around the bend. Always be aware of this and you'll be better prepared to deal with it if you need to.

Question 4.71

You should not overtake when

Mark three answers

☒ intending to turn left shortly afterwards

☒ in a one-way street

☒ approaching a junction

☒ driving up a long hill

☒ the view ahead is blocked.

Answers

☒ **intending to turn left shortly afterwards**

☒ **approaching a junction**

☒ **the view ahead is blocked**

Before you overtake you should ask youself if it's really necessary. Getting there safely is more important than taking unnecessary risks.

This section looks at judgement and hazard perception.

The questions will ask you about

- anticipation
- hazard awareness
- attention
- speed and distance
- reaction time
- the effects of alcohol and drugs
- tiredness.

Question 5.1

You see this sign on the rear of a slow-moving lorry that you want to pass. It is travelling in the middle lane of a three lane motorway. You should

Mark one answer

[ ] cautiously approach the lorry then pass on either side

[ ] follow the lorry until you can leave the motorway

[ ] wait on the hard shoulder until the lorry has stopped

[ ] approach with care and keep to the left of the lorry.

Answer

☒ **approach with care and keep to the left of the lorry**

This sign indicates that you should keep to the left of the vehicle. If you wish to overtake then you should do so on the left. Be aware that there might be workmen in the area.

Question 5.2

Where would you expect to see these markers?

Mark two answers

[ ] On a motorway sign.

[ ] At the entrance to a narrow bridge.

[ ] On a large goods vehicle.

[ ] On a builder's skip placed on the road.

Answers

☒ **On a large goods vehicle.**

☒ **On a builder's skip placed on the road.**

These markers are reflective so that they show up at night. If you see them ahead then you should be aware that there might be a stationary, slow or long vehicle.

What does this signal from a police officer, mean to oncoming traffic?

Mark one answer

- [X] Go ahead.
- [X] Stop.
- [X] Turn left.
- [X] Turn right.

Answer

 Stop.

Police officers might be found at a point where there's heavy traffic or a breakdown of traffic lights. Check your copy of *The Highway Code* for the signals that they use.

What is the main hazard shown in this picture?

Mark one answer

- [X] Vehicles turning right.
- [X] Vehicles doing U-turns.
- [X] The cyclist crossing the road.
- [X] Parked cars around the corner.

Answer

 The cyclist crossing the road.

Look at the picture carefully and try to imagine you're there.

The cyclist in this picture isn't crossing the road in the correct place. You must be able to deal with the unexpected, especially when you're planning your approach to a hazardous junction. There will be several things to think about on your approach so look well ahead to give yourself time to deal with them.

Question 5.5

Which road user has caused a hazard?

Mark one answer

- ☒ The parked car (arrowed A).
- ☒ The pedestrian waiting to cross (arrowed B).
- ☒ The moving car (arrowed C).
- ☒ The car turning (arrowed D).

Answer

☒ **The parked car (arrowed A).**

The car has parked on the approach to a pedestrian crossing. The road is marked with white zigzag lines. Don't park on these – they're there for a reason. Parking here will

- block the view for pedestrians wishing to cross the road
- restrict the view of the crossing for traffic approaching.

Question 5.6

When approaching a hazard your FIRST reaction should be to

Mark one answer

- ☒ use your footbrake
- ☒ change direction
- ☒ release the accelerator
- ☒ check the mirrors.

Answer

☒ **check the mirrors**

Look well ahead and around so that you're as ready as possible for hazards that occur. Be aware of what's behind you. You might need to indicate that you're slowing down or changing direction.

What should the driver of the car approaching the crossing do?

Answer

❌ **Slow down and get ready to stop.**

Look well ahead to see if any hazards are developing. This will give you more time to deal with them in the correct way. The man in the picture is clearly intending to cross the road. You should be travelling at a speed that allows you to check your mirror, slow down and stop in good time. You shouldn't have to brake harshly.

Mark one answer

☒ Continue at the same speed.

☒ Sound the horn.

☒ Drive through quickly.

☒ Slow down and get ready to stop.

What should the driver of the red car do?

Answer

❌ **Wait for the pedestrian in the road to cross.**

Some people might take longer to cross the road. They may be elderly or have a disability. Be patient and don't hurry them by showing your impatience. They might have poor eyesight or not be able to hear traffic approaching.

Don't signal or wave the pedestrian to cross the road. Other road users may not have seen your signal and this could lead the pedestrian into a hazardous situation.

Mark one answer

☒ Wave the pedestrians who are waiting to cross.

☒ Wait for the pedestrian in the road to cross.

☒ Quickly drive behind the pedestrian in the road.

☒ Tell the pedestrian in the road she should not have crossed.

Question 5.9

What THREE things should the driver of the grey car be specially aware of?

Mark three answers

- ☒ Pedestrians stepping out between cars.
- ☒ The bumpy road surface.
- ☒ Empty parking spaces.
- ☒ Other cars behind the grey car.
- ☒ Cars leaving parking spaces.
- ☒ Parked cars' doors opening.

Answers

- ☒ **Pedestrians stepping out between cars.**
- ☒ **Cars leaving parking spaces.**
- ☒ **Parked cars' doors opening.**

Your awareness in hazardous situations is very important. In a busy street like the one in the picture there are many potential dangers. You might not be able to see a pedestrian crossing from between the parked vehicles. A driver or passenger of a parked car might open a door.

Drive or ride at a speed that will allow you to stop in good time if a hazard suddenly appears. It could happen at any time.

Question 5.10

What should the driver of the red car (arrowed) do?

Mark one answer

- ☒ Sound the horn to tell other drivers where he is.
- ☒ Squeeze through the gap.
- ☒ Wave the driver of the white car to go on.
- ☒ Wait until the car blocking the way has moved.

Answer

- ☒ **Wait until the car blocking the way has moved.**

If you're moving in slow-moving traffic think ahead so that you don't block junctions or stop others' progress. Don't

- force others to give way to you
- sound the horn to gain priority
- flash your lights to gain or give prority
- give any other misleading signal.

What should the driver of the grey car (arrowed) do?

Mark one answer

☒ Cross if the way is clear.

☒ Reverse out of the box junction.

☒ Wait in the same place until the lights are green.

☒ Wait until the lights are red then cross.

Answer

☒ **Cross if the way is clear.**

Yellow markings are marked on the road to prevent busy junctions becoming blocked with traffic. Don't enter the box unless your exit road is clear.

When turning right you can wait in the box if your exit road is clear but you can't proceed due to the oncoming traffic.

What should the driver of a car coming up to this level crossing do?

Mark one answer

☒ Drive through quickly.

☒ Drive through carefully.

☒ Stop before the barrier.

☒ Switch on hazard warning lights.

Answer

☒ **Stop before the barrier.**

Approach and cross level crossings with care. If you need to stop, wait patiently. In this picture there's a junction on the left, before the crossing; keep clear of the defined road markings. Don't

- try to beat the barrier by driving through
- drive or ride onto the crossing unless the road is clear on the other side
- drive or ride nose-to-tail over it
- stop on or just over the crossing.

Question 5.13

What are TWO main hazards a driver should be aware of when driving along this street?

Mark two answers

- ☒ Glare from the sun.
- ☒ Car doors opening suddenly.
- ☒ Lack of road markings.
- ☒ The headlights on parked cars being switched on.
- ☒ Large goods vehicles.
- ☒ Children running out from between vehicles.

Question 5.14

What is the main hazard a driver should be aware of when following this cyclist?

Mark one answer

- ☒ The cyclist may move into the left and dismount.
- ☒ The cyclist may swerve out into the road.
- ☒ The contents of the cyclist's carrier may fall onto the road.
- ☒ The cyclist may wish to turn right at the end of the road.

Answers

- ☒ **Car doors opening suddenly.**
- ☒ **Children running out from between vehicles.**

When driving or riding on roads where there are many parked vehicles you must take extra care. Always be ready for the unexpected and drive or ride accordingly.

Children are small and you might not be able to see them about to emerge from between cars. Drivers may be getting in and out of their vehicles, providing another potential hazard. If the road is narrow, as it is in this picture, you'll also need to look well down the road. This will help you to deal with any oncoming traffic safely.

Answer

- ☒ **The cyclist may swerve out into the road.**

When following a cyclist be aware that they also have to deal with the hazards around them. They may wobble or swerve to avoid a pot-hole in the road. They might see a potential hazard and change direction suddenly.

Don't drive or ride very close to them or rev your engine impatiently. This will only add to their perception of a hazard and may rush them into a dangerous decision.

The driver of which car has caused a hazard?

Answer

❌ **Car A.**

The driver of car A has forced the approaching vehicle to the right onto the hatch-marked area of the road. It's also blocked the view of the other vehicle trying to emerge.

When dealing with busy junctions consider the other road users around you. Your actions must not put any other driver or rider at risk.

Mark one answer

❌ Car A.

❌ Car B.

❌ Car C.

❌ Car D.

You think the driver of the vehicle in front has forgotten to cancel his right indicator. You should

Mark one answer

❌ sound your horn before overtaking

❌ overtake on the left if there's room

❌ flash your lights to alert the driver

❌ stay behind and not overtake.

Answer

❌ **stay behind and not overtake**

The driver may be unsure of the location of a junction and suddenly turn. Be cautious.

Question 5.17

What is the main hazard the driver of the red car (arrowed) should be most aware of?

Mark one answer

- ☒ Glare from the sun may affect the driver's vision.
- ☒ The black car may stop suddenly.
- ☒ The bus may move out into the road.
- ☒ Oncoming vehicles will assume the driver is turning right.

Answer

❌ **The bus may move out into the road.**

You should try to anticipate the actions of the other road users around you. The driver of the red car should have made a mental note that the bus was at the bus stop. If you do this you'll be prepared for the bus pulling out. Look and see how many more passengers are waiting to board. If the last one has just got on, the bus is likely to move off.

Question 5.18

In heavy motorway traffic you are being followed closely by the vehicle behind. How can you lower the risk of an accident?

Mark one answer

- ☒ Increase your distance from the vehicle in front.
- ☒ Tap your foot on the brake pedal.
- ☒ Switch on your hazard lights.
- ☒ Move onto the hard shoulder and stop.

Answer

❌ **Increase your distance from the vehicle in front.**

On a busy motorway, traffic might still travel at high speeds although the weight of traffic means the vehicles are close together. Don't follow too close to the vehicle in front. If a driver behind seems to be 'pushing' you, increase your distance from the car in front by easing off the accelerator. This will lessen the risk of an accident involving several vehicles.

You are driving along this dual carriageway. Why may you need to slow down?

Mark one answer

☒ There is a broken white line in the centre.

☒ There are solid white lines either side.

☒ There are roadworks ahead of you. ˙

☒ There are no footpaths.

Answer

 There are roadworks ahead of you.

Look well ahead and read any road signs as you drive. They are there to inform you of what is ahead. In this case you may need to slow right down and change direction. Make sure you are well prepared for the hazard.

What does the solid white line at the side of the road indicate?

Mark one answer

☒ Traffic lights ahead.

☒ Edge of the carriageway.

☒ Footpath on the left.

☒ Cycle path.

Answers

 Edge of the carriageway.

This road marking gives you a warning. This is especially useful in bad weather when visibility is restricted.

Question 5.21

You see this sign ahead. You should expect the road to

Mark one answer

- [ ] go steeply uphill
- [ ] go steeply downhill
- [ ] bend sharply to the left
- [ ] bend sharply to the right.

Answer

❌ **bend sharply to the left**

Adjust your speed in good time so that you are able to select the correct gear for the bend. Driving too fast into the bend will lead to lack of control.

Question 5.22

You are approaching this cyclist. You should

Mark one answer

- [ ] overtake before the cyclist gets to the junction
- [ ] flash your headlights at the cyclist
- [ ] slow down and allow the cyclist to turn
- [ ] overtake the cyclist on the left-hand side.

Answer

❌ **slow down and allow the cyclist to turn**

Keep well back and allow the cyclist room to take up the correct position for the turn. Don't drive up close behind or try to squeeze past through a narrow gap.

You have just been overtaken by this
motorcyclist who is cutting in sharply. You
should

Mark one answer

☒ sound the horn

☒ brake firmly

☒ keep a safe gap

☒ remember to flash your lights.

Answer

☒ **keep a safe gap**

If you need to, take your foot off the
accelerator and drop back to allow a safe
separation distance. Try not to react by
braking sharply as you could lose control.
Any vehicles behind you will have to react
in the same way, and it could lead to an
accident.

Why must you take extra care when turning
right at this junction?

Mark one answer

☒ Road surface is poor.

☒ Footpaths are narrow.

☒ Road markings are faint .

☒ There is reduced visibility.

Answer

☒ **There is reduced visibility.**

You may have to pull forward slowly until
you can see down the road. Be aware that
the traffic approaching the junction can't see
you either. If you don't know that it's clear,
don't go.

Question 5.25

What is the main hazard in this picture?

Mark one answer

- ☒ The pedestrian.
- ☒ The parked cars.
- ☒ The junction on the left.
- ☒ The driveway on the left.

Answer

✖ **The pedestrian.**

As you drive make a mental note of pedestrians on the pavement. They could suddenly decide to cross the road or step off the kerb.

Question 5.26

You are driving towards this parked lorry. What is the first hazard you should be aware of?

Mark one answer

- ☒ The lorry moving off.
- ☒ The narrowing road.
- ☒ The pedestrian crossing.
- ☒ The vehicles ahead.

Answer

✖ **The pedestrian crossing.**

Pedestrian crossings are usually provided in shopping areas like the one in the picture. As you approach consider that you may have to slow down and stop to allow pedestrians to cross.

Question 5.27

This yellow sign on a vehicle indicates this is

Answer

✗ a school bus

Buses which carry children to and from school stop at places other than scheduled bus stops. Be aware that they might pull over to allow children to get on or off. This will normally be in rush hours when traffic is heavy.

Mark one answer

- ☒ a vehicle broken down
- ☒ a school bus
- ☒ an ice cream van
- ☒ a private ambulance.

Question 5.28

You are driving towards this level crossing. What would be the first warning of an approaching train?

Answer

✗ A steady amber light.

This will be followed by a twin flashing red light which gives you a further warning. There is also a sound alarm to alert you. You must obey the lights. Stop.

Mark one answer

- ☒ Both half barriers down.
- ☒ A steady amber light.
- ☒ One half barrier down.
- ☒ Twin flashing red lights.

Question 5.29

You are driving along this motorway. It is raining. When following this lorry you should

Mark two answers

- [ ] allow at least a two-second gap
- [ ] move left and drive on the hard shoulder
- [ ] allow at least a four-second gap
- [ ] be aware of spray reducing your vision
- [ ] move right and stay in the right hand lane.

Answers

✖ **allow at least a four-second gap**

✖ **be aware of spray reducing your vision**

The two-second time gap will increase to four seconds when the roads are wet. If you stay well back you will increase your

- vision around the vehicle
- visibility through the windscreen
- degree of safety.

Question 5.30

You are behind this cyclist. When the traffic lights change, what should you do?

Mark one answer

- [ ] Try to move off before the cyclist.
- [ ] Allow the cyclist time and room.
- [ ] Turn right but give the cyclist room.
- [ ] Tap your horn and drive through first.

Answer

✖ **Allow the cyclist time and room.**

Hold back and allow the cyclist to move off. In some towns, junctions have special areas across the front of the traffic lane to allow cyclists to wait for the lights to change.

Question 5.31

You are driving towards this left hand bend. What dangers should you be aware of?

Mark one answer

 A vehicle overtaking you.

No white lines in the centre of the road.

No sign to warn you of the bend.

Pedestrians walking towards you.

Answer

✖ **Pedestrians walking towards you.**

Pedestrians walking on a road with no pavement will walk against the direction of the traffic. You can't see around this bend; there may be hidden dangers. Always consider this so you give yourself time to react to them.

Question 5.32

When approaching this bridge you should give way to

Mark one answer

bicycles

buses

motorcycles

cars.

Answer

✖ **buses**

A double-decker bus will have to take up a position in the centre of the road so that it can clear the bridge. There is normally a sign to indicate this. Look well down the road, through the bridge and consider that you may have to stop and give way to any bus approaching.

Question 5.33

What type of vehicle could you expect to meet in the middle of the road?

Mark one answer

- ☒ Lorry.
- ☒ Bicycle.
- ☒ Car.
- ☒ Motorcycle.

Answer

- ☒ **Lorry.**

A large vehicle might have to take up all the road to allow the top of the vehicle to clear the bridge. The arch of the bridge is at its highest point in the centre.

Question 5.34

As the driver of this vehicle, why should you slow down?

Mark two answers

- ☒ Because of the bend.
- ☒ Because its hard to see to the right.
- ☒ Because of approaching trains.
- ☒ Because of animals crossing.
- ☒ Because of the level crossing.

Answers

- ☒ **Because of the bend.**
- ☒ **Because of the level crossing.**

There are two hazards clearly signed in this picture. You should be preparing for the bend by slowing down and selecting the correct gear. You might also have to stop for the level crossing, so be alert and be prepared.

While driving, you see this sign ahead. You should

Answer

 slow, but continue around the bend

Drive around the bend at a steady speed in the correct gear. Be aware that you might have to stop for approaching trains.

Mark one answer

☒ stop at the sign

☒ slow, but continue around the bend ✗

☒ slow to a crawl and continue

☒ stop and look for open farm gates.

Why should the junction on the left be kept clear?

Answer

✗ **To allow vehicles to enter and emerge.**

If you are waiting in traffic look well down the queue. Judge stopping so that you are able to leave a gap allowing traffic to flow in and out of the junction.

Mark one answer

☒ To allow vehicles to enter and emerge. ✗

☒ To allow the bus to reverse.

☒ To allow vehicles to make a 'U' turn.

☒ To allow vehicles to park.

Question 5.37

What is the first hazard shown in this picture?

Mark one answer

- ☒ Standing traffic.
- ☒ Oncoming traffic.
- ☒ Junction on the left.
- ☒ Pedestrians.

Answer

❌ **Junction on the left.**

There may be traffic waiting to emerge, or traffic approaching waiting to turn right into the junction. If there is a queue ahead leave a gap so that traffic can proceed.

Question 5.38

You are driving in the left lane but want to turn right at the traffic lights. You should

Mark one answer

- ☒ check your mirrors, signal and move to the right
- ☒ weave into the middle and then to the right lane
- ☒ drive up to the lights then turn right
- ☒ stay in your lane and find another way back.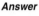

Answer

❌ **stay in your lane and find another way back**

Don't disrupt the flow of traffic by cutting across the lanes. Look out for direction signs as you drive and get into the correct lane in good time.

When the traffic lights change to green the white car should

Mark one answer

☒ wait for the cyclist to pull away ✗

☒ move off quickly and turn in front of the cyclist

☒ move close up to the cyclist to beat the lights

☒ sound the horn to warn the cyclist.

You intend to turn left at the traffic lights. Just before turning you should

Mark one answer

☒ check your right mirror

☒ move close up to the white car

☒ straddle the lanes

☒ check for bicycles on your left.

Answer

✗ wait for the cyclist to pull away

Before you move away check all around, cyclists often filter along the nearside of waiting traffic. Allow the cyclist to move off safely.

Answer

✗ check for bicycles on your left

This is especially important if you have been stationary and are about to move off. Cyclists do often try to filter passed vehicles in this way. You should always check your nearside.

Question 5.41

You should reduce your speed when driving along this road because

Answer

❌ **there is a staggered junction ahead**

Traffic could be turning off to the left or right ahead of you. They will be slowing right down or stopping to allow oncoming traffic to clear. Be prepared for this situation as you might have to slow down or stop behind them.

Mark one answer

☒ there is a staggered junction ahead ✗

☒ there is a low bridge ahead

☒ there is a change in the road surface

☒ the road ahead narrows.

Question 5.42

An approaching motorcyclist is easier to see when

Mark three answers

☒ the rider is wearing bright clothing ✗

☒ the rider has a white helmet ✗

☒ the headlight is on ✗

☒ the motorcycle is moving slowly.

☒ the motorcycle is moving quickly

☒ the rider has a passenger.

Answers

❌ **the rider is wearing bright clothing**

❌ **the rider has a white helmet**

❌ **the headlight is on**

These precautions are sensible measures which can increase the chances of other road users seeing the motorcyclist. As a driver you should not assume that all other vehicles are the width of a car. Motorcyclists can filter between traffic and approach junctions from behind queueing or parked cars. Watch out for them.

Question 5.43

You are driving at 60 mph. As you approach this hazard you should

Mark one answer

☒ maintain your speed

☒ reduce your speed ✗

☒ take the next right turn

☒ take the next left turn.

Answer

☒ **reduce your speed**

There could be stationery traffic ahead, waiting to turn right. Other traffic could be emerging and they will take time to gather speed.

Question 5.44

The traffic ahead of you in the left lane is slowing. You should

Mark two answers

☒ be wary of cars on your right cutting in ✗

☒ accelerate past the vehicles in the left lane

☒ pull up on the left hand verge

☒ move across and continue in the right hand lane

☒ slow down keeping a safe separation distance. ✗

Answers

☒ **be wary of cars on your right cutting in**

☒ **slow down keeping a safe separation distance**

Allow the traffic to merge into the nearside lane. Leave enough room so that your separation distance is not shortened drastically if a vehicle pulls into the left hand lane ahead of you.

Question 5.45

What might you expect to happen in this situation?

Mark one answer

- ☒ Traffic will move into the right-hand lane.
- ☒ Traffic speed will increase.
- ☒ Traffic will move into the left-hand lane. ✗
- ☒ Traffic will not need to change position.

Answer

✗ **Traffic will move into the left-hand lane.**

Be courteous and allow the traffic to merge into the left-hand lane. Try not to cut the vehicle off so that the driver has to steer sharply at the end of the lane.

Question 5.46

You are driving on a road with several lanes. You see these signs above the lanes. What do they mean?

Mark one answer

- ☒ The two right lanes are open.
- ☒ The two left lanes are open. ✗
- ☒ Traffic in the left lanes should stop.
- ☒ Traffic in the right lanes should stop.

Answer

✗ **The two left lanes are open.**

If you see a red cross above your lane it means that there is an obstruction ahead. You will have to move into the lane which is showing the green light. If all the lanes are showing a red cross, then you must stop.

At this blind junction you must stop

Mark one answer

☒ behind the line, then edge forward to see clearly ✗

☒ beyond the line at a point where you can see clearly

☒ only if there is traffic on the main road

☒ only if you are turning to the right.

Answer

✗ **behind the line, then edge forward to see clearly**

The stop sign has been put here because it is a dangerous junction. You must stop. It will not be possible to assess the situation on the move, however slowly.

When must you stop at this junction?

Mark one answer

☒ During rush hour only.

☒ Only when the area is busy.

☒ When turning right only.

☒ At all times. ✗

Answer

✗ **At all times.**

Attempting to emerge from this junction without stopping is highly dangerous. Even the most experienced driver would not be able to assess the situation without stopping.

Question 5.49

As a provisional licence holder, you must not drive a motor car

Mark two answers

☒ at more than 50 mph

☒ on your own

☒ on the motorway

☒ under the age of 18 years of age at night

☒ with passengers in the rear seats.

Answers

❌ **on your own**

❌ **on the motorway**

When you have passed your practical test you will be able to drive on a motorway. It is recommended that you have instruction on motorway driving before you venture out on your own. Ask your instructor about this.

Question 5.50

To drive you must be able to read a number plate from what distance?

Mark one answer

☒ 10 metres (33 feet).

☒ 15 metres (49 feet).

☒ 20.5 metres (67 feet).

☒ 205 metres (673 feet).

Answer

❌ **20.5 metres (67 feet).**

When you take your practical test your examiner will ask you to read a number plate from a distance of 20.5 metres (67 feet). This is a legal requirement to ensure that you see situations around you on the road.

Question 5.51

A driver can only read a number plate at the required distance with glasses on. The glasses should be worn

Mark one answer

- [ ] all the time when driving
- [ ] only when driving long distances
- [ ] only when reversing
- [ ] only in poor visibility.

Answer

✖ all the time when driving

You might find you need glasses or contact lenses to read number plates. This is fine, but you must then wear them when you drive or ride.

Question 5.52

You are about to drive home. You cannot find the glasses you need to wear when driving. You should

Mark one answer

- [ ] drive home slowly, keeping to quiet roads
- [ ] borrow a friend's glasses and drive home
- [ ] drive home at night, so that the lights will help you
- [ ] find a way of getting home without driving. ✖

Answer

✖ find a way of getting home without driving

Don't be tempted to drive if you've lost or forgotten your glasses. It's obvious that you must be able to see clearly when driving.

Question 5.53

You must wear glasses or contact lenses when driving on public roads if

Mark one answer

- [ ] you are the holder of an orange badge
- [ ] you cannot read a vehicle number plate from a distance of 36 metres (120 feet) without them
- [ ] there is an eyesight problem in your family
- [ ] you cannot read a vehicle number plate from a distance of 20.5 metres (67 feet) without them. ✖

Answer

✖ you cannot read a vehicle number plate from a distance of 20.5 metres (67 feet) without them

When you take your practical test your examiner will test your eyesight. You can wear glasses or contact lenses to do this but then you must wear them every time you drive.

Question 5.54

As a driver you find that your eyesight has become very poor. Your optician says he cannot help you. The law says that you should tell

Mark one answer

- [ ] the licensing authority
- [ ] your own doctor
- [ ] the local police station
- [ ] another optician.

Answer

- ☒ **the licensing authority**

This will have a serious affect on your judgement and concentration. The Driver and Vehicle Licencing Agency can be contacted by telephoning

0179 277 2151

Question 5.55

After passing your driving test, you suffer from ill health. This affects your driving. You **must**

Mark one answer

- [ ] inform your local police station
- [ ] get on as best you can
- [ ] not inform anyone as you hold a full licence
- [ ] inform the licensing authority.

Answer

- ☒ **inform the licensing authority**

The licencing authority won't automatically take away your licence without investigation. Contact the Driver and Vehicle Licencing Agency for advice.

Question 5.56

Which THREE result from drinking alcohol and driving?

Mark three answers

- [ ] Less control.
- [ ] A false sense of confidence.
- [ ] Faster reactions.
- [ ] Poor judgement of speed.
- [ ] Greater awareness of danger.

Answers

- ☒ **Less control.**
- ☒ **A false sense of confidence.**
- ☒ **Poor judgement of speed.**

From the start you must understand the dangers of mixing alcohol with driving or riding. One drink is too many if you're going to drive or ride. Alcohol will reduce your ability to drive or ride safely.

Which THREE of these are likely effects of drinking alcohol on driving?

Mark three answers

☒ Reduced co-ordination.

☒ Increased confidence.

☒ Poor judgement.

☒ Increased concentration.

☒ Faster reactions.

☒ Colour blindness.

Answers

☒ **Reduced co-ordination.**

☒ **Increased confidence.**

☒ **Poor judgement.**

Alcohol can increase confidence to a point where a driver or rider's behaviour might become 'out of character'. Someone who normally behaves sensibly suddenly takes risks and enjoys it. Never let yourself or your friends get into this situation.

You find that you need glasses to read vehicle number plates. When must you wear them?

Mark one answer

☒ Only in bad weather conditions.

☒ At all times when driving.

☒ Only when you think it necessary.

☒ Only in bad light or at night time.

Answer

☒ **At all times when driving.**

Have your eyesight tested before you start your practical training. Then, throughout your driving life, have periodical checks to ensure that your eyes haven't deteriorated.

Question 5.59

What is the **maximum** fine when causing death by careless driving whilst under the influence of alcohol?

Mark one answer

- ☒ A fine of £500.
- ☒ An unlimited fine.
- ☒ A fine of £2000.
- ☒ A fine of £5000.

Answer

☒ **An unlimited fine.**

This could result in a very expensive night out. Not only in financial terms but, more importantly, in terms of peoples lives.

Question 5.60

Drinking any amount of alcohol is likely to

Mark three answers

- ☒ reduce your ability to react to hazards
- ☒ increase the speed of your reactions
- ☒ worsen your judgement of speed
- ☒ increase your awareness of danger
- ☒ give a false sense of confidence.

Answers

☒ **reduce your ability to react to hazards**

☒ **worsen your judgement of speed**

☒ **give a false sense of confidence**

Never drink if you are going to drive. It's always the safest option not to drink at all. Don't be tempted, it's not worth it.

Question 5.61

You are invited to a pub lunch. You know that you will have to drive in the evening. What is your best course of action?

Mark one answer

- ☒ Avoid mixing your alcoholic drinks.
- ☒ Not drink any alcohol at all.
- ☒ Have some milk before drinking alcohol.
- ☒ Eat a hot meal with your alcoholic drinks.

Answer

☒ **Not drink any alcohol at all.**

Alcohol will stay in the body for this length of time. Drinking during the day will affect your performance at work or study. Avoid drinking at all even if you have not planned to drive in the evening.

Question 5.62

What else can seriously affect your concentration when driving, other than alcoholic drinks?

Mark three answer

- [x] Drugs.
- [x] Tiredness.
- [x] Tinted windows.
- [x] Contact lenses.
- [x] Loud music.

Answers

- [x] **Drugs.**
- [x] **Tiredness.**
- [x] **Loud music.**

The least distraction can allow your concentration to drift. Think about your driving, and that only, to stay in full control of your vehicle.

Question 5.63

How does alcohol affect your driving?

Mark one answer

- [x] It speeds up your reactions.
- [x] It increases your awareness.
- [x] It improves your co-ordination.
- [x] It reduces your concentration.

Answer

- [x] **It reduces your concentration.**

Concentration and good judgement at all times are needed to be a good, safe driver.

Question 5.64

After drinking alcohol heavily you should not drive the following day. Why is this?

Mark two answers

- [x] You may still be over the legal limit.
- [x] Your concentration will not be badly affected.
- [x] You will be well under the legal limit.
- [x] Your concentration may still be badly affected.

Answers

- [x] **You may still be over the legal limit.**
- [x] **Your concentration may still be badly affected.**

Think about this before you go to get into your car for work. You might still be over the limit, this means that your judgement and decision making will still be impaired.

Question 5.65

You have been convicted of driving whilst unfit through drink or drugs. You will find this is likely to cause the cost of one of the following to rise considerably. Which one?

Mark one answer

- [ ] Road fund licence.
- [ ] Insurance premiums.
- [ ] Vehicle test certificate.
- [ ] Driving licence.

Answer

✗ Insurance premiums.

You have proved yourself to a be risk to yourself and others on the road. For this reason insurance companies may charge you a high premium.

Question 5.66

What advice should you give to a driver who has had a few alcoholic drinks at a party?

Mark one answer

- [ ] Have a strong cup of coffee and then drive home.
- [ ] Drive home carefully and slowly.
- [ ] Go home by public transport.
- [ ] Wait a short while and then drive home.

Answer

✗ Go home by public transport.

Drinking black coffee or waiting a few hours won't make any difference. Alcohol takes time to leave the body. You might even be unfit to drive or ride the following morning.

Question 5.67

A driver attends a social event. What precaution should the driver take?

Mark one answer

- ☒ Drink plenty of coffee after drinking alcohol.
- ☒ Avoid busy roads after drinking alcohol.
- ☒ Avoid drinking alcohol completely.
- ☒ Avoid drinking alcohol on an empty stomach.

Answer

 Avoid drinking alcohol completely.

This is always going to be the safest option. One drink could be too many.

Question 5.68

It is eight hours since you last had an alcoholic drink. Which of the following applies?

Mark two answers

- ☒ You will certainly be under the legal limit.
- ☒ You will have no alcohol in your system.
- ☒ You may still be unfit to drive.
- ☒ You may still be over the legal limit.

Answers

 You may still be unfit to drive.

You may still be over the legal limit.

Alcohol can take several hours to leave the body. You may feel alright to drive, but it's effect will last for several hours.

Question 5.69

Your doctor has given you a course of medicine. Why should you ask if it is OK to drive?

Mark one answer

- ☒ Drugs make you a better driver by quickening your reactions.
- ☒ You will have to let your insurance company know about the medicine.
- ☒ Some types of medicine can cause your reactions to slow down.
- ☒ The medicine you take may affect your hearing.

Answer

☒ **Some types of medicine can cause your reactions to slow down.**

Always check the label of any medication container. The contents might affect your driving. If you aren't sure, ask your doctor or pharmacist.

Question 5.70

You have been taking medicine for a few days which made you feel drowsy. Today you feel better but still need to take the medicine. You should only drive

Mark one answer

☒ if your journey is necessary

☒ at night on quiet roads

☒ if someone goes with you

☒ after checking with your doctor.

Answer

☒ **after checking with your doctor**

Take care, it's not worth taking risks. Always check to be really sure. The medicine may have an affect on you later in the day.

Question 5.71

You are about to return home from holiday when you become ill. A doctor prescribes drugs which are likely to affect your driving. You should

Mark one answer

☒ drive only if someone is with you

☒ avoid driving on motorways

☒ not drive yourself

☒ never drive at more than 30 mph.

Answer

☒ **not drive yourself**

Find another way to get home. This may be very inconvenient, but it isn't worth the risk to other road users, your passengers or yourself.

Question 5.72

During periods of illness your ability to drive may be impaired. You must

Mark two answers

☒ see your doctor each time before you drive

☒ only take smaller doses of any medicines

☒ be medically fit to drive

☒ not drive after taking certain medicines

☒ take all your medicines with you when you drive.

Answers

☒ **be medically fit to drive**

☒ **not drive after taking certain medicines**

Medication can affect your concentration and your judgement when dealing with hazards. This of course is highly dangerous; be responsible.

Question 5.73

You are not sure if your cough medicine will affect your driving. What TWO things could you do?

Mark two answers

☒ Ask your doctor.

☒ Check the medicine label.

☒ Drive if you feel alright.

☒ Ask a friend or relative for advice.

Answers

✖ **Ask your doctor.**

✖ **Check the medicine label.**

If you're taking medicine or drugs prescribed by your doctor, check to ensure that they won't make you drowsy. If you forget to ask at the time of your visit to the surgery, check with your pharmacist.

Question 5.74

You take some cough medicine given to you by a friend. What must you do before driving?

Mark one answer

☒ Drink some strong coffee.

☒ Ask your friend if taking the medicine affected their driving.

☒ Check the label to see if the medicine will affect your driving.

☒ Make a short journey to see if the medicine is affecting your driving.

Answer

✖ **Check the label to see if the medicine will affect your driving.**

Never drive or ride having taken drugs you don't know about. They might affect your judgement and perception, and therefore endanger lives.

Question 5.75

You have taken medication that may make you feel drowsy. Your friends tell you it is safe to drive. What should you do?

Mark one answer

☒ Take their advice and drive.

☒ Ignore your friends' advice and do not drive.

☒ Only drive if they come with you.

☒ Drive for short distances only.

Answer

✖ **Ignore your friends' advice and do not drive.**

Friends may have their own reasons for wanting you to drive. Don't take the risk; it's never worth it.

Question 5.76

You feel drowsy when driving. You should

Mark two answers

- [ ] stop and rest as soon as possible
- [ ] turn the heater up to keep you warm and comfortable
- [ ] make sure you have a good supply of fresh air
- [ ] continue with your journey but drive more slowly
- [ ] close the car windows to help you concentrate.

Answers

✗ stop and rest as soon as possible

✗ make sure you have a good supply of fresh air

You will be putting other road users at risk if you continue to drive. Pull over and stop in a safe place. If you are driving a long distance think about finding some accommodation in order to get some sleep before continuing your journey.

Question 5.77

You are driving along a motorway and become tired. You should

Mark two answers

- [ ] stop at the next service area and rest
- [ ] leave the motorway at the next exit and rest
- [ ] increase your speed and turn up the radio volume
- [ ] close all your windows and set heating to warm
- [ ] pull up on the hard shoulder and change drivers.

Answers

✗ stop at the next service area and rest

✗ leave the motorway at the next exit and rest

If you have planned your journey properly, to include rest stops, you will arrive at your destination in good time.

Question 5.78

You are taking drugs that are likely to affect your driving. What should you do?

Mark one answer

☒ Seek medical advice before driving.

☒ Limit your driving to essential journeys.

☒ Only drive if accompanied by a full licence-holder.

☒ Drive only for short distances.

Answer

✖ **Seek medical advice before driving.**

Check with your doctor or pharmacist if you think that the drugs you're taking are likely to make you feel drowsy.

Question 5.79

You are about to drive home. You feel very tired and have a severe headache. You should

Mark one answer

☒ wait until you are fit and well before driving

☒ drive home, but take a tablet for headaches

☒ drive home if you can stay awake for the journey

☒ wait for a short time, then drive home slowly.

Answer

✖ **wait until you are fit and well before driving**

All your concentration should be on your driving. Any pain you feel will distract you. Change your plans and be safe.

Question 5.80

If you are feeling tired it is best to stop as soon as you can. Until then you should

Mark one answer

☒ increase your speed to find a stopping place quickly

☒ ensure a supply of fresh air

☒ gently tap the steering wheel

☒ keep changing speed to improve concentration.

Answer

✖ **ensure a supply of fresh air**

If you're travelling on a long journey plan your route before you leave. This will help you to

• be decisive at intersections and junctions

• plan your rest stops

• know approximately how long the journey will take.

Make sure that the vehicle you're travelling in is well ventilated. A warm, stuffy atmosphere can make you drowsy, which will impair your judgement and perception.

Question 5.81

Your reactions will be much slower when driving

Mark one answer

⊠ if tired

⊠ in fog

⊠ too quickly

⊠ in rain.

Answer

❌ **if tired**

Try to prevent becoming tired by

- taking plenty of rest stops
- allowing fresh air into the vehicle.

Question 5.82

You are driving on a motorway. You feel tired. You should

Mark one answer

⊠ carry on but drive slowly

⊠ leave the motorway at the next exit

⊠ complete your journey as quickly as possible

⊠ stop on the hard shoulder.

Answer

❌ **leave the motorway at the next exit**

If you do feel tired and there's no service station for many miles, leave the motorway at the next exit. Find a road off the motorway where you can pull up and stop.

How often should you stop on a long journey?

Mark one answer

☒ When you need petrol.

☒ At least every four hours.

☒ At least every two hours.

☒ When you need to eat.

Answer

✖ **At least every two hours.**

Your judgement and perception will be affected if you aren't alert. Tiredness could endanger your passengers and other road users as well as yourself.

If your motorway journey seems boring and you feel drowsy whilst driving you should

Mark one answer

☒ open a window and drive to the next service area

☒ stop on the hard shoulder for a sleep

☒ speed up to arrive at your destination sooner

☒ slow down and let other drivers overtake.

Answer

✖ **open a window and drive to the next service area**

Never stop on the hard shoulder to rest. If there is not a service station for several miles, then leave the motorway at the next exit.

You are planning a long journey. It should take about six hours. Do you need to plan rest stops?

Mark one answer

☒ Yes, you should plan to stop after about four hours driving.

☒ Yes, regular stops help concentration.

☒ No, you will be less tired if you get there as soon as possible.

☒ No, only fuel stops will be needed.

Answer

✖ **Yes, regular stops help concentration.**

Try to plan your journey so that you can take two rest stops. You will need to stop for something to eat within this six hours in order to keep up your energy level. If this is allowed to drop you will become tired and lose concentration.

Question 5.86

Driving long distances can be tiring. You can prevent this by

Mark three answers

- [x] stopping every so often for a walk
- [x] opening a window for some fresh air
- [x] ensuring plenty of refreshment breaks
- [x] playing loud music on the radio
- [x] completing the journey without stopping
- [x] eating a large meal before driving.

Answers

- [x] **stopping every so often for a walk**
- [x] **opening a window for some fresh air**
- [x] **ensuring plenty of refreshment breaks**

A stuffy, warm vehicle will cause you to feel tired. Playing loud music could prevent you hearing the approach of an emergency vehicle.

Question 5.87

To help concentration on long journeys you should stop frequently and

Mark one answer

- [x] have a rest
- [x] fill up with fuel
- [x] eat a meal
- [x] have a drink.

Answer

- [x] **have a rest**

Feeling tired will affect your ability to concentrate fully. This could have dangerous results leading to injury or even death.

Question 5.88

Which TWO things would help to keep you alert during a long journey?

Mark two answers

- [x] Finishing your journey as fast as you can.
- [x] Keeping off the motorways and using country roads.
- [x] Making sure that you get plenty of fresh air.
- [x] Making regular stops for refreshments.

Answers

- [x] **Making sure that you get plenty of fresh air.**
- [x] **Making regular stops for refreshments.**

Make sure that the vehicle you're driving is well ventilated. A warm, stuffy atmosphere will make you feel drowsy. Open a window or turn down the heating.

Question 5.89

Which THREE are likely to make you lose concentration while driving?

Mark three answers

- ☒ Looking at road maps.
- ☒ Listening to loud music.
- ☒ Using your windscreen washers.
- ☒ Looking in your wing mirror.
- ☒ Using a mobile phone.

Answers

- ☒ **Looking at road maps.**
- ☒ **Listening to loud music.**
- ☒ **Using a mobile phone.**

Looking at road maps while driving is very dangerous. If you aren't sure of your route stop in a safe place and check the map. You must not allow anything to take your attention away from the road.

If you wish to use a mobile phone, stop in a safe place before doing so. If you use a mobile phone frequently have a 'hands free' phone fitted in your vehicle.

Question 5.90

You have not worn suitable riding gear and get cold and wet when riding. Which TWO are likely effects?

Mark two answers

- ☒ You may lose concentration.
- ☒ Your visor may freeze up.
- ☒ You may slide off the seat.
- ☒ Your reaction times may slow.
- ☒ Your helmet may loosen.

Answers

- ☒ **You may lose concentration.**
- ☒ **Your reaction times may slow.**

If you're riding a motorcycle you should ensure that you're wearing suitable clothing. If you become cold and uncomfortable this could cause you to lose concentration.

Question 5.91

A correct seating position will enable you to

Mark three answers

- ☒ rest your head against the head restraint
- ☒ comfortably reach the pedals
- ☒ have good visability through the windows
- ☒ talk to all your passengers
- ☒ have a suitable grip on the steering wheel
- ☒ rest your hand on the gear lever.

Answers

- ☒ **comfortably reach the pedals**
- ☒ **have good visibility through the windows**
- ☒ **have a suitable grip on the steering wheel**

You need to be in control of your vehicle at all times. You should be able to reach all the controls comfortably, without stretching. Also, check the position of the mirrors and adjust them if you need to.

Question 5.92

A driver pulls out of a side road in front of you. You have to brake hard. You should

Mark one answer

☒ ignore the error and stay calm

☒ flash your lights to show your annoyance

☒ sound your horn to show your annoyance

☒ overtake as soon as possible.

Answer

☒ **ignore the error and stay calm**

If you're driving or riding where there are a number of side roads, be alert. Drivers approaching or emerging from the side road might not be able to see you. Be especially careful if there are a lot of parked vehicles. If a vehicle does emerge and you have to stop quickly

- try to be tolerant
- learn from the experience.

Question 5.93

A car driver pulls out causing you to brake. You should

Mark one answer

☒ keep calm and not retaliate

☒ overtake and sound your horn

☒ drive close behind and sound your horn

☒ flag the driver down and explain the mistake.

Answer

☒ **keep calm and not retaliate**

You have to understand that others on the road might disobey the rules or make an error of judgement at times. Try to accept this calmly and learn from other people's mistakes.

Question 5.94

Another driver does something that upsets you. You should

Mark one answer

☒ try not to react

☒ let them know how you feel

☒ flash your headlamps several times

☒ sound your horn.

Answer

☒ **try not to react**

There are occasions when other drivers or riders make a misjudgement or a mistake. If this happens try not to let it worry you. Don't react by showing anger. Sounding the horn, flashing the headlamps or shouting at the other driver won't help the situation. Good anticipation will help to prevent these incidents becoming accidents.

Another driver's behaviour has upset you.
It may help if you

Mark one answer

☒ stop and take a break

☒ shout abusive language

☒ gesture to them with your hand

☒ follow their car, flashing the headlights.

Answer

✗ **stop and take a break**

Tiredness may make you more irritable than
you would be normally. You might react
differently to situations because of it. If you
feel yourself becoming tense, take a break.

Just before driving you have had an argument
with a member of your family. This has made
you angry and late for an appointment. You
should

Mark one answer

☒ drive as quickly as possible to make up
time

☒ drive normally, thinking how to calm
things down later

☒ take a quick drink to calm you down

☒ take time to compose yourself before
driving.

Answer

✗ **take time to compose yourself before
driving**

We all get annoyed at times. Rushing in a
temper will make you feel even worse. Wait a
while, the problem will seem quite small
when you have calmed down.

Question 5.97

An older person's driving ability could be affected because they may be unable to

Mark one answer

- understand road signs
- obtain car insurance
- react very quickly
- give signals correctly

Answer

 react very quickly

Poor eyesight and hearing could affect their judgement of speed and distances. This may cause them to be more hesitant. Be tolerant of other drivers on the road and allow them time and room.

Question 5.98

You enter a one-way street by mistake. You should

Mark one answer

- reverse out of the road
- turn round in the school entrance
- continue to the end of the road
- reverse into a driveway.

Answer

 continue to the end of the road

Never reverse or turn your vehicle around in a one-way street. This is highly dangerous. Carry on and find another route checking the direction signs as you drive.

If you need to check a map, stop in a safe place.

This section looks at the risks when dealing with vulnerable road users

The questions will ask you about

- pedestrians
- children
- elderly drivers
- disabled people
- cyclists
- motorcycles
- animals
- new drivers.

Question 6.1

You should not ride too closely behind a lorry because

Mark one answer

☒ you will breathe in the lorry's exhaust fumes

☒ wind from the lorry will slow you down

☒ drivers behind you may not be able to see you

☒ it will reduce your view ahead.

Answer

☒ it will reduce your view ahead

If you're following a large vehicle your view beyond it will be restricted. Drop back. This will help you to see more of the road ahead.

Question 6.2

You are riding in fast-flowing traffic. The vehicle behind is following too closely. You should

Mark one answer

☒ slow down gradually to increase the gap' in front of you

☒ slow down as quickly as possible by braking

☒ accelerate to get away from the vehicle behind you

☒ apply the brakes briefly to warn the driver behind.

Answer

☒ slow down gradually to increase the gap in front of you

Vehicles travelling too close together are dangerous. Increase the safety margin by dropping back.

Question 6.3

You are riding along a main road with many side roads. Why should you be particularly careful?

Mark one answer

☒ Gusts of wind from the side roads may push you off course.

☒ Drivers coming out from side roads may not see you.

☒ The road will be more slippery where cars have been turning.

☒ Drivers will be travelling slowly when they approach a junction.

Answer

☒ Drivers coming out from side roads may not see you.

If you're riding along a main road where there are many side roads be alert. Drivers approaching or emerging from side roads may not be able to see you. Be especially careful if there are a lot of parked vehicles.

Always drive at a speed that will enable you to slow down and stop in good time. If you look well ahead and anticipate the actions of other road users you'll avoid having to brake suddenly or harshly.

Question 6.4

You are driving on a country road. What should you expect to see coming towards you on YOUR side of the road?

Mark one answer

 Motorcycles.

Bicycles.

Pedestrians.

Horse riders.

Answer

❌ **Pedestrians.**

On a quiet country road always be aware that there may be a hazard just around the next bend, such as a slow-moving vehicle or pedestrians. There might not be a pavement and people may be walking on your side of the road.

Question 6.5

Which sign means that there may be people walking along the road?

Mark one answer

Answer

Always check the road signs as you drive. They'll keep you informed of hazards ahead and help you to anticipate any problems.

There are different types of signs showing pedestrians. Learn the meaning of each one. This will help you to be aware of the hazard ahead.

Question 6.6

What does this sign mean?

Mark one answer

Pedestrian crossing.

Pedestrians in the road ahead.

No pedestrians.

Route for pedestrians.

Answer

 No pedestrians.

Always be aware that, although the sign restricts pedestrians, there may be some about.

Question 6.7

You are turning left into a side road. Pedestrians are crossing the road near the junction. You must

Mark one answer

☒ wave them on

☒ sound your horn

☒ switch on your hazard lights

☒ wait for them to cross.

Answer

☒ **wait for them to cross**

Before you turn into a junction check that it's clear. Check the pavement in each direction. If there are pedestrians crossing let them cross in their own time.

Question 6.8

You are turning left at a junction. Pedestrians have started to cross the road. You should

Mark one answer

☒ go on, giving them plenty of room

☒ stop and wave at them to cross

☒ blow your horn and proceed

☒ give way to them.

Answer

☒ **give way to them**

If you're turning into a side road you should give way to pedestrians already crossing. They have priority. Don't

- wave them across the road
- sound your horn
- flash your lights
- give any other misleading signal – other road users may misinterpret your signal and you might lead the pedestrian into a dangerous situation.

If a pedestrian is slow or indecisive be patient and wait. Don't hurry them across by revving the engine.

Question 6.9

You are turning left from a main road into a side road. People are already crossing the road into which you are turning. You should

Mark one answer

- [ ] continue, as it is your right of way
- [ ] signal to them to continue crossing
- [ ] wait and allow them to cross
- [ ] sound your horn to warn them of your presence.

Answer

 wait and allow them to cross

Always check the road you're turning into. Approaching at the correct speed will allow you enough time to observe and react.

Question 6.10

You are at a road junction, turning into a minor road. There are pedestrians crossing the minor road. You should

Mark one answer

- [ ] stop and wave the pedestrians across
- [ ] sound your horn to let the pedestrians know that you are there
- [ ] give way to the pedestrians who are already crossing
- [ ] carry on; the pedestrians should give way to you.

Answer

 give way to the pedestrians who are already crossing

Always look into the road you're turning into. If there are pedestrians crossing, be considerate, but don't wave or signal to them to cross. Signal your intention to turn as you approach.

Question 6.11

You are turning left into a side road. What hazards should you be especially aware of?

Mark one answer

☒ One way street.

☒ Pedestrians.

☒ Traffic Congestion.

☒ Parked vehicles.

Answer

☒ **Pedestrians.**

Make sure that you have reduced you speed and are in the correct gear for the turn. Look into the road before you turn and always give way to any pedestrians who are crossing.

Question 6.12

You want to reverse into a side road. You are not sure that the area behind your car is clear. What should you do?

Mark one answer

☒ Look through the rear window only.

☒ Get out and check.

☒ Check the mirrors only.

☒ Carry on, assuming it is clear.

Answer

☒ **Get out and check.**

It's always safer to be sure. You may not be able to see a small child close behind your car. The shape and size of your vehicle can restrict visibility.

Question 6.13

You are about to reverse into a side road. A pedestrian wishes to cross behind you. You should

Mark one answer

☒ wave to the pedestrian to stop

☒ give way to the pedestrian

☒ wave to the pedestrian to cross

☒ reverse before the pedestrian starts to cross.

Answer

☒ **give way to the pedestrian**

If you need to reverse into a side road try to find a place that's free from traffic and pedestrians.

Look all around before and during the manoeuvre. Always stop and give way to any pedestrians who wish to cross behind you. Don't

- wave them across the road
- sound the horn
- flash your lights
- give any other misleading signal – other road users may not have seen your signal and you might lead the pedestrian into a dangerous situation.

Question 6.14

You are reversing from a driveway and cannot see clearly. There are many pedestrians around. You should

Mark one answer

- [ ] continue whilst sounding your horn
- [ ] continue with your hazard lights on
- [ ] get someone to guide you
- [ ] continue; it is your right of way.

Answer

☒ **get someone to guide you**

If you can't see clearly it's safer to get help from someone outside the vehicle. They'll be in a better position to see all around the vehicle and along the pavement.

Question 6.15

Who is especially in danger of not being seen as you reverse your car?

Mark one answer

- [ ] Motorcyclists.
- [ ] Car drivers.
- [ ] Cyclists.
- [ ] Children.

Answer

☒ **Children.**

As you look through the rear of your vehicle you will not be able to see a small child. Be aware of this before you reverse. If there are children about, get out and check if it is clear.

Question 6.16

You intend to turn right into a side road. Just before turning you should check for motorcyclists who might be

Mark one answer

- [ ] overtaking on your left
- [ ] following you closely
- [ ] emerging from the side road
- [ ] overtaking on your right.

Answer

☒ **overtaking on your right**

Never attempt to change direction to the right without checking your right-hand mirror. A motorcyclist might not have seen your signal, it could be hidden by the car behind you. This action should become a matter of routine.

Question 6.17

You are reversing around a corner when you notice a pedestrian walking behind you. What should you do?

Mark one answer

- [ ] Slow down and wave the pedestrian across.
- [ ] Continue reversing and steer round the pedestrian.
- [ ] Stop and give way.
- [ ] Continue reversing and sound your horn.

Answer

☒ **Stop and give way.**

Wait until the pedestrian has passed, then look around again before you start to reverse. Don't forget that you may not be able to see a small child directly behind your vehicle. Be aware of the possibility of hidden dangers.

Question 6.18

You want to turn right from a junction but your view is restricted by parked vehicles. What should you do?

Mark one answer

☒ Move out quickly, but be prepared to stop.

☒ Sound your horn and pull out if there is no reply.

☒ Stop, then move slowly forward until you have a clear view.

☒ Stop, get out and look along the main road to check.

Answer

☒ **Stop, then move slowly forward until you have a clear view.**

If you want to turn right from a junction and your view's restricted STOP. Ease forward until you can see – there might be something approaching.

IF YOU DON'T KNOW, DON'T GO.

Question 6.19

You are at the front of a queue of traffic waiting to turn right into a side road. Why is it important to check your right mirror just before turning?

Mark one answer

☒ To look for pedestrians about to cross.

☒ To check for overtaking vehicles.

☒ To make sure the side road is clear.

☒ To check for emerging traffic.

Answer

☒ **To check for overtaking vehicles.**

There could be a motorcyclist riding along the outside of the queue. Always check your mirror, situations behind you can change in the time you have been waiting to turn.

Question 6.20

In which THREE places would parking your vehicle cause danger or obstruction to other road users?

Mark three answers

☒ In front of a property entrance.

☒ At or near a bus stop.

☒ On your driveway.

☒ In a marked parking space.

☒ On the approach to a level crossing

Answers

☒ **In front of a property entrance.**

☒ **At or near a bus stop.**

☒ **On the approach to a level crossing.**

Don't park your vehicle where parking restrictions apply. Think carefully before you slow down and stop. Look at road markings and signs to ensure that you aren't parking illegally.

Question 6.21

In which three places would parking cause an obstruction to others ?

Mark three answers

- [ ] Near the brow of a hill.
- [ ] In a lay-by.
- [ ] Where the kerb is raised.
- [ ] Where the kerb has been lowered for wheelchairs.
- [ ] At or near a bus stop.

Answers

- [x] **Near the brow of a hill.**
- [x] **Where the kerb has been lowered for wheelchairs.**
- [x] **At or near a bus stop.**

Think about the affect your parking will have on other road users. Don't forget that not all vehicles are the size of a car. Large vehicles will need more room to pass and might need more time to do so. Leaving the traffic unsighted, as before the brow of a hill, causes unecessary risks. Think before you park your car.

Question 6.22

What must a driver do at a pelican crossing when the amber light is flashing?

Mark one answer

- [ ] Signal the pedestrian to cross.
- [ ] Always wait for the green light before proceeding.
- [ ] Give way to any pedestrians on the crossing.
- [ ] Wait for the red-and-amber light before proceeding.

Answer

- [x] **Give way to any pedestrians on the crossing.**

The flashing amber light allows pedestrians already on the crossing to get to the other side before a green light shows to the traffic. Let them to do this at their own pace.

Question 6.23

You have stopped at a pelican crossing. A disabled person is crossing slowly in front of you. The lights have now changed to green. You should

Mark two answers

- [ ] allow the person to cross
- [ ] ride in front of the person
- [ ] ride behind the person
- [ ] sound your horn
- [ ] be patient
- [ ] edge forward slowly.

Answers

- [x] **allow the person to cross**
- [x] **be patient**

At a pelican crossing the green light means you may proceed as long as the crossing is clear. If someone hasn't finished crossing be patient and wait for them.

DSA THEORY TEST for car drivers and motorcyclists

Question 6.24

A toucan crossing is different from other crossings because

Mark one answer

- ☒ moped riders can use it
- ☒ it is controlled by a traffic warden
- ☒ it is controlled by two flashing lights
- ☒ cyclists can use it.

Answer

☒ cyclists can use it

Pedestrians and cyclists are shown the green light together. The signals are push button operated and there is no flashing amber phase.

Question 6.25

At toucan crossings

Mark two answers

- ☒ there is no flashing amber light
- ☒ cyclists are not permitted
- ☒ there is a continuously flashing amber beacon
- ☒ pedestrians and cyclists may cross
- ☒ you only stop if someone is waiting to cross.

Answers

☒ there is no flashing amber light
☒ pedestrians and cyclists may cross

There are some crossings where cycle routes lead the cyclists to cross at the same place as pedestrians. Always look out for cyclists, as they're likely to be approaching faster than pedestrians.

Question 6.26

What type of crossing is this?

Mark one answer

- ☒ A zebra crossing.
- ☒ A pelican crossing.
- ☒ A puffin crossing.
- ☒ A toucan crossing.

Answer

☒ A toucan crossing.

This crossing is similar to a pelican crossing. Cyclists share the crossing with pedestrians without the need to dismount. Watch out for cyclists as they will approach the crossing faster than pedestrians.

When may you stop on a pedestrian crossing?

Mark one answer

☒ Not at any time.

☒ To avoid an accident.

☒ When there is a queue of traffic in front of you.

☒ Between the hours of 11 pm and 7 am.

Answer

☒ **To avoid an accident.**

Don't stop directly on a pedestrian crossing. If you're moving in a queue look well ahead and try to judge the flow of traffic. Leave a gap for pedestrians to cross.

Look at this picture. What is the danger you should be most aware of?

Mark one answer

☒ The ice cream van may move off.

☒ The driver of the ice cream van may get out.

☒ The car on the left may move off.

☒ The child may run out into the road.

Answer

☒ **The child may run out into the road.**

Extra care must be taken when there are children about. Look out for them at all times but especially

- in residential areas
- near parks
- near schools.

Where there are crossing places used by children be extra cautious. Don't

- overtake
- drive at high speed.

If you see an ice cream van ask yourself, 'Where are the children?' They might run across the road to it. Their small size may prevent you seeing them emerging from behind parked vehicles.

You are driving past parked cars. You notice a wheel of a bicycle sticking out between them. What should you do?

Mark one answer

☒ Accelerate past quickly and sound your horn.

☒ Slow down and w   e the cyclist across.

☒ Brake sharply and flash your headlights.

☒ Slow down and be prepared to stop for a cyclist.

Answer

☒ **Slow down and be prepared to stop for a cyclist.**

Scan the road as you drive. Try to anticipate hazards by being aware of the places where they are likely to occur. You'll then be able to react in good time, if necessary.

Question 6.30

You are driving past a line of parked cars. You notice a ball bouncing out into the road ahead. What should you do?

Mark one answer

- [ ] Continue driving at the same speed and sound your horn.
- [ ] Continue driving at the same speed and flash your headlights.
- [ ] Slow down and be prepared to stop for children.
- [ ] Stop and wave the children across to fetch their ball.

Answer

❌ **Slow down and be prepared to stop for children.**

Beware of children playing in the street and running out into the road. If a ball bounces out from the pavement slow down and stop. Don't encourage anyone to retrieve it. Other road users may not see your signal and you might lead a child into a dangerous situation.

Question 6.31

What does this sign tell you?

Mark one answer

- [ ] No cycling.
- [ ] Cycle route ahead.
- [ ] Route for cycles only.
- [ ] End of cycle route.

Answer

❌ **Cycle route ahead.**

With people's concern today for the environment, cycle routes are being created in our towns and cities. These can be defined by road markings and signs. Don't straddle or drive in them. Respect the presence of cyclists on the road and give them plenty of room if you need to pass.

What does this sign warn you to look for?

Mark one answer

☒ A school crossing patrol.

☒ A pedestrian crossing.

☒ A park.

☒ School children.

Answer

✗ **School children.**

Look out for road signs as you drive. There could be a sign to warn you that children may be about. If you're driving near a school take extra care, as children can be impulsive and might dart out into the road without warning. Drive at an appropriately slow speed and try to anticipate their actions.

How will a school crossing patrol signal you to stop?

Mark one answer

☒ By pointing to children on the opposite pavement.

☒ By displaying a red light.

☒ By displaying a stop sign.

☒ By giving you an arm signal.

Answer

✗ **By displaying a stop sign.**

If someone steps out into the road with a school crossing sign you must stop. Don't

• wave anyone across the road

• get impatient or rev your engine.

What warning may you see before a school 'lollipop' warden ?

Mark one answer

☒ One flashing amber light.

☒ Two flashing amber lights.

☒ Two flashing red lights.

☒ One flashing red light.

Answer

✗ **Two flashing amber lights.**

You are likely to be driving in a built-up area; you should already be anticipating hazards such as pedestrians and parked cars. The lights give you an extra warning that it is the time of day when children will be leaving school. Watch out for them.

Question 6.35

You see someone step into the road holding this sign. What must you do?

Mark one answer

☒ Slow down and look out for children.

☒ Signal the person to cross.

☒ Drive carefully round the person.

☒ Pull up before the person.

Answer

✖ **Pull up before the person.**

Check the road signs as you drive. If you see a sign for a school there might be a school crossing patrol ahead, especially if amber flashing lights show beneath it.

Question 6.36

You are approaching a school crossing patrol. When this sign is held up you must

Mark one answer

☒ stop and allow any children to cross

☒ stop and beckon the children to cross

☒ stop only if the children are on a pedestrian crossing

☒ stop only when the children are actually crossing the road.

Answer

✖ **stop and allow any children to cross**

If you see a school sign anticipate that there might be a school crossing patrol. Always drive carefully where there might be ch''dren.

A school crossing patrol shows this sign. What must you do?

Mark one answer

☒ Continue if it is safe to do so.

☒ Slow down and be ready to stop.

☒ Stop ONLY if children are crossing.

☒ Stop at all times.

Answer

✖ **Stop at all times.**

Where would you see this sign?

Mark one answer

☒ In the window of a car taking children to school.

☒ At the side of the road.

☒ At playground areas.

☒ On the rear of a school bus or coach.

Answer

✖ **On the rear of a school bus or coach.**

Vehicles that are used to carry children to and from school will be travelling at busy times of the day. If you're following a vehicle with this sign be prepared for it to make frequent stops. It might pick up or set down passengers in places other than normal bus stops.

Question 6.39

Where would you see this sign?

Mark one answer

⊠ On the approach to a school crossing.

⊠ At a playground entrance.

⊠ On a school bus.

⊠ At a 'pedestrians only' area.

Answer

❌ **On a school bus.**

Watch out for children crossing the road from the other side of the bus.

Question 6.40

You are parking your vehicle in the street. The car parked in front of you is displaying an orange badge. You should

Mark one answer

⊠ park close to it to save road space

⊠ allow room for a wheelchair

⊠ wait until the orange-badge holder returns

⊠ park with two wheels on the pavement.

Answer

❌ **allow room for a wheelchair**

Think about the room that's needed to open the rear of the vehicle and lift a chair in. Room might be needed to manoeuvre a chair between the two cars.

Question 6.41

Are you allowed to block the pavement when parking your vehicle?

Mark one answer

⊠ No, unless to pick up passengers.

⊠ Yes, when on a narrow road.

⊠ No, not at any time.

⊠ Yes, when you think it is safe to do so.

Answer

❌ **No, not at any time.**

Parking on the pavement can obstruct and cause problems for pedestrians.

People who are in wheel chairs, are visually impaired or pushing pushchairs might not be able to pass.

You are following a car driven by an elderly driver. You should

Mark one answer

 expect the driver to drive badly

flash your lights and overtake

be aware that the driver's reactions may not be as fast as yours

stay close behind and drive carefully.

Answer

 be aware that the driver's reactions may not be as fast as yours

You must show consideration to other road users. Their reactions may be slower and they might need more time to deal with a situation. Be tolerant and don't lose patience or show your annoyance.

Which sign tells you that pedestrians may be walking in the road as there is no pavement?

Mark one answer

Answer

If you have to pass pedestrians who are walking at the side of the road, you must give them plenty of room. The draught caused by your vehicle could unsteady them, or they could turn around when they hear your car engine and step sideways into the road.

Which sign means there may be elderly pedestrians likely to cross the road ?

Mark one answer

Answer

You will often find this sign where there is a nursing home or retirement accommodation. Be patient if elderly people are crossing the road. They will need more time. Be aware that they might be deaf, or there vision is limited.

Question 6.45

What does this sign mean?

Mark one answer

- ☒ No route for pedestrians and cyclists.
- ☒ A route for pedestrians only.
- ☒ A route for cyclists only.
- ☒ A route for pedestrians and cyclists.

Answer

☒ **A route for pedestrians and cyclists.**

This shared route is for pedestrians and cyclists only. Be aware that when it ends the cyclists will be rejoining the main road.

Question 6.46

You see a pedestrian carrying a white stick. This shows that the person is

Mark one answer

- ☒ disabled
- ☒ deaf
- ☒ elderly
- ☒ blind.

Answer

☒ **blind**

If you see a pedestrian carrying a white stick it will mean that the person is partially sighted or blind. Make allowances for their hesitation at crossings or junctions.

Question 6.47

You see a pedestrian with a white stick and two red reflective bands. This means that the person is

Mark one answer

- ☒ physically disabled
- ☒ deaf only
- ☒ blind only
- ☒ deaf and blind.

Answer

☒ **deaf and blind**

If the person is deaf as well as blind the stick will have two red reflective bands. You can't tell if a pedestrian is deaf. Don't assume everyone can hear you approaching.

You are driving towards a pedestrian crossing. Waiting to cross is a person in a wheelchair. You should

Mark one answer

 be prepared to stop

 wave to the person to cross

wave to the person to wait

continue on your way.

Answer

 be prepared to stop

As you would with an able bodied pedestrian, you should prepare to slow down and stop. Don't wave the pedestrian across as they, due to their seated position, might not be able to see traffic beyond in a right hand lane. There might be a motorcyclist on your offside.

What action would you take when elderly people are crossing the road?

Mark one answer

 Wave them across so they know that you have seen them.

 Be patient and allow them to cross in their own time.

 Rev the engine to let them know that you are waiting.

 Tap the horn in case they are hard of hearing.

Answer

 Be patient and allow them to cross in their own time.

Don't hurry elderly people across the road by driving up close to them or revving the engine. Be aware that they might take longer to cross. They might also be hard of hearing and not able to hear your approach.

You see two elderly pedestrians about to cross the road ahead. You should

Mark one answer

 expect them to wait for you to pass

 speed up to get past them quickly

 stop and wave them across the road

 be careful, they may misjudge your speed.

Answer

be careful, they may misjudge your speed

Their concentration, judgement, hearing and/or vision could be impaired. Be aware that if they proceed to cross they will take more time to do so.

Question 6.51

Why should you be more careful when following elderly drivers?

Mark one answer

☒ Their passengers may be talking to them.

☒ Their reactions may be quicker than yours.

☒ Their reactions may not be as quick as yours.

☒ Their car may be very old.

Answer

✖ **Their reactions may not be as quick as yours.**

Drivers in the age range of 17–25 are more likely to have a road accident. So although elderly drivers may react more slowly they may react correctly. Quick reactions do not necessarily mean right decisions.

Question 6.52

As you approach a pelican crossing the lights change to green. Elderly people are halfway across. You should

Mark one answer

☒ wave them to cross as quickly as they can

☒ rev your engine to make them hurry

☒ flash your lights in case they have not heard you

☒ wait because they will take longer to cross.

Answer

✖ **wait because they will take longer to cross**

Even if the lights turn to red, wait for them to clear the crossing. Allow them to cross the road in their own time.

Question 6.53

You are following a motorcyclist on an uneven road. You should

Mark one answer

☒ allow less room to ensure that you can be seen in their mirrors

☒ overtake immediately

☒ allow extra room in case they swerve to avoid pot-holes

☒ allow the same room as normal because motorcyclists are not affected by road surfaces.

Answer

✖ **allow extra room in case they swerve to avoid pot-holes**

Pot-holes in the road can unsteady a motorcyclist. For this reason the rider might swerve to avoid an uneven road surface. Watch out at places where this is likely to occur.

What does this sign mean?

Mark one answer

☒ Contra-flow pedal cycle lane.

☒ With-flow pedal cycle lane.

☒ Pedal cycles and buses only.

☒ No pedal cycles or buses.

Answer

✖ **With-flow pedal cycle lane.**

This will be marked on the road, sometimes with a different colour surface. Leave these clear for cyclists and don't pass too closely when you overtake.

You should NEVER attempt to overtake a cyclist

Mark one answer

☒ just before you turn left

☒ just before you turn right

☒ on a one-way street

☒ on a dual carriageway.

Answer

✖ **just before you turn left**

If you want to turn left and there's a cyclist in front of you, hold back. Wait until the cyclist has passed the junction and then turn left behind them.

You are driving behind a cyclist. You wish to turn left just ahead. You should

Mark one answer

☒ overtake the cyclist before the junction

☒ pull alongside the cyclist and stay level until after the junction

☒ hold back until the cyclist has passed the junction

☒ go around the cyclist on the junction.

Answer

✖ **hold back until the cyclist has passed the junction**

When driving or riding make allowances for cyclists. Allow them plenty of room. If you're following a cyclist be aware that they also have to deal with hazards around them. They might swerve or change direction suddenly to avoid an uneven road surface.

Question 6.57

You are coming up to a roundabout. A cyclist is signalling to turn right. What should you do?

Mark one answer

☒ Overtake on the right.

☒ Give a horn warning.

☒ Signal the cyclist to move across.

☒ Give the cyclist plenty of room.

Answer

 Give the cyclist plenty of room.

If you're following a cyclist who's signalling to turn right at a roundabout leave plenty of room. Give them space and time to get into the correct lane.

Question 6.58

You are driving behind two cyclists. They approach a roundabout in the left-hand lane. In which direction should you expect the cyclists to go?

Mark one answer

☒ Left.

☒ Right.

☒ Any direction.

☒ Straight ahead.

Answer

 Any direction.

If you're following a cyclist into a roundabout be aware of them as they might not be taking the exit you anticipate. Cyclists approaching in the left-hand lane may be turning right but may not have been able to get into the correct lane due to the heavy traffic. Give them room.

Question 6.59

You are approaching this roundabout and see the cyclist signal right. Why is the cyclist keeping to the left?

Mark one answer

☒ It is a quicker route for the cyclist.

☒ The cyclist is going to turn left instead.

☒ The cyclist thinks *The Highway Code* does not apply to bicycles.

☒ The cyclist is slower and more vulnerable.

Answer

☒ **The cyclist is slower and more vulnerable.**

Cycling in today's heavy traffic can be hazardous. Some cyclists may not feel happy about crossing the path of traffic to take up a position in an outside lane. Be aware of this and understand that, although in the left-hand lane, the cyclist might be turning right.

Question 6.60

When you are overtaking a cyclist you should leave as much room as you would give to a car. Why is this?

Mark one answer

☒ The cyclist might change lanes.

☒ The cyclist might get off the bike.

☒ The cyclist might swerve.

☒ The cyclist might have to make a right turn.

Answer

☒ **The cyclist might swerve.**

If you intend to overtake a cyclist look at the road ahead. Check if the cyclist needs to change direction for a parked vehicle or an uneven road surface. When you have a safe place to overtake leave as much room as you would for a car. Don't cut in sharply or pass too closely.

Question 6.61

Which TWO should you allow extra room when overtaking?

Mark two answers

☒ Motorcycles.

☒ Tractors.

☒ Bicycles.

☒ Road-sweeping vehicles.

Answers

☒ **Motorcycles.**

☒ **Bicycles.**

Don't pass riders too closely as this may cause them to lose balance. Always leave as much room as you would for a car, and don't cut in.

Question 6.62

Why should you allow extra room when overtaking a motorcyclist on a windy day?

Mark one answer

☒ The rider may turn off suddenly to get out of the wind.

☒ The rider may be blown across in front of you.

☒ The rider may stop suddenly.

☒ The rider may be travelling faster than normal.

Answer

☒ **The rider may be blown across in front of you.**

A motorcyclist's position on the road can be affected by high winds. If you're driving or riding on a windy day be aware that the conditions might force a motorcyclist to swerve or wobble. Take this into consideration if you're following or wish to overtake.

Question 6.63

Which type of vehicle is most affected by strong winds?

Mark one answer

☒ Tractor.

☒ Motorcycle.

☒ Car.

☒ Tanker.

Answer

☒ **Motorcycle.**

Pass a motocyclist leaving plenty of room. Allow space in case the wind blows the motorcyclist across the lane.

Question 6.64

Why should you look particularly for motorcyclist and cyclists at junctions ?

Mark one answer

☒ They may want to turn into the side road.

☒ They may slow down to let you turn.

☒ They are harder to see.

☒ They might not see you turn.

Answer

❌ **They are harder to see.**

These road users could be hazards that are hidden from your view. Parked cars could cause you to lose sight of them. Consider that cyclists may need more time to make a turn.

Question 6.65

You are waiting to come out of a side road. Why should you watch carefully for motorcycles?

Mark one answer

☒ Motorcycles are usually faster than cars.

☒ Police patrols often use motorcycles.

☒ Motorcycles are small and hard to see.

☒ Motorcycles have right of way.

Answer

❌ **Motorcycles are small and hard to see.**

If you're waiting to emerge from a side road watch out for motorcyclists. They're smaller and more difficult to see. Be especially careful if there are parked vehicles restricting your view. There might be a motorcyclist appoaching.

IF YOU DON'T KNOW, DON'T GO.

Question 6.66

Where should you take **particular** care to look out for motorcyclists and cyclists?

Mark one answer

☒ On dual carriageways.

☒ At junctions.

☒ At zebra crossings.

☒ On one-way streets.

Answer

❌ **At junctions.**

Motorcyclists and cyclists may be more difficult to see on the road. This is especially the case at junctions. You may not be able to see a motorcyclist approaching a junction if your view's blocked by other traffic. Be aware of the possibility. A motorcycle may be travelling as fast as a car, or faster. Make sure that you judge speeds correctly before you emerge.

In daylight, an approaching motorcyclist is using a dipped headlight. Why?

Mark one answer

☒ So that the rider can be seen more easily.

☒ To stop the battery over-charging.

☒ To improve the rider's vision.

☒ The rider is inviting you to proceed.

Answer

 So that the rider can be seen more easily.

A motorcycle can be lost out of sight behind another vehicle. The use of the headlight helps to make it more conspicuous and therefore more easily seen.

Question 6.68

Where in particular should you look out for motorcyclists?

Mark one answer

☒ In a filling station.

☒ At a road junction.

☒ Near a service area.

☒ When entering a car park.

Answer

 At a road junction.

Always look ahead and try to make use of the information you see. This will enable you to anticipate possible hazards, and give you more time to deal with them as they occur.

Question 6.69

Motorcycle riders are vulnerable because they

Mark one answer

☒ are easy for other road users to see

☒ are difficult for other road users to se'

☒ are likely to have breakdowns

☒ cannot give arm signals.

Answer

 are difficult for other road users to see

Motorcyclists don't always wear bright clothing. Look out for them and expect to see them at junctions.

Motorcyclists should wear bright clothing mainly because

Mark one answer

- [ ] they must do so by law
- [ ] it helps keep them cool in summer
- [ ] the colours are popular
- [ ] drivers often do not see them.

Answer

✗ drivers often do not see them

Although they're advised to wear clothing that's bright or reflective motorcyclists often wear black. This means that they're difficult to see. Look out for them.

Motorcyclists ride in daylight with their headlights switched on because

Mark one answer

- [ ] it is a legal requirement
- [ ] there is a speed trap ahead
- [ ] they need to be seen
- [ ] there are speed humps ahead.

Answer

✗ they need to be seen

Motorcyclists using their headlights in this way aren't indicating any priority. They want you to see them. Riding with the headlight on warns of their approach.

There is a slow-moving motorcyclist ahead of you. You are unsure what the rider is going to do. You should

Mark one answer

- [ ] pass on the left
- [ ] pass on the right
- [ ] stay behind
- [ ] move closer.

Answer

✗ stay behind

Be patient. The motorcyclist might be turning right or changing direction.

Question 6.73

You are driving behind a moped. You want to turn left just ahead. You should

Mark one answer

☒ overtake the moped before the junction

☒ pull alongside the moped and stay level until just before the junction

☒ sound your horn as a warning and pull in front of the moped

☒ stay behind until the moped has passed the junction.

Answer

✗ **stay behind until the moped has passed the junction**

Passing the moped and turning into the junction could mean that you cut across the front of the rider. This might force them to slow down, stop or even lose control.

Question 6.74

Motorcyclists will often look round over their right shoulder just before turning right. This is because

Mark one answer

☒ they need to listen for following traffic

☒ motorcycles do not have mirrors

☒ looking around helps them balance as they turn

☒ they need to check for traffic in their blind area.

Answer

✗ **they need to check for traffic in their blind area**

If you're behind a motorcyclist who makes a quick glance over their shoulder expect them to be changing direction. They should do this before turning. By observing this you'll get an early signal of their intention.

Question 6.75

At road juctions which of the following are most vulnerable?

Mark three answers

☒ Cyclists.

☒ Motorcyclists.

☒ Pedestrians.

☒ Car drivers.

☒ Lorry drivers.

Answers

✗ **Cyclists.**

✗ **Motorcyclists.**

✗ **Pedestrians.**

Good effective observation, coupled with appropriate action, can save lives.

Question 6.76

When emerging from a side road into a queue of traffic which vehicles can be especially difficult to see?

Mark one answer

- [ ] Motorcycles.
- [ ] Tractors.
- [ ] Milk floats.
- [ ] Cars.

Answer

☒ **Motorcycles.**

Your view of the road in both directions can be obscured by parked cars, overgrown hedges or a bend in the road. As you're waiting to emerge don't just expect cars to approach. Look out for other road users too.

Question 6.77

You want to turn right from a main road into a side road. Just before turning you should

Mark one answer

- [ ] cancel your right-turn signal
- [ ] select first gear
- [ ] check for traffic overtaking on your right
- [ ] stop and set the handbrake.

Answer

☒ **check for traffic overtaking on your right**

Motorcyclists often overtake queues of vehicles. Always make that last check in the mirror to avoid turning across their path.

Question 6.78

Motorcyclists are particularly vulnerable

Mark one answer

- [ ] when moving off
- [ ] on dual carriageways
- [ ] when approaching junctions
- [ ] on motorways

Answer

☒ **when approaching junctions**

Another road user failing to see a motorcyclist at a junction is a major cause of collision accidents. Wherever streams of traffic join or cross there's the potential for this type of accident to occur.

Question 6.79

Which of the following are hazards motorcyclists present in queues of traffic?

Mark three answers

☒ Cutting in just in front of you.

☒ Riding in single file.

☒ Passing very close to your car.

☒ Riding with their headlamp on dipped beam.

☒ Filtering between the lanes.

Answers

☒ **Cutting in just in front of you.**

☒ **Passing very close to your car.**

☒ **Filtering between the lanes.**

Where there's more than one lane of queuing traffic motorcyclists use the opportunity to make progress by riding between the lanes. Be aware that they may be passing on either side. Check your mirrors before you move off.

Question 6.80

You are driving on a main road. You intend to turn right into a side road. Just before turning you should

Mark one answer

☒ adjust your interior mirror

☒ flash your headlamps

☒ steer over to the left

☒ check for traffic overtaking on your offside.

Answer

☒ **check for traffic overtaking on your offside**

A last check in the offside mirror will allow you sight of any cyclist or motorcyclist passing on your offside.

Question 6.81

When driving, ahead of you there is a vehicle with a flashing amber beacon. This means it is

Mark one answer

☒ slow moving

☒ broken down

☒ a doctor's car

☒ a school crossing patrol.

Answer

☒ **slow moving**

As you approach the vehicle assess the situation. Due to it's slow progress you will need to judge whether it is safe to overtake.

Question 6.82

You are driving in slow-moving queues of traffic. Just before changing lane you should

Mark one answer

☒ sound the horn

☒ look for motorcyclists filtering through the traffic

☒ give a 'slowing down' arm signal

☒ change down to first gear.

Answer

☒ **look for motorcyclists filtering through the traffic**

In this situation motorcyclists could be passing you on either side. Always check before you change lanes or change direction.

Question 6.83

Which of the following are a major cause of motorcycle collisions?

Mark one answer

☒ Car drivers.

☒ Moped riders.

☒ Sunny weather conditions.

☒ Traffic lights.

Answer

☒ **Car drivers.**

Motorcycles might be hidden from view by other vehicles. Always be aware that a rider might be there.

Question 6.84

An injured motorcyclist is lying unconscious in the road. You should

Mark one answer

☒ remove the crash helmet

☒ seek medical assistance

☒ move the person off the road

☒ remove the leather jacket

Answer

☒ **seek medical assistance**

In an injury situation the earlier proper medical attention is given the better. Either send someone to phone for help or go yourself. Only move an injured person if further danger is threatened.

Do **not** remove the crash helmet.

Question 6.85

You are riding on a country lane. You see cattle on the road. You should

Mark three answers

☒ slow down

☒ stop if necessary

☒ give plenty of room

☒ rev your engine

☒ sound your horn

☒ ride up close behind them.

Answers

☒ **slow down**

☒ **stop if necessary**

☒ **give plenty of room**

Try not to startle the animals. They can be easily frightened by noise or by traffic passing too closely.

You are driving in town. There is a bus at the bus stop on the other side of the road. Why should you be careful?

Mark one answer

☒ The bus may have broken down.

☒ Pedestrians may come from behind the bus.

☒ The bus may move off suddenly.

☒ The bus may remain stationary.

Answer

☒ **Pedestrians may come from behind the bus.**

If you see a bus ahead watch out for pedestrians. They may not be able to see you if they're crossing behind the bus.

You are about to overtake horse riders. Which of the following could scare the horses?

Mark two answers

☒ Sounding your horn.

☒ Giving arm signals.

☒ Riding slowly.

☒ Revving your engine.

Answers

☒ **Sounding your horn.**

☒ **Revving your engine.**

When passing horses allow plenty of space and slow down. Animals can become frightened by sudden or loud noises so don't sound your horn or rev the engine.

Which THREE should you do when passing sheep on a road?

Mark three answers

☒ Allow plenty of room.

☒ Drive very slowly.

☒ Pass quickly but quietly.

☒ Be ready to stop.

☒ Briefly sound your horn.

Answers

☒ **Allow plenty of room.**

☒ **Drive very slowly.**

☒ **Be ready to stop.**

If you see animals in the road ahead slow down and be ready to stop. Animals are easily frightened by

• noise

• vehicles passing too close to them.

Stop if signalled to do so by the person in charge. Switch off your engine if the animals are taking a long time to clear the road.

How should you overtake horse riders?

Mark one answer

☒ Drive up close and overtake as soon as possible.

☒ Speed is not important but allow plenty of room.

☒ Use your horn just once to warn them.

☒ Drive slowly and leave plenty of room.

Answer

☒ **Drive slowly and leave plenty of room.**

If you're driving or riding on a country road then take extra care. Be ready for

• farm animals

• horses

• pedestrians

• farm vehicles.

Always be prepared to slow down or stop.

You notice horse riders in front. What should you do FIRST?

Answer

![X] **Be prepared to slow down.**

When you're driving or riding you must always look well ahead and be ready to deal with hazards as they occur.

Mark one answer

☒ Pull out to the middle of the road.

☒ Be prepared to slow down.

☒ Accelerate around them.

☒ Signal right.

As you are driving along you meet a group of horses and riders from a riding school. Why should you be extra cautious?

Mark one answer

☒ They will be moving in single file.

☒ They will be moving slowly.

☒ Many of the riders may be learners.

☒ The horses will panic more because they are in a group.

Answer

![X] **Many of the riders may be learners.**

If you see a group of horses ahead be extra cautious, especially if they're being ridden by children. The riders might be learners and may not be able to control their animals if they're startled.

Question 6.92

You are driving on a narrow country road. Where would you find it most difficult to see horses and riders ahead of you?

Mark one answer

☒ On left-hand bends.

☒ When travelling downhill.

☒ When travelling uphill.

☒ On right-hand bends.

Answer

✖ **On left-hand bends.**

You're more likely to come across horses on country roads. These roads can be narrow so extra care must be taken when approaching left-hand bends as your view of the road ahead will be restricted.

Question 6.93

A horse rider is in the left-hand lane approaching a roundabout. The driver behind should expect the rider to

Mark one answer

☒ go in any direction

☒ turn right

☒ turn left

☒ go ahead.

Answer

✖ **go in any direction**

Horses and their riders will move more slowly than other road users. They might not have time to cut across busy traffic to take up positions in the offside lane. For this reason a horse and rider may approach a roundabout in the left-hand lane, even though they're turning right.

Question 6.94

You are approaching a roundabout. There are horses just ahead of you. You should

Mark two answers

☒ be prepared to stop

☒ treat them like any other vehicle

☒ give them plenty of room

☒ accelerate past as quickly as possible

☒ sound your horn as a warning.

Answers

✖ **be prepared to stop**

✖ **give them plenty of room**

Horse riders often keep to the outside of the roundabout even if they are turning right. Give them room in case they have to cross lanes of traffic.

You see some horse riders as you approach a roundabout. They are signalling right but keeping well to the left. You should

Answer

 stay well back

Allow the riders to enter and exit the roudabout in their own time. Don't drive up close behind or alongside them, this could disturb the horses .

Mark one answer

☒ proceed as normal

☒ keep close to them

☒ cut in front of them

☒ stay well back.

What is the most common factor in causing road accidents?

Mark one answer

☒ Weather conditions.

☒ Driver error.

☒ Road conditions.

☒ Mechanical failure.

Answer

 Driver error.

Bad weather and different conditions will increase the risks so you must drive accordingly.

Be aware of the distance it will take you to stop

- in good conditions
- during wet or icy weather
- when you're tired
- when you don't concentrate or are distracted. (Your thinking distance will increase.)

Question 6.97

You have a collision whilst your car is moving. What is the FIRST thing you MUST do?

Mark one answer

☒ Stop only if there are injured people.

☒ Call the emergency services.

☒ Stop at the scene of the accident.

☒ Call your insurance company.

Answer

✖ **Stop at the scene of the accident.**

It is the law. Apart from taking responsibility for any mistake you have made, the incident will have shaken you. You will need time to take stock before you drive on.

Question 6.98

Riders are more likely to have a serious accident if they

Mark one answer

☒ wear glasses or contact lenses

☒ have recently passed their test

☒ are carrying pillion passengers

☒ have not taken a theory test.

Answer

✖ **have recently passed their test**

It takes time to experience different situations on the road. Develop safe habits and a responsible attitude from the start. This will help you to become a better rider.

Question 6.99

You have just passed your driving test. How likely are you to have an accident, compared with other drivers?

Mark one answer

☒ More likely.

☒ It depends on your age.

☒ Less likely.

☒ About the same.

Answer

✖ **More likely.**

When you pass your practical driving test you'll have demonstrated that you're safe to drive or ride without supervision. It takes experience to become a good driver. Even then, try to learn from your experiences. This will increase your ability to anticipate the actions of other drivers and therefore help to make you a safer driver. Discuss further training with your Approved Driving Instructor (ADI).

How would you react to other drivers who appear to be inexperienced?

Mark one answer

☒ Sound your horn to warn them of your presence.

☒ Be patient and prepared for them to react more slowly. ✗

☒ Flash your headlights to indicate that it is safe for them to proceed.

☒ Overtake them as soon as possible.

Answer

✗ **Be patient and prepared for them to react more slowly.**

Learners might not have confidence when they first start to drive. Allow them plenty of room and don't react adversely to their hesitation. We all learn from experience, but new drivers will have had less practice in dealing with all the situations that might occur.

As a new driver, how can you decrease your risk of accidents on the motorway?

Mark one answer

☒ By keeping up with the car in front.

☒ By never driving over 45 mph.

☒ By driving only in the nearside lane.

☒ By taking further training. ✗

Answer

✗ **By taking further training.**

You're more likely to have an accident in the first year after taking your test. Lack of experience means that you might not react to hazards as quickly as a more experienced driver or rider. Further training will help you to become safer on the roads.

If you're a motorcyclist ask your Compulsory Basic Training (CBT) instructor about this.

Which age group is most likely to be involved in a road accident?

Mark one answer

☒ 36 to 45-year-olds.

☒ 55-year-olds and over.

☒ 46 to 55-year-olds.

☒ 17 to 25-year-olds. ✗

Answer

✗ **17 to 25-year-olds.**

Statistics show that if you're between the ages of 17 and 25 you're more likely to be involved in a road accident. There are several reasons contributing to this, but in most cases accidents are due to driver or rider error.

Question 6.103

You are following a learner driver who stalls at a junction. You should

Mark one answer

☒ be patient as you expect them to make mistakes ✗

☒ drive up close behind and flash your headlamps

☒ start to rev your engine if they take too long to re-start

☒ immediately steer around them and drive on.

Answer

☒ **be patient as you expect them to make mistakes**

Learning is a process of practice and experience. Try to understand this and tolerate others who are at the beginning of this process.

Question 6.104

A learner driver has begun to emerge into your path from a side road on the left. You should

Mark one answer

☒ be ready to slow down and stop ✗

☒ let them emerge then ride close behind

☒ turn into the side road

☒ brake hard, then wave them out.

Answer

☒ **be ready to slow down and stop**

If you see another vehicle begin to emerge into your path you should ride defensively. Always be ready to slow down or stop if necessary.

Question 6.105

A friend wants to teach you to drive a car. They must

Mark one answer

☒ be over 21 and have held a full licence for at least two years

☒ be over 18 and hold an advanced driver's certificate

☒ be over 18 and have fully comprehensive insurance

☒ be over 21 and have held a full licence for at least three years ✗

Answer

☒ **be over 21 and have held a full licence for at least three years**

Teaching someone to drive is a responsible task. You're advised to contact a qualified Approved Driving Instructor (ADI) about learning to drive. This will ensure that you're taught the correct procedures from the start.

Your vehicle hits a pedestrian at 40 mph. The pedestrian will

Mark one answer

 certainly be killed

 certainly survive

 probably be killed

 probably survive.

Answer

 probably be killed

If you're a car driver ask your Approved Driving Instructor (ADI) about the Pass Plus scheme. This is a course designed to give you further instruction, which includes driving

- in town
- out of town
- in all weathers
- at night
- on dual carriageways
- on motorways.

Taking further training with a professional will help you to gain experience and positive driving skills. Taking the Pass Plus course may also provide you with cheaper insurance.

Whether driving or riding you must always be aware that there may be others on the road who are particularly vulnerable. Always be on the lookout for danger and adjust your speed accordingly.

At night you see a pedestrian wearing reflective clothing and carrying a bright red light. What does this mean?

Mark one answer

☒ You are approaching roadworks.

☒ You are approaching an organised march.

☒ You are approaching a slow-moving vehicle.

☒ You are approaching an accident black spot.

Answer

 You are approaching an organised march.

The people involved in the march should be keeping to the left, but this can't be assumed. Pass slowly, ensuring that you have the time to do so safely. Be aware that the pedestrians have their backs to you and might not know that you're there.

Question 6.108

You are dazzled at night by a vehicle behind you. You should

Mark one answer

- ☒ set your mirror to anti dazzle
- ☒ set your mirror to dazzle the other driver
- ☒ brake sharply to a stop
- ☒ switch your rear lights on and off.

Answer

☒ **set your mirror to anti dazzle**

Most modern vehicles have this facility. The interior mirror of your vehicle can be set to the anti-dazzle position. This prevents distraction from the lights of traffic behind you. You will still be able to see the lights but the dazzle will be greatly reduced.

Question 6.109

A pedestrian steps out into the road just ahead of you. What should you do FIRST?

Mark one answer

- ☒ Sound your horn.
- ☒ Check your mirror.
- ☒ Flash your headlights.
- ☒ Press the brake.

Answer

☒ **Press the brake.**

You should always react quickly to avoid a pedestrian. The normal slowing-down procedure might result in injury in this case. The vehicle behind you should have left enough room to stop safely, and you must act to protect vulnerable road users.

Question 6.110

The vehicle ahead is being driven by a learner. You should

Mark one answer

- ☒ keep calm and be patient
- ☒ ride up close behind
- ☒ put your headlight on full beam
- ☒ sound your horn and overtake.

Answer

☒ **keep calm and be patient**

Learners might take longer to react to traffic situations. Don't unnerve them by riding up close behind.

SECTION 7 OTHER TYPES OF VEHICLE

This section looks at the risks when dealing with different types of vehicle.

The questions will ask you about

- motorcycles
- lorries
- buses.

Question 7.1

The road is wet. Why might a motorcyclist steer round drain covers on a bend?

Mark one answer

☒ To avoid puncturing the tyres on the edge of the drain covers. ✗

☒ To prevent the motorcycle sliding on the metal drain covers.

☒ To help judge the bend using the drain covers as marker points.

☒ To avoid splashing pedestrians on the pavement.

Answer

☒ **To prevent the motorcycle sliding on the metal drain covers.**

The actions other drivers take may be due to the size or characteristics of their vehicle. If you understand this it will help you to anticipate their actions.

Motorcyclists will be checking the road ahead for uneven or slippery surfaces, especially in wet weather. They may need to move across their lane to avoid road surface hazards.

Question 7.2

It is very windy. You are behind a motorcyclist who is overtaking a high-sided vehicle. What should you do?

Mark one answer

☒ Overtake the motorcyclist immediately.

☒ Keep well back. ✗

☒ Stay level with the motorcyclist.

☒ Keep close to the motorcyclist.

Answer

☒ **Keep well back.**

Motorcyclists are affected more by windy weather than other vehicles. Keep well back as they could be blown off course.

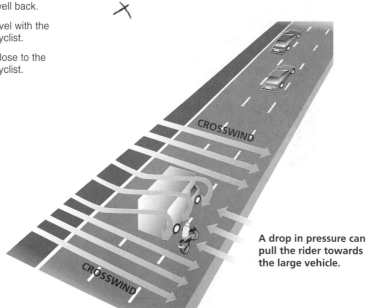

CROSSWIND

CROSSWIND

A drop in pressure can pull the rider towards the large vehicle.

Question 7.3

It is very windy. You are about to overtake a motorcyclist. You should

Mark one answer

☒ overtake slowly

☒ allow extra room

☒ sound your horn

☒ keep close as you pass.

Answer

☒ **allow extra room**

Side winds can blow a cyclist across the lane. Passing too close could also cause a draught, unsteadying the rider.

Question 7.4

You are about to overtake a slow-moving motorcyclist. Which one of these signs would make you take special care?

Mark one answer

☒

☒

☒

Answer

☒

In windy weather watch out for motorcyclists, as they can be blown sideways and veer into your path. Pass them leaving plenty of room and check your mirror as you pass and pull back in.

Question 7.5

You are waiting to emerge left from a minor road. A large vehicle is approaching from the right. You have time to turn, but you should wait. Why?

Mark one answer

☒ The large vehicle can easily hide an overtaking vehicle.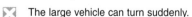

☒ The large vehicle can turn suddenly.

☒ The large vehicle is difficult to steer in a straight line.

☒ The large vehicle can easily hide vehicles from the left.

Answer

☒ **The large vehicle can easily hide an overtaking vehicle.**

Don't only consider the hazards you can see. The hidden, possible hazards are the most dangerous as they are often unexpected. By considering the possible dangers when emerging, you can lessen the risk.

Question 7.6

You are following a large articulated vehicle. It is going to turn left into a narrow road. What action should you take?

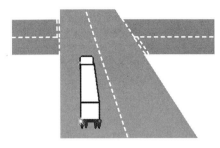

Answer

✖ Be prepared to stop behind.

Lorries are larger and longer than other vehicles. This will affect their position when approaching junctions – especially when turning left. They need more room so that they don't cut in and mount the kerb when turning.

Mark one answer

☒ Move out and overtake on the offside.

☒ Pass on the left as the vehicle moves out.

☒ Be prepared to stop behind. ✗

☒ Overtake quickly before the lorry moves out.

Question 7.7

You are following a long vehicle. It approaches a crossroads and signals left, but moves out to the right. You should

Mark one answer

☒ get closer in order to pass it quickly

☒ stay well back and give it room ✗

☒ assume the signal is wrong and it is really turning right

☒ overtake as it starts to slow down.

Answer

✖ stay well back and give it room

Approaching a left turn a lorry may swing out to the right. This is to allow the rear wheels to clear the kerb as it turns. If you see a gap on the nearside don't try to filter through.

You are riding behind a long vehicle. There is a mini-roundabout ahead. The vehicle is signalling left, but positioned to the right. You should

Mark one answer

 sound your horn

☒ overtake on the left

☒ keep well back

☒ flash your headlights.

Answer

■ **keep well back**

The long vehicle needs more room to make the left turn. Don't overtake on the left. Staying well back will also give you a better view around the vehicle.

You are following a long vehicle approaching a crossroads. The driver signals right but moves close to the left-hand kerb. What should you do?

Mark one answer

☒ Warn the driver of the wrong signal.

☒ Wait behind the long vehicle.

☒ Report the driver to the police.

☒ Overtake on the right-hand side.

Answer

■ **Wait behind the long vehicle**

When a long vehicle is going to turn right it may need to keep close to the left-hand kerb. This is to prevent the rear end of the trailer cutting the corner. You need to be aware of how long vehicles behave in such situations. Don't overtake the lorry because it could turn as you're alongside. Stay behind and give plenty of room.

Question 7.10

You are approaching a mini-roundabout. The long vehicle in front is signalling left but positioned over to the right. You should

Mark one answer

- [ ] sound your horn
- [ ] overtake on the left
- [ ] follow the same course as the lorry
- [ ] keep well back.

Answer

 keep well back

At mini-roundabouts there isn't much room for a long vehicle to manoeuvre. It will have to swing out wide so that it can complete the turn safely. Keep well back and allow plenty of room. Don't drive or ride along its nearside.

Question 7.11

You are following a large vehicle. Side and end markers are being displayed. This means the load

Mark one answer

- [ ] is higher than normal
- [ ] may be flammable
- [ ] is in two parts
- [ ] overhangs at the rear.

Answer

 overhangs at the rear

Always keep a safe distance from the vehicle in front. In this case you should judge your separation distance from the extreme rear of the load the vehicle is carrying.

Question 7.12

You are towing a caravan. Which is the safest type of rear view mirror to use?

Mark one answer

☒ Interior wide-angle-view mirror.

☒ Extended-arm side mirrors.

☒ Ordinary door mirrors.

☒ Ordinary interior mirror.

Answer

☒ **Extended-arm side mirrors.**

Towing a large trailer or caravan can greatly reduce your view of the road. The correct equipment will help you to get a better view behind and around the unit.

Question 7.13

You keep well back while waiting to overtake a large vehicle. Another car fills the gap. You should

Mark one answer

☒ sound your horn

☒ drop back further

☒ flash your headlights

☒ start to overtake.

Answer

☒ **drop back further**

It's very frustrating when your separation distance is shortened by another car. React positively and consider your own and your passengers' safety.

Question 7.14

Before overtaking a large vehicle you should keep well back. Why is this?

Mark one answer

☒ To give acceleration space to overtake quickly on blind bends.

☒ To get the best view of the road ahead.

☒ To leave a gap in case the vehicle stops and rolls back.

☒ To offer other drivers a safe gap if they want to overtake you.

Answer

☒ **To get the best view of the road ahead.**

When following a large vehicle keep well back. If you're too close

* you won't be able to see the road ahead
* the driver of the long vehicle might not be able to see you in his mirrors.

Question 7.15

You wish to overtake a long, slow-moving vehicle on a busy road. You should

Mark one answer

☒ wait behind until the driver waves you past

☒ flash your headlights for the oncoming traffic to give way

☒ follow it closely and keep moving out to see the road ahead

☒ keep well back until you can see that it is clear.

Answer

☒ **keep well back until you can see that it is clear**

If you wish to overtake a long vehicle stay well back so that you can see the road ahead. Don't

- get up close to the vehicle – this will restrict your view of the road ahead
- get impatient – overtaking on a busy road calls for sound judgement
- take a gamble – only overtake when you can see that you can safely complete the manoeuvre
- flash your headlights – this could confuse and mislead other traffic
- sound your horn.

Question 7.16

You are driving downhill. There is a car parked on the other side of the road. Large, slow lorries are coming towards you. You should

Mark one answer

☒ keep going because you have the right of way

☒ slow down and give way

☒ speed up and get past quickly

☒ pull over on the right behind the parked car.

Answer

☒ **slow down and give way**

Large vehicles need several gear changes to build up speed and this takes time, especially on an uphill gradient. You should keep this in mind and give way so that they can maintain momentum up the hill.

When about to overtake a long vehicle you should

Mark one answer

☒ sound the horn to warn the driver that you are there

☒ stay well back from the lorry to obtain a better view ✗

☒ drive close to the lorry in order to pass more quickly

☒ flash your lights and wait for the driver to signal when it is safe.

Answer

☒ **stay well back from the lorry to obtain a better view**

If you're thinking about overtaking ask yourself if it's really necessary. An unladen large vehicle can make surprisingly good progress.

You are driving in the right lane of a dual carriageway at 70 mph. You catch up to a lorry which is overtaking another vehicle. You should

Mark one answer

☒ maintain your speed

☒ slow down and keep well back ✗

☒ slow down, but flash your headlamps

☒ maintain your speed and sound your horn.

Answer

☒ **slow down and keep well back**

If the lorry is carrying a heavy load it will take longer to overtake than a car. Be patient, keep well back and don't endanger yourself by driving up too close.

Why is passing a lorry more risky than passing a car?

Mark one answer

☒ Lorries are longer than cars. ✗

☒ Lorries may suddenly pull up.

☒ The brakes of lorries are not as good.

☒ Lorries climb hills more slowly.

Answer

☒ **Lorries are longer than cars.**

Hazards to watch for include

• oncoming traffic

• junctions

• bends or dips, which could restrict your view

• any signs or road markings prohibiting overtaking.

Never begin to overtake unless you can see that it's safe to complete the manoeuvre.

Question 7.20

The FIRST thing you should do when you want to overtake a large lorry is

Mark one answer

☒ move close behind so that you can pass quickly

☒ keep in close to the left-hand side

☒ flash your headlights and wait for the driver to wave you on

☒ stay well back to get a better view. ✗

Answer

☒ **stay well back to get a better view**

When you're planning to overtake a large vehicle take its length into account. It will take you longer to pass a lorry or coach than another car. You'll need to look further ahead.

Question 7.21

As a driver, why should you be more careful where trams operate?

Mark two answers

☒ Because they do not have a horn.

☒ Because they do not stop for cars.

☒ Because they are silent. ✗

☒ Because they cannot steer to avoid you. ✗

☒ Because they do not have lights.

Answers

☒ **Because they are silent.**

☒ **Because they cannot steer to avoid you.**

You should take extra care when you first encounter trams. You will have to get used to dealing with a different traffic system. As well as being silent, they can travel very quickly.

You are driving along a road and you see this signal. It means

Mark one answer

☒ cars must stop

☒ trams must stop ✗

☒ both trams and cars must stop

☒ both trams and cars can continue.

You are travelling behind a bus that pulls up at a bus stop. What should you do?

Mark two answers

☒ Accelerate past the bus sounding your horn.

☒ Watch carefully for pedestrians. ✗

☒ Be ready to give way to the bus. ✗

☒ Pull in closely behind the bus.

You are driving in town. Ahead of you a bus is at a bus stop. Which two of the following should you do?

Mark two answers

☒ Be prepared to give way if the bus suddenly moves off. ✗

☒ Continue at the same speed but sound your horn as a warning.

☒ Watch carefully for the sudden appearance of pedestrians. ✗

☒ Pass the bus as quickly as you possibly can.

Answer

☒ **trams must stop**

Trams are popular in some cities, not least because they don't create fumes so they're cleaner. You may not live in an area that has trams but you should still learn the signs. You never know when you might drive through a town that has them.

Answers

☒ **Watch carefully for pedestrians.**

☒ **Be ready to give way to the bus.**

There might be pedestrians crossing from in front of the bus. Look out for them if you intend to pass. Consider staying back and waiting.

How many people are waiting to get on the bus? Check the queue if you can. The bus might be moving off straight away.

Answers

☒ **Be prepared to give way if the bus suddenly moves off.**

☒ **Watch carefully for the sudden appearance of pedestrians.**

As you approach, look out for any signal the driver might make. If you pass the vehicle watch out for pedestrians attempting to cross the road from the other side of the bus. They will be hidden from view until the last moment.

Question 7.25

When you approach a bus signalling to move off from a bus stop you should

Mark one answer

☒ get past before it moves

☒ allow it to pull away, if it is safe to do so ✗

☒ flash your headlamps as you approach

☒ signal left and wave the bus on.

Answer

✗ **allow it to pull away, if it is safe to do so**

Give way to buses whenever you can do so safely, especially when they signal to pull away from bus stops. Look out for people who've got off the bus and may try to cross the road. Don't

* try to accelerate past before it moves away
* flash your lights – other road users may be misled by this signal.

Question 7.26

In which THREE places could a strong crosswind affect your course?

Mark three answers

☒ After overtaking a large vehicle. ✗

☒ When passing gaps in hedges. ✗

☒ On exposed sections of roadway. ✗

☒ In towns.

☒ In tunnels.

☒ When passing parked vehicles.

Answers

✗ **After overtaking a large vehicle.**

✗ **When passing gaps in hedges.**

✗ **On exposed sections of roadway.**

Crosswinds affect some vehicles more than others. The worst affected vehicles are

* high-sided vehicles
* caravans
* motorcycles
* cycles.

It's important to be aware which types of vehicles are affected so that you can anticipate their actions.

Question 7.27

Which of these vehicles is LEAST likely to be affected by crosswinds?

Mark one answer

☒ Cyclists.

☒ Motorcyclists.

☒ High-sided vehicles.

☒ Cars. ✗

Answer

☒ **Cars.**

Crosswinds can take you by surprise

- after overtaking a large vehicle
- when passing gaps between hedges or buildings
- on exposed sections of road.

Question 7.28

What does 'tailgating' mean?

Mark one answer

☒ When a vehicle delivering goods has its tailgate down.

☒ When a vehicle is travelling with its back doors open.

☒ When a driver is following another vehicle too closely. ✗

☒ When stationary vehicles are too close in a queue.

Answer

☒ **When a driver is following another vehicle too closely.**

This can often be seen on motorways, when traffic is travelling at high speeds. Tailgating is a highly dangerous practice and could lead to a serious multiple accident.

Question 7.29

You are following a large lorry on a wet road. Spray makes it difficult to see. You should

Mark one answer

☒ drop back until you can see better ✗

☒ put your headlights on full beam

☒ keep close to the lorry, away from the spray

☒ speed up and overtake quickly.

Answer

☒ **drop back until you can see better**

In the wet, large vehicles may throw up a lot of spray. This will make it difficult to see ahead. Dropping back further will

- move you out of the spray and so allow you to see further
- increase your separation distance. It takes longer to stop in the wet and you need to allow more room.

Don't

- get up close behind
- overtake, unless you can see the way ahead is clear.

Question 7.30

You are driving on a wet motorway with surface spray. You should

Mark one answer

☒ use your hazard flashers

☒ use dipped headlights ✗

☒ use your rear fog lights

☒ drive in any lane with no traffic.

Answer

☒ use dipped headlights

When surface spray reduces visibility switch on your dipped headlights. This will help other road users to see you.

Question 7.31

You are driving in heavy traffic on a wet road. Spray makes it difficult to be seen. You should use your

Mark two answers

☒ full headlights

☒ rear fog lights if visibility is less than 100 ✗ metres (328 feet)

☒ rear fog lights if visibility is more than 100 metres (328 feet)

☒ dipped headlights ✗

☒ side lights only.

Answers

☒ rear fog lights if visibility is less than 100 metres (328 feet)

☒ dipped headlights

You must ensure that you can be seen by others on the road. Use your lights during the day if the visibility is bad. If you use your rear foglights, don't forget to turn them off when the visibility improves.

Question 7.32

Some two way roads are divided into three lanes. Why are these particularly dangerous ?

Mark one answer

☒ Traffic in both directions can use the middle lane to overtake. ✗

☒ Traffic can travel faster in poor weather conditions.

☒ Traffic can overtake on the left.

☒ Traffic uses the middle lane for emergencies only.

Answer

☒ Traffic in both directions can use the middle lane to overtake.

If you intend to overtake you must consider that approaching traffic could be intending the same manoeuvre. When you have considered, judge the situation and have decided it is safe, indicate your intentions early. This will show the approaching traffic that you intend to pull out.

This section looks at the handling of your vehicle in different conditions.

The questions will ask you about

- weather conditions

- road conditions

- the time of day

- speed

- traffic calming.

Question 8.1

When you are seated on a stationary motorcycle, your position should allow you to

Mark one answer

☒ just touch the ground with your toes

☒ place both feet on the ground ✗

☒ operate the centre stand

☒ reach the switches by stretching.

Answer

☒ **place both feet on the ground**

When sitting astride a stationary motorcycle you should be able to place both feet on the ground for maximum control and stability.

Question 8.2

As a safety measure before starting your engine, you should

Mark two answers

☒ push the motorcycle forward to check the rear wheel turns freely ✗

☒ engage first gear and apply the rear brake

☒ engage first gear and apply the front brake

☒ glance at the neutral light on your instrument panel. ✗

Answers

☒ **push the motorcycle forward to check the rear wheel turns freely**

☒ **glance at the neutral light on your instrument panel**

Before starting the engine you should ensure the motorcycle is in neutral. This can be done by

• moving the motorcycle to see the rear wheel turns freely

• checking the neutral lamp is lit when the ignition is turned on.

Question 8.3

You should not ride with your clutch in for longer than necessary because it

Mark one answer

☒ increases wear on the gearbox

☒ increases petrol consumption

☒ reduces your control of the motorcycle ✗

☒ reduces the grip of the tyres.

Answer

☒ **reduces your control of the motorcycle**

Coasting

• gives you less steering control

• reduces the traction on the road surface

• causes the machine to pick up speed.

If you're travelling downhill your machine will gather speed quickly. The engine won't be able to assist the braking.

Question 8.4

What are TWO main reasons why coasting downhill is wrong?

Mark two answers

- ☒ Petrol consumption will be higher.
- ☒ The vehicle will pick up speed.
- ☒ It puts more wear and tear on the tyres.
- ☒ You have less braking and steering control.
- ☒ It damages the engine.

Answers

- ☒ **The vehicle will pick up speed.**
- ☒ **You have less braking and steering control.**

It's especially important that you don't coast your vehicle

- at junctions
- approaching hazards
- on bends.

Question 8.5

Hills can affect the performance of your vehicle. Which two apply when driving up steep hills?

Mark two answers

- ☒ Higher gears will pull better.
- ☒ You will slow down sooner.
- ☒ Overtaking will be easier.
- ☒ The engine will work harder.
- ☒ The steering will feel heavier.

Answers

- ☒ **You will slow down sooner.**
- ☒ **The engine will work harder.**

The engine will need more power to pull the vehicle up the hill. When approaching a steep hill you should select a lower gear to maintain your speed. You should do this without hesitation, so that you don't lose too much speed.

Question 8.6

Why is coasting wrong?

Mark one answer

- ☒ It will cause the car to skid.
- ☒ It will make the engine stall.
- ☒ The engine will run faster.
- ☒ There is no engine braking.

Answer

- ☒ **There is no engine braking.**

Try to look ahead and read the road. Plan your approach to junctions and select the correct gear in good time. This will give you the control you need to deal with any hazards that occur.

You'll coast a little every time you change gear. This can't be avoided, but it should be kept to a minimum.

Question 8.7

You should not drive with your foot on the clutch for longer than necessary because it

Mark one answer

- ☒ increases wear on the gearbox
- ☒ increases petrol consumption
- ☒ reduces your control of the vehicle
- ☒ reduces the grip of the tyres.

Answer

- ☒ **reduces your control of the vehicle**

Pressing down the clutch pedal or riding with the clutch in for longer than necessary is referred to as coasting. Coasting your vehicle or machine will

- cause the vehicle or machine to pick up speed
- give you less steering and braking control
- make selecting the correct gear difficult.

Question 8.8

Which THREE of the following will affect your stopping distance?

Mark three answers

- [x] How fast you are going.
- [x] The tyres on your vehicle. ✗
- [ ] The time of day.
- [x] The weather. ✗
- [ ] The street lighting.

Answers

- [x] **How fast you are going.**
- [x] **The tyres on your vehicle.**
- [x] **The weather.**

You should be aware that there are several factors that can affect the distance it takes to stop your vehicle.

Your stopping distance in wet weather will increase. You should double the separation distance from the car in front. Your tyres will have less grip on the road and therefore need more time to stop. Always drive in accordance with the conditions.

Question 8.9

You are approaching a bend at speed. You should begin to brake

Mark one answer

- [ ] on the bend
- [ ] after the bend
- [ ] after changing gears
- [x] before the bend. ✗

Answer

- [x] **before the bend**

Full control of the vehicle is essential at all times. Adjust your speed before the bend. Change gear if necessary and drive round it under gentle acceleration.

Question 8.10

The safest way to brake is

Mark one answer

- [ ] by using the rear brake first and then the front
- [ ] when the machine is being turned or ridden through a bend
- [ ] by pulling in the clutch before using the front brake
- [x] when the machine is upright and moving in a straight line. ✗

Answer

- [x] **when the machine is upright and moving in a straight line**

A motorcycle is most stable when it's upright and moving in a straight line. This is the best time to brake and normally both brakes should be used with the front brake being applied just before the rear.

Question 8.11

When coming to a normal stop on a motorcycle, you should

Mark one answer

☒ only apply the front brake

☒ rely just on the rear brake

☒ apply both brakes smoothly ✗

☒ apply any one of the brakes gently.

Answer

☒ **apply both brakes smoothly**

In normal riding you should always use both brakes. Harsh or poorly-controlled use of the brakes can cause loss of control and skidding.

Question 8.12

You are following a vehicle at a safe distance on a wet road. Another driver overtakes you and pulls into the gap you have left. What should you do?

Mark one answer

☒ Flash your headlights as a warning.

☒ Try to overtake safely as soon as you can.

☒ Drop back to regain a safe distance. ✗

☒ Stay close to the other vehicle until it moves on.

Answer

☒ **Drop back to regain a safe distance.**

The weather will affect the way your vehicle or machine behaves. It will increase the time it takes for you to stop and can affect your control.

Drive at a speed that will allow you to stop safely and in good time.

If another vehicle pulls into the gap you've left, ease back until you've regained your stopping distance. Don't flash your lights or drive up close to it.

Question 8.13

Why is pressing the clutch down for long periods a bad habit?

Mark one answer

☒ It reduces the car's speed when going downhill.

☒ It causes the engine to wear out more quickly.

☒ It reduces the driver's control of the vehicle. ✗

☒ It causes the engine to use more fuel.

Answer

☒ **It reduces the driver's control of the vehicle.**

'Coasting' means that although your vehicle or machine is moving it isn't being driven by the engine. This could be because

- the clutch is down or being held in
- the vehicle or machine isn't in gear (i.e., it's in neutral).

Question 8.14

You should avoid 'coasting' your vehicle because it could

Mark one answer

- ☒ damage the suspension
- ☒ increase tyre wear
- ☒ flatten the battery
- ☒ reduce steering control. ✗

Answer

☒ **reduce steering control**

Coasting your vehicle or machine will

- cause it to pick up speed
- give you less steering and braking control
- make selecting the correct gear difficult.

Question 8.15

You are driving in the left-hand lane of a dual carriageway. Another vehicle overtakes and pulls in front of you leaving you without enough separation distance. You should

Mark one answer

- ☒ move to the right lane
- ☒ continue as you are
- ☒ drop back ✗
- ☒ sound your horn.

Answer

☒ **drop back**

Dual carriageways have at least two lanes in each direction. There will be a central reserve where there may be a safety barrier.

If you're overtaken by another vehicle and it cuts in too closely don't react by flashing your lights or giving any other signal. Gradually increase your distance from the vehicle so that you have a safe gap if you need to stop.

Question 8.16

You are driving on the motorway in windy conditions. When passing high-sided vehicles you should

Mark one answer

- ☒ increase your speed
- ☒ be wary of a sudden gust
- ☒ drive alongside very closely
- ☒ expect normal conditions.

Answer

☒ **be wary of a sudden gust**

The draught caused by other vehicles could be strong enough to push you out of your lane. Keep both hands on the steering wheel to maintain full control.

Question 8.17

You wish to overtake on a dual carriageway. You see in your mirror that the car behind has pulled out to overtake you. You should

Mark one answer

- [X] not signal until the car has passed
- [X] signal and pull out to overtake
- [X] signal to tell the driver behind that you also want to overtake
- [X] touch the brakes to show your brake lights.

Answer

[X] **not signal until the car has passed**

Before you overtake ask yourself, 'Is it really necessary?'

Look well ahead to check for hazards. Check in your mirror. If there's a vehicle about to overtake you, wait until it's passed before you signal to pull out. Then do so safely.

Question 8.18

In which THREE of these situations may you overtake another vehicle on the left?

Mark three answers

- [X] When you are in a one-way street.
- [X] When approaching a motorway slip road where you will be turning off.
- [X] When the vehicle in front is signalling to turn right.
- [X] When a slower vehicle is travelling in the right-hand lane of a dual carriageway.
- [X] In slow-moving traffic queues when traffic in the right-hand lane is moving more slowly.

Answers

[X] **When you are in a one-way street.**

[X] **When the vehicle in front is signalling to turn right.**

[X] **In slow-moving traffic queues when traffic in the right-hand lane is moving more slowly.**

At certain times of the day traffic might be heavy. If traffic is moving in queues and vehicles in the right-hand lane are moving more slowly you may overtake on the left. Don't keep changing lanes to try and beat the queue.

Question 8.19

You are travelling in very heavy rain. Your overall stopping distance is likely to be

Mark one answer

- [X] doubled
- [X] halved
- [X] up to ten times greater
- [X] no different

Answer

[X] **doubled**

Apart from the lack of visibility the road will be extremely wet. This will lessen the grip the tyres have on the road and increase the distance it takes to stop. Double your separation distance.

Question 8.20

You are riding in heavy rain. What clears the water between your tyres and the road surface to prevent aquaplaning?

Mark one answer

- [ ] Tread depth.
- [ ] Your speed.
- [ ] Your mudguards.
- [ ] Harsh braking.

Answer

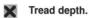 **Tread depth.**

When riding in the wet you rely on the tyres' tread to allow the water to clear and let the tyres grip the road. As tread wears it cannot clear the water as quickly, so increasing the risk of aquaplaning.

Question 8.21

Give two reasons for using an additive in the windscreen washer reservoir.

Mark two answers

- [ ] To prevent freezing in winter.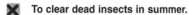
- [ ] To wipe off leaves in autumn.
- [ ] To help prevent mould growth.
- [ ] To clear dead insects in summer.
- [ ] To prevent corrosion.

Answers

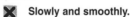 **To prevent freezing in winter.**
To clear dead insects in summer.

Make sure that your washers are working, and keep the reservoir filled. It's important that you maintain full vision through the windscreen.

Question 8.22

How should you drive around a bend on ice?

Mark one answer

- [ ] Using the clutch and brake together.
- [ ] In first gear.
- [ ] Braking as you enter the bend.
- [ ] Slowly and smoothly.

Answer

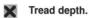 **Slowly and smoothly.**

When the weather is cold and the roads are icy you must be aware that your vehicle or machine will handle differently. The tyres will lose much of their grip on the road, which will greatly affect your steering control. If you're driving around bends in icy weather do so slowly and smoothly.

Motorcyclists are more at risk from other road users because they

Mark one answer

☒ are less experienced than other drivers

☒ are more likely to break down than other motorists

☒ are always faster than other drivers

☒ are more difficult to see than other drivers.

Answer

☒ **are more difficult to see than other drivers**

A motorcycle is one of the smallest motor vehicles on our roads. Being small they are not always easy to see. This makes them more at risk from other road users who may not see them, particularly at junctions.

You are approaching this junction. As the motorcyclist you should

Mark two answers

☒ prepare to slow down

☒ sound your horn

☒ keep near the left kerb

☒ speed up to clear the junction

☒ stop, as the car has right of way.

Answers

☒ **prepare to slow down**
☒ **sound your horn**

Look out for road signs indicating side roads, even if you aren't turning off. A driver emerging might not be able to see you due to parked cars or heavy traffic. Always be prepared, and stop if it's necessary. Remember, no one has priority at unmarked crossroads.

What can you do to improve your safety on the road as a motorcyclist?

Mark one answer

☒ Anticipate the actions of others.

☒ Stay just above the speed limits.

☒ Keep positioned close to the kerbs.

☒ Remain well below speed limits.

Answer

☒ **Anticipate the actions of others.**

Always ride defensively. This means looking and planning ahead as well as anticipating the actions of other road users.

Question 8.26

Which FOUR types of road surface increase the risk of skidding for motorcyclists?

Mark four answers

- [x] White lining.
- [x] Dry tarmac.
- [x] Tar banding.
- [x] Yellow grid lining.
- [x] Loose chippings.

Answers

- White lining.
- Tar banding.
- Yellow grid lining.
- Loose chippings.

If you're riding a motorcycle you must look at the road surface ahead. The stability of your machine will depend on it. Also, look out for

- pot-holes
- drain covers (especially in the wet)
- oily surfaces
- road markings
- tram tracks
- wet mud and leaves.

Question 8.27

You have to brake sharply and your machine starts to skid. You should

Mark one answer

- [x] continue braking and select a low gear
- [x] apply the brakes harder for better grip
- [x] select neutral and use the front brake only
- [x] release the brakes and re-apply.

Answer

- release the brakes and re-apply

If you skid as a result of too much braking you need to

- release the brakes to stop the skid
- re-apply them progressively to stop.

Question 8.28

Which THREE of these can cause skidding?

Mark three answers

- [x] Braking too gently.
- [x] Leaning too far over when cornering.
- [x] Staying upright when cornering.
- [x] Braking too hard.
- [x] Changing direction suddenly.

Answers

- Leaning too far over when cornering.
- Braking too hard.
- Changing direction suddenly.

In order to keep control of your vehicle and prevent skidding you must plan well ahead to prevent harsh, late braking. Take the road and weather conditions into consideration and ride accordingly.

Question 8.29

It is very cold and the road looks wet. You cannot hear any road noise. You should

Mark two answers

- ☒ continue riding at the same speed
- ☒ ride slower in as high a gear as possible ✗
- ☒ ride in as low a gear as possible
- ☒ keep revving your engine
- ☒ slow down as there may be black ice. ✗

Answers

☒ **ride slower in as high a gear as possible**

☒ **slow down as there may be black ice**

Rain freezing on roads as it falls is called black ice and isn't clearly visible. The first indication that you might have of it is when the steering becomes very light. You need to keep your speed down and ride according to the weather conditions.

Question 8.30

You are approaching a road with a surface of loose chippings. What should you do?

Mark one answer

- ☒ Ride normally.
- ☒ Speed up.
- ☒ Slow down.
- ☒ Stop.

Answer

☒ **Slow down.**

You should

- ride at an appropriate speed
- apply both front and rear brakes evenly
- brake when travelling in a straight line and your machine is upright.

Don't make sudden changes of direction unless you are avoiding an accident.

The handling of your machine will be greatly affected by the road surface that you're riding on. Look at the road ahead and be alert if the road looks uneven or has loose chippings. Slow down in good time – braking harshly here will cause you to skid.

Question 8.31

When snow is falling heavily you should

Mark one answer

- ☒ drive as long as your headlights are used
- ☒ not drive unless you have a mobile phone
- ☒ drive only when your journey is short
- ☒ not drive unless it is essential. ✗

Answer

☒ **not drive unless it is essential**

Consider if the increased risk is worth it. If the weather conditions are bad and your journey isn't essential, then stay at home.

Question 8.32

How can you best control your vehicle when driving in snow?

Mark one answer

By driving slowly in as high a gear as possible. ✗

By staying in low gear and gripping the steering wheel tightly.

By driving in first gear.

By keeping the engine revs high and slipping the clutch.

Answer

 By driving slowly in as high a gear as possible.

If the ground is covered with snow move off in as high a gear as possible. This will lessen the chance of skidding by reducing the power to the driven wheels.

Question 8.33

You are driving on an icy road. What distance should you drive from the car in front?

Mark one answer

Eight times the normal distance.

Six times the normal distance.

Ten times the normal distance. ✗

Four times the normal distance.

Answer

✗ **Ten times the normal distance.**

Think about how far this is. It's a long way; probably further than you imagine.

Question 8.34

To correct a rear-wheel skid you should

Mark one answer

not turn at all

turn away from it

turn into it ✗

apply your handbrake.

Answer

✗ **turn into it**

Prevention is better than cure, so it's important that you take every precaution to prevent a skid. If you do feel your vehicle beginning to skid, try to steer to recover control. Don't brake suddenly – this will only make the situation worse.

You are driving in very wet weather. Your vehicle begins to slide. This effect is called

Mark one answer

☒ hosing

☒ weaving

☒ aquaplaning ✗

☒ fading.

Answer

☒ **aquaplaning**

Water can build up between the tyres and the road. This means that the tyres might not have contact with the road. Your vehicle could slide on the film of water, causing the steering to feel light and you to lose proper control.

Question 8.36

Why should you test your brakes after this hazard?

Mark one answer

☒ Because you will be driving on a slippery road.

☒ Because your brakes will be soaking ✗ wet.

☒ Because you will have driven down a long hill.

☒ Because you will have just crossed a long bridge.

Answer

☒ **Because your brakes will be soaking wet.**

A ford is a crossing over a stream that's shallow enough to drive through. If you've driven through a ford or a deep puddle the water can affect your brakes. Be sure you check that they're working before returning to normal speed.

Question 8.37

You have to make a journey in fog. What are the TWO most important things you should do before you set out?

Mark two answers

☒ Top up the radiator with antifreeze.

☒ Make sure that you have a warning triangle in the vehicle.

☒ Check that your lights are working. ✗

☒ Check the battery.

☒ Make sure that the windows are clean. ✗

Answers

☒ **Check that your lights are working.**

☒ **Make sure that the windows are clean.**

Don't drive in fog unless you really have to. Drive in accordance with the conditions.

Question 8.38

When riding a motorcycle you should wear full protective clothing

Mark one answer

☒ at all times

☒ only on faster, open roads

☒ just on long journeys

☒ only during bad weather.

Answer

☒ **at all times**

You should wear suitable clothing to protect you from injury and bad weather at all times.

Question 8.39

You have to make a journey in fog. What are the TWO most important things you should do before you set out?

Mark two answers

☒ Fill up with fuel.

☒ Make sure that you have a warm drink with you.

☒ Check that your lights are working. ✕

☒ Check the battery.

☒ Make sure that your visor is clean. ✕

Answers

☒ **Check that your lights are working.**

☒ **Make sure that your visor is clean.**

If you're riding a motorcycle keep your visor as clean as possible to give you a clear view of the road. It's a good idea to carry a clean, damp cloth in a polythene bag for this purpose. When the weather is foggy or misty ensure that your lights are clean and can be seen clearly by other road users.

Question 8.40

You have to make a journey in foggy conditions. You should

Mark one answer

☒ follow closely other vehicles' tail lights

☒ never use demisters and windscreen wipers

☒ leave plenty of time for your journey ✕

☒ keep two seconds behind other vehicles.

Answer

☒ **leave plenty of time for your journey**

If you're planning to make a journey in foggy conditions listen to the weather reports on the radio or television. Don't drive if visibility is very low or your journey isn't necessary. If you do travel, leave plenty of time for your journey. If there's someone expecting you at the other end of your journey let them know that you'll be taking longer than normal to arrive. Take your time and don't hurry.

Question 8.41

When travelling home the weather becomes foggy. Your daytime visibility is reduced to 80 metres (262 feet). You should

Mark one answer

☒ switch on side lights only

☒ switch on hazard warning lights

☒ leave lights switched off unless conditions worsen

☒ switch on dipped headlights and rear fog lamps. ✗

Answer

☒ **switch on dipped headlights and rear fog lamps**

Rear fogs lights are fitted to all modern vehicles. They will only work when the headlights are on. Inside the vehicle there should be an indicator light to show you when they are on. Make sure you switch them off, when the weather improves.

Question 8.42

You are following other vehicles in fog with your lights on. How else can you reduce the chances of being involved in an accident?

Mark one answer

☒ Keep close to the vehicle in front.

☒ Use your main beam instead of dipped headlights.

☒ Keep together with the faster vehicles.

☒ Reduce your speed and increase the gap. ✗

Answer

☒ **Reduce your speed and increase the gap.**

Always ensure that you have your lights on and that you're seen by all other road users. Use dipped headlights. If visibility is below 100 metres (330 feet) use fog lights and high-intensity rear lights. Drive at a sensible speed and don't follow the car in front too closely. You'll need to adjust your stopping distance as the road is likely to be wet and slippery.

Question 8.43

Why should you always reduce your speed when driving in fog?

Mark one answer

☒ Because the brakes do not work as well.

☒ Because you could be dazzled by other people's fog lights.

☒ Because the engine's colder.

☒ Because it is more difficult to see events ahead. ✗

Answer

☒ **Because it is more difficult to see events ahead.**

Driving in fog is hazardous. Only travel if it's really necessary. To drive or ride safely you must always look well ahead. In fog this won't be possible and you'll have less time to react to any hazards. You must reduce your speed.

Question 8.44

You are driving in fog. The car behind seems to be very close. You should

Mark one answer

☒ switch on your hazard warning lights

☒ pull over and stop immediately

☒ speed up to get away

☒ continue cautiously.

Answer

☒ **continue cautiously**

If the car behind seems to be too close to you, the driver's probably using your rear lights as a guide through the fog. This isn't advisable. A good separation distance will be even more important on a wet road surface. Don't react to this but continue cautiously.

Question 8.45

You are driving in fog. Why should you keep well back from the vehicle in front?

Mark one answer

☒ In case it changes direction suddenly.

☒ In case its fog lights dazzle you.

☒ In case it stops suddenly.

☒ In case its brake lights dazzle you.

Answer

☒ **In case it stops suddenly.**

If you're following another road user in fog stay well back. The driver in front won't be able to see hazards until they're close and might brake suddenly. You'll need a good separation distance as the road surface is likely to be wet and slippery.

Question 8.46

You should switch your rear fog lights on when visibility drops below

Mark one answer

☒ your overall stopping distance

☒ ten car lengths

☒ 10 metres (33 feet)

☒ 100 metres (330 feet).

Answer

☒ **100 metres (330 feet)**

This will help other road users to see you. Don't forget to turn off fog lights once visibility is clear. Their brightness might be mistaken for brake lights.

Question 8.47

You are driving in poor visibility. You can see more than 100 metres (330 feet) ahead. How can you make sure that other drivers can see you?

Mark one answer

- ☒ Turn on your dipped headlights. ✗
- ☒ Follow the vehicle in front closely.
- ☒ Turn on your rear fog lights.
- ☒ Keep well out towards the middle of the road.

Answer

☒ **Turn on your dipped headlights.**

You should always use your headlights in fog. They should be on dipped beam to prevent the light reflecting back off the fog.

Question 8.48

You should only use rear fog lights when you cannot see further than about

Mark one answer

- ☒ 100 metres (330 feet) ✗
- ☒ 200 metres (660 feet)
- ☒ 250 metres (800 feet)
- ☒ 150 metres (495 feet).

Answer

☒ **100 metres (330 feet)**

This will help other road users to see you. Don't forget to switch them off when visibility improves. Driving with them on at other times, such as in heavy rain, can dazzle the car behind.

Question 8.49

Whilst driving, the fog clears and you can see more clearly. You must remember to

Mark one answer

- ☒ switch off the fog lights ✗
- ☒ reduce your speed
- ☒ switch off the demister
- ☒ close any open windows.

Answer

☒ **switch off the fog lights**

Bright rear fog lights might be mistaken for brake lights and could be misleading for the traffic behind.

Question 8.50

You have to park on the road in fog. You should

Mark one answer

- ☒ leave sidelights on
- ☒ leave dipped headlights and fog lights on
- ☒ leave dipped headlights on
- ☒ leave main beam headlights on.

Answer

☒ **leave sidelights on**

If you have to park your vehicle in foggy conditions it's important that it can be seen by other road users.

Try to find a place to park off the road. If this isn't possible leave it facing in the same direction as the traffic. Make sure that your lights are clean and that you leave your sidelights on.

Question 8.51

On a foggy day you unavoidably have to park your car on the road. You should

Mark one answer

- ☒ leave your headlights on
- ☒ leave your fog lights on
- ☒ leave your sidelights on
- ☒ leave your hazard lights on.

Answer

☒ **leave your sidelights on**

Ensure that your vehicle can be seen by other traffic. If possible, park your car off the road in a car park or driveway to avoid the extra risk to other road users.

Question 8.52

The best place to park your motorcycle is

Mark one answer

- ☒ on soft tarmac
- ☒ on bumpy ground
- ☒ on grass
- ☒ on firm, level ground.

Answer

☒ **on firm, level ground**

Parking your machine on soft ground might cause the stand to sink and the bike to fall over. The ground should also be even and level to ensure that the bike is stable. If possible, park your machine off the road.

Question 8.53

You are driving on a motorway in fog. The left-hand edge of the motorway can be identified by reflective studs. What colour are they?

Mark one answer

- ☒ Green.
- ☒ Amber.
- ☒ Red.
- ☒ White.

Answer

☒ **Red.**

Be especially careful if you're driving on a motorway in fog. You must be able to stop well within the distance that you can see to be clear. Keep in the left-hand lane.

Reflective studs are used on motorways to help you in poor visibility. The studs are coloured so that you'll know which lane you're in and where slip roads join or leave the motorway.

Question 8.54

When riding in windy conditions, you should

Mark one answer

- ☒ stay close to large vehicles
- ☒ keep your speed up
- ☒ keep your speed down
- ☒ stay close to the gutter.

Answer

☒ **keep your speed down**

Strong winds can blow motorcycles off course and even across the road. In windy conditions you need to

- slow down
- avoid riding on exposed roads
- watch for gaps in buildings and hedges where you may be affected by a sudden blast of wind.

Question 8.55

In normal riding your position on the road should be

Mark one answer

- ☒ about a foot from the kerb
- ☒ about central in your lane
- ☒ on the right of your lane
- ☒ near the centre of the road.

Answer

☒ **about central in your lane**

If you're riding a motorcycle it's very important to ride where other road users can see you. In normal weather you should ride in the centre of your lane. This will

- help you to be seen in the mirror of the vehicle in front
- avoid uneven road surfaces in the gutter
- allow others to overtake on the right if they wish.

Question 8.56

Should lights be used when travelling at night on a well lit motorway?

Mark one answer

- ☒ Yes, but only sidelights are needed.
- ☒ Yes, dipped headlights are needed.
- ☒ No, unless the weather is bad.
- ☒ No, lights are not needed.

Answer

☒ **Yes, dipped headlights are needed.**

Due to the higher speeds on a motorway you must ensure that your vehicle can be seen much earlier. Use your dipped headlights during the day if there is bad visibility. Some motorways are only lit in parts, this can throw you into pools of darkness when you drive into an unlit stretch of the motorway.

Question 8.57

You are driving on a well-lit motorway at night. You must

Mark one answer

☒ use only your sidelights

☒ always use your headlights

☒ always use rear fog lights

☒ use headlights only in bad weather.

Answer

☒ **always use your headlights**

If you're driving on a motorway at night you must always use your headlights, even if the road is well lit. The vehicles in front must be able to see you in their mirrors.

Question 8.58

You are driving on a motorway at night. You MUST have your headlights switched on unless

Mark one answer

☒ there are vehicles close in front of you

☒ you are travelling below 50 mph

☒ the motorway is lit

☒ your vehicle is broken down on the hard shoulder

Answer

☒ **your vehicle is broken down on the hard shoulder**

Always use your headlights at night on a motorway unless you're stopped on the hard shoulder. If you break down and have to stop on the hard shoulder switch off the main beam. Leave the sidelights on so that other road users can see your vehicle or machine.

Question 8.59

You are travelling on a motorway at night with other vehicles just ahead of you. Which lights should you have on?

Mark one answer

☒ Front fog lights.

☒ Main beam headlights.

☒ Sidelights only.

☒ Dipped headlights.

Answer

☒ **Dipped headlights.**

If you're driving or riding behind other traffic at night on the motorway

- leave a two-second time gap
- dip your headlights.

Full beam will dazzle the driver ahead. Your light beam should fall short of the vehicle in front.

Question 8.60

Which TWO of the following are correct?
When overtaking at night you should

Mark two answers

- [x] wait until a bend so that you can see the oncoming headlights
- [x] sound your horn twice before moving out
- [x] be careful because you can see less
- [x] beware of bends in the road ahead
- [x] put headlights on full beam.

Answers

- [x] **be careful because you can see less**
- [x] **beware of bends in the road ahead**

Only overtake the vehicle in front if it's really necessary. At night the risks are increased due to the poor visibility. Don't overtake if there's a possibility of

- road junctions
- bends ahead
- the brow of a bridge or hill, except on a dual carriageway
- pedestrian crossings
- double white lines ahead
- vehicles changing direction
- any other potential hazard.

Question 8.61

You are overtaking a car at night. You must be sure that

Mark one answer

- [x] you flash your headlamps before overtaking
- [x] your rear fog lights are switched on
- [x] you have switched your lights to full beam before overtaking
- [x] you do not dazzle other road users.

Answer

- [x] **you do not dazzle other road users**

If you wish to overtake at night ensure that your lights don't reflect in the mirror of the car in front. Wait until you've overtaken before switching to full beam.

Question 8.62

You are driving at night. Why should you be extra careful of your speed?

Mark one answer

- [x] Because you might need to stop within the distance that you can see.
- [x] Because it uses more petrol.
- [x] Because driving with the lights on runs down the battery.
- [x] Because you may be late.

Answer

- [x] **Because you might need to stop within the distance that you can see.**

You can't see as far at night as in daylight. Therefore, you need to be aware that you can't safely drive as fast at night. There will be more unseen hazards.

Question 8.63

When riding at night you should

Mark two answers

☒ wear fluorescent clothing

☒ ride closer to the vehicle in front

☒ keep your goggles or visor clean

☒ ride well to the left

☒ use your headlight.

Answers

☒ **keep your goggles or visor clean**

☒ **use your headlight**

Always make sure that you can see clearly and that other road users can see you. Make sure that your visor or goggles don't have any scratches, which might distort your view or cause dazzle. Wearing bright clothing is a good idea, but remember, only **reflective** clothing will adequately show up at night.

Question 8.64

You are travelling at night. You are dazzled by headlights coming towards you. You should

Mark one answer

☒ pull down your sun visor

☒ slow down or stop

☒ switch on your main beam headlights

☒ put your hand over your eyes.

Answer

☒ **slow down or stop**

If you're driving at night there will be extra hazards to deal with. The lights of oncoming vehicles can often distract. If you're dazzled by them don't

• close your eyes

• flash your headlights. This will only distract the other driver too.

Question 8.65

You are dazzled by oncoming headlights when driving at night. What should you do?

Mark one answer

☒ Slow down or stop.

☒ Brake hard.

☒ Drive faster past the oncoming car.

☒ Flash your lights.

Answer

☒ **Slow down or stop.**

Let your eyes readjust. Speed and distance are more difficult to judge at night. You won't be able to see as far as in daylight so less information will be available. Don't take risks, especially if you're considering overtaking the vehicle in front.

Question 8.66

You are parking on a two way road at night.
The speed limit is 40 mph. You should park on
the

Mark one answer

☒ left with sidelights on

☒ left with no lights on

☒ right with sidelights on

☒ right with dipped headlights on.

Answer

 left with sidelights on

On a two way road you may only park at
night without lights on

- if the road has a speed limit of 30 mph
  or less
- you're at least 10 metres (32 feet) away
  from a junction
- you're facing in the direction of the
  traffic flow.

Question 8.67

When driving towards a bright setting sun,
glare can be reduced by

Mark one answer

☒ closing one eye

☒ dipping the interior mirror

☒ wearing dark glasses

☒ looking sideways.

Answer

 wearing dark glasses

Dark glasses are often used as a fashion item
but they do have their practical uses. Low
sun in the early morning or evening can
dazzle and distract. Lessen the risk by
reducing the glare. Wear dark glasses if they
help you to see better.

Question 8.68

You are on a narrow road at night. A slower-
moving vehicle ahead has been signalling
right for some time. What should you do?

Mark one answer

☒ Overtake on the left.

☒ Flash your headlights before overtaking.

☒ Signal right and sound your horn.

☒ Wait for the signal to be cancelled
before overtaking.

Answer

☒ **Wait for the signal to be cancelled
before overtaking.**

If the vehicle in front has been indicating
right for some time, but has made no
attempt to turn, wait for the signal to be
cancelled. The other driver may have
misjudged the distance to the road junction
or there might be a hidden hazard.
Whenever you overtake don't

- flash your headlights
- sound your horn
- do so without being able to see well
  down the road.

Question 8.69

A rumble device is designed to

Mark two answers

- ☒ give directions
- ☒ prevent cattle escaping
- ☒ alert drivers to low tyre pressure
- ☒ alert drivers to a hazard
- ☒ encourage drivers to reduce speed.

Answers

- ☒ **alert drivers to a hazard**
- ☒ **encourage drivers to reduce speed**

A rumble device is usually raised markings or strips on the road's surface. These strips are in places where traffic has constantly ignored warning or restriction signs. They're there for a good reason. Slow down and be ready to deal with a hazard.

Question 8.70

Which TWO are correct? The passing places on a single-track road are

Mark two answers

- ☒ for taking a rest from driving
- ☒ to pull into if an oncoming vehicle wants to proceed
- ☒ for stopping and checking your route
- ☒ to turn the car around in, if you are lost
- ☒ to pull into if the car behind wants to overtake.

Answers

- ☒ **to pull into if an oncoming vehicle wants to proceed**
- ☒ **to pull into if the car behind wants to overtake**

If you're driving on a single-track road be prepared to pull over and let other road users pass. There are passing places to enable you to do this. These shouldn't be used for parking or turning your car around.

Question 8.71

You see a vehicle coming towards you on a single-track road. You should

Mark one answer

- ☒ reverse back to the main road
- ☒ do an emergency stop
- ☒ stop at a passing place
- ☒ put on your hazard flashers.

Answer

- ☒ **stop at a passing place**

You must take extra care when driving on single-track roads. You may not be able to see around bends due to high hedges or fences. Drive with caution and expect to meet oncoming vehicles around the next bend. If you do, pull over into or opposite a passing place.

Question 8.72

Your motorcycle is parked on a two-way road. You should get on from the

Mark one answer

☒ right and apply the rear break

☒ left and leave the brakes alone

☒ left and apply the front brake

☒ right and leave the brakes alone.

Answer

☒ **left and apply the front brake**

When you get onto a motorcycle you should

- get on from the left side to avoid putting yourself in danger from passing traffic

- apply the front brake to prevent the machine rolling either forwards or backwards.

Question 8.73

When may you wait in a box junction?

Mark one answer

☒ When you are stationary in a queue of traffic.

☒ When approaching a pelican crossing.

☒ When approaching a zebra crossing.

☒ When oncoming traffic prevents you turning right.

Answer

☒ **When oncoming traffic prevents you turning right.**

The purpose of this road marking is to keep the junction clear by preventing traffic from stopping in the path of crossing traffic. If there is already a vehicle waiting to turn right you're free to enter behind it and wait to turn right.

Question 8.74

Which of the following may apply when dealing with this hazard?

Mark four answers

☒ It could be more difficult in winter.

☒ Use a low gear and drive slowly.

☒ Use a high gear to prevent wheelspin

☒ Test your brakes afterwards.

☒ Always switch on fog lamps.

☒ There may be a depth gauge.

Answers

☒ **It could be more difficult in winter.**

☒ **Use a low gear and drive slowly.**

☒ **Test your brakes afterwards.**

☒ **There may be a depth gauge.**

During the winter the stream is likely to flood. It is also possible that, in extreme weather it could ice over. Assess the situation carefully before you drive through. If you drive a vehicle with low suspension you will have to be extra cautious.

Question 8.75

Which of these plates normally appear with this road sign?

Mark one answer

☒ Humps for
   1₂ mile

☒ Hump Bridge

☒ Low Bridge

☒ Soft Verge

Answer

☒ Humps for
      1₂ mile

These are in place to slow down the traffic. You should be aware that they are in places where there are often pedestrians, such as

• shopping areas
• near schools
• residential areas

Watch out for people close to the kerb or crossing the road.

Question 8.76

How should a scooter be left when parking for some time in a town centre?

Mark three answers

☒ On firm and level ground.   ^

☒ By using the side stand leaning over the kerb.

☒ On the centre stand if fitted.   ┌   ─

☒ Secure and with the fuel tap off.

☒ On any very wide pavement.

Answers

☒ **On firm and level ground.**

☒ **On the centre stand if fitted.**

☒ **Secure and with the fuel tap off.**

When parking a motorcycle always try to park

• on firm level ground
• on the centre stand
• with the fuel tap turned off.

You should always secure your vehicle using any steering lock or imobiliser fitted by the manufacturer. Any additional visible motorcycle lock that helps to deter thieves is recommended.

Question 8.77

To gain basic skills in how to ride a motorcycle you should

Mark one answer

☒ practice off-road with an approved   ∿ training body

☒ ride on the road on the first dry day

☒ practice off road in a public park or in a quiet cul-de-sac

☒ ride on the road as soon as possible.

Answer

☒ **practice off-road with an approved training body**

All new motorcyclists must complete a course of basic training with an approved training body before going on the road. This training is given on a site which has been authorised by the Driving Standards Agency as suitable for off-road training.

This section looks at motorway rules.

The questions will ask you about

- speed limits
- lane discipline
- stopping
- lighting
- parking.

Question 9.1

Which of the following CAN travel on a motorway?

Mark one answer

☒ Cyclists.

☒ Vans.

☒ Farm tractors.

☒ Learner drivers.

Answer

☒ **Vans.**

Motorways are designed to help traffic travel quickly. Traffic can only travel safely at high speed if the road is clear. Any slow-moving road user would be a danger to themselves and passing traffic. For this reason there are restrictions on who can use the motorway.

Question 9.2

As a provisional licence-holder you should not drive a car

Mark one answer

☒ over 50 mph

☒ at night

☒ on the motorway

☒ with passengers in rear seats.

Answer

☒ **on the motorway**

When you've passed your practical test ask your instructor to take you for a lesson on the motorway. You'll need to get used to the speed of traffic and how to deal with multiple lanes.

Question 9.3

Which FOUR of these must not use motorways?

Mark four answers

☒ Learner car drivers.

☒ Motorcycles over 50cc.

☒ Double-decker buses.

☒ Farm tractors.

☒ Horse riders.

☒ Cyclists.

Answers

☒ **Learner car drivers.**

☒ **Farm tractors.**

☒ **Horse riders.**

☒ **Cyclists.**

In addition, motorways MUST NOT be used by

- pedestrians
- motorcycles under 50cc
- certain slow-moving vehicles, without permission
- invalid carriages not weighing more than 254kg (560 lbs).

Question 9.4

Which FOUR of these must NOT use motorways?

Mark four answers

- ☒ Learner car drivers.
- ☒ Motorcycles over 50cc.
- ☒ Double-decker buses.
- ☒ Farm tractors.
- ☒ Learner motorcyclists.
- ☒ Cyclists.

Answers

- ☒ **Learner car drivers.**
- ☒ **Farm tractors.**
- ☒ **Learner motorcyclists.**
- ☒ **Cyclists.**

When you've passed your practical driving test it's a good idea to have some lessons on motorway driving. Statistically, motorways are safer than other roads, but they have rules that you need to know before you venture out for the first time. Check with your instructor about this.

Question 9.5

A motorcycle is not allowed on a motorway if it has an engine size smaller than

Mark one answer

- ☒ 50cc
- ☒ 125cc
- ☒ 150cc
- ☒ 250cc.

Answer

 50cc

The restricted speed of a small machine will cause a hazard to other motorway users. If you're riding a machine with a small engine choose another route.

Question 9.6

To ride on a motorway your motorcycle must be over

Mark one answer

- ☒ 100cc
- ☒ 125cc
- ☒ 250cc
- ☒ 50cc.

Answer

☒ **50cc**

Traffic on motorways travels at high speeds. Vehicles need to be capable of keeping up with the flow of traffic. For this reason low-powered vehicles are prohibited.

Question 9.7

Why is it particularly important to carry out a check on your vehicle before making a long motorway journey?

Mark one answer

☒ You will have to do more harsh braking on motorways.

☒ Motorway service stations do not deal with breakdowns.

☒ The road surface will wear down the tyres faster.

☒ Continuous high speeds may increase the risk of your vehicle breaking down.

Answer

☒ **Continuous high speeds may increase the risk of your vehicle breaking down.**

Before you start your journey make sure that your vehicle can cope with the demands of high-speed driving. Before starting a motorway journey check your vehicle's

- oil
- water
- tyres.

Plan your rest stops if you're travelling a long way.

Question 9.8

Immediately after joining a motorway you should normally

Mark one answer

☒ try to overtake

☒ readjust your mirrors

☒ position your vehicle in the centre lane

☒ keep in the left lane

Answer

☒ **keep in the left lane**

Wait until you've built up speed and only move into the centre lane if you intend to overtake.

Question 9.9

You are joining a motorway. Why is it important to make full use of the slip road?

Mark one answer

☒ Because there is space available to reverse if you need to.

☒ To allow you direct access to the overtaking lanes.

☒ To build up a speed similar to traffic on the motorway.

☒ Because you can continue on the hard shoulder.

Answer

☒ **To build up a speed similar to traffic on the motorway.**

Try to join the motorway without affecting the progress of the traffic already travelling on it. At busy times this could also mean slowing down to merge into slow-moving traffic.

Question 9.10
You are joining a motorway from a slip road on the left. You should

Mark one answer

☒ adjust your speed to the speed of the traffic on the motorway

☒ accelerate as quickly as you can and ride straight out

☒ ride onto the hard shoulder until a gap appears

☒ give a left signal to join the motorway.

Answer

☒ **adjust your speed to the speed of the traffic on the motorway**

Give way to the traffic already on the motorway and join where there's a suitable gap in the traffic. Try to avoid stopping at the end of the slip road. This might not be avoidable, however, if the motorway is exceptionally busy and there isn't a clear gap in the traffic.

Question 9.11
When joining a motorway you must always

Mark one answer

☒ use the hard shoulder

☒ stop at the end of the acceleration lane

☒ come to a stop before joining the motorway

☒ give way to traffic already on the motorway.

Answer

☒ **give way to traffic already on the motorway**

The traffic may be travelling at high speed so you should adjust your speed and emerge when it's safe to do so.

Question 9.12
You have just joined a motorway. Which lane would you normally stay in to get used to the higher speeds?

Mark one answer

☒ Hard shoulder.

☒ Right hand lane.

☒ Centre lane.

☒ Left hand lane.

Answer

☒ **Left hand lane.**

Don't force your way into the stream of traffic or drive along the hard shoulder. Give yourself time to judge and adjust to the faster speed of the moving traffic.

Question 9.13
You are riding on a motorway. Unless signs show otherwise you must NOT exceed

Mark one answer

☒ 50 mph

☒ 60 mph

☒ 70 mph

☒ 80 mph.

Answer

☒ **70 mph**

Ride in accordance with the conditions. Bad weather, heavy traffic or roadworks will limit your speed.

Question 9.14

What is the national speed limit for cars and motorcycles in the centre lane of a three-lane motorway?

Mark one answer

☒ 40 mph.

☒ 50 mph.

☒ 60 mph.

☒ 70 mph.

Answer

 70 mph.

Unless otherwise indicated the speed limit for the motorway applies to all the lanes. Be on the lookout for any indication of speed limit changes due to roadworks or traffic flow control.

Question 9.15

What is the national speed limit on motorways for cars and motorcycles?

Mark one answer

☒ 30 mph.

☒ 50 mph.

☒ 60 mph.

☒ 70 mph.

Answer

 70 mph.

Speed limits may be altered due to weather conditions. Look out for signs on the central reserve or above your lane.

Question 9.16

You are towing a trailer on a motorway. What is your maximum speed limit?

Mark one answer

☒ 40 mph.

☒ 50 mph.

☒ 60 mph.

☒ 70 mph.

Answer

 60 mph.

Don't forget that you're towing a trailer. If you're towing a small, light trailer it won't reduce your vehicle's performance by very much. Strong winds or buffeting from large vehicles might cause it to snake from side to side. Be aware of your speed and don't exceed the lower limit imposed.

Question 9.17

You are driving a car on a motorway. Unless signs show otherwise you must NOT exceed

Mark one answer

- ☒ 50 mph
- ☒ 60 mph
- ☒ 70 mph
- ☒ 80 mph.

Answer

☒ **70 mph**

The national speed limit for a car or motorcycle on the motorway is 70 mph.

Lower speed limits may be in force so look out for the signs. There might be a variable speed limit in operation to control a very busy motorway. The speed limit may change depending on the volume of traffic. There may be roadworks enforcing a low speed

Question 9.18

On a three-lane motorway which lane should you use for normal driving?

Mark one answer

- ☒ Left.
- ☒ Right.
- ☒ Centre.
- ☒ Either the right or centre.

Answer

☒ **Left.**

On a three-lane motorway you should travel in the left-hand lane unless you're overtaking. This applies regardless of the speed you're travelling at.

Question 9.19

A basic rule when driving on motorways is

Mark one answer

- ☒ use the lane that has least traffic
- ☒ keep to the left lane unless overtaking
- ☒ overtake on the side that is clearest
- ☒ try to keep above 50 mph to prevent congestion.

Answer

☒ **keep to the left lane unless overtaking**

When you've overtaken, move back into the left-hand lane as soon as it's safe to do so. Don't cut across in front of the vehicle that you're overtaking.

Question 9.20

On a three-lane motorway why should you normally ride in the left lane?

Mark one answer

- ☒ The lanes on the right are for overtaking.
- ☒ The left lane is for motorcycles only.
- ☒ The left lane is only for slower vehicles.
- ☒ Motorcycles are not allowed in the far right lane.

Answer

☒ **The lanes on the right are for overtaking.**

Change lane only if necessary. When you do change lane observe, signal and manoeuvre in good time. Always remember your 'lifesaver' check. This is a final, quick rearward glance before you manoeuvre.

Question 9.21

You are driving on a three-lane motorway at 70 mph. There is no traffic ahead. Which lane should you use?

Mark one answer

- ☒ Any lane.
- ☒ Middle lane.
- ☒ Right lane.
- ☒ Left lane.

Answer

☒ **Left lane.**

Use the left-hand lane if it's free, regardless of the speed you're travelling at.

Question 9.22

The left-hand lane on a three-lane motorway is for use by

Mark one answer

- ☒ any vehicle
- ☒ large vehicles only
- ☒ emergency vehicles only
- ☒ slow vehicles only.

Answer

☒ **any vehicle**

On a motorway all traffic should use the left-hand lane unless overtaking. If you need to overtake use the centre or right-hand lanes.

Make sure that you move back to the left-hand lane when you've finished overtaking. Don't stay in the middle or right-hand lanes if the left-hand lane is free.

The left-hand lane of a motorway should be used for

Mark one answer

☒ breakdowns and emergencies only

☒ overtaking slower traffic in the other lanes

☒ slow vehicles only

☒ normal driving.

Answer

 normal driving

You must be aware that large vehicles aren't allowed into the right-hand lane to overtake. Don't impede their progress by staying in the middle lane. Move back into the left-hand lane as soon as it is safe to do so.

What is the right hand-lane used for on a three-lane motorway?

Mark one answer

☒ Emergency vehicles only.

☒ Overtaking.

☒ Vehicles towing trailers.

☒ Coaches only.

Answer

 Overtaking.

You should keep to the left and only use the right-hand lane if you're passing slower-moving traffic.

Which of the these IS NOT allowed to travel in the right-hand lane of a three-lane motorway?

Mark one answer

☒ A small delivery van.

☒ A motorcycle.

☒ A vehicle towing a trailer.

☒ A motorcycle and side-car.

Answer

✖ A vehicle towing a trailer.

A vehicle with a trailer is restricted to 60 mph. For this reason it isn't allowed in the right-hand lane as it might hold up the faster-moving traffic that wishes to overtake in that lane.

Question 9.26

For what reason may you use the right-hand lane of a motorway?

Mark one answer

☒ For keeping out of the way of lorries.

☒ For driving at more than 70 mph.

☒ For turning right.

☒ For overtaking other vehicles. ʹ

Answer

☒ **For overtaking other vehicles.**

The right-hand lanes of the motorway are for overtaking. Sometimes you may be directed into a right-hand lane as a result of roadworks or an accident.
Be guided by the signs or police directing the traffic.

Question 9.27

On motorways you should never overtake on the left UNLESS

Mark one answer

☒ you can see well ahead that the hard shoulder is clear

☒ the traffic in the right-hand lane is signalling right

☒ you warn drivers behind by signalling left

☒ there is a queue of traffic to your right that is moving more slowly

Answer

☒ **there is a queue of traffic to your right that is moving more slowly**

Only overtake on the left if traffic is moving slowly in queues and the traffic on the right is moving slower..

Question 9.28

On a motorway you may ONLY stop on the hard shoulder

Mark one answer

☒ in an emergency

☒ if you feel tired and need to rest

☒ if you accidentally go past the exit that you wanted to take

☒ to pick up a hitchhiker.

Answer

☒ **in an emergency**

Don't stop on the hard shoulder to

- have a rest or a picnic
- pick up hitchhikers
- answer a mobile phone
- check a road map.

Never reverse along the hard shoulder if you accidentally go past the exit you wanted.

Question 9.29

You are travelling on a motorway. You decide you need a rest. You should

Mark two answers

☒ stop on the hard shoulder

☒ go to a service area

☒ park on the slip road

☒ park on the central reservation

☒ leave at the next exit.

Answers

☒ **go to a service area**

☒ **leave at the next exit**

Stopping on the motorway in any circumstances other than an emergency or traffic queue will cause a major hazard. You should plan your journey so that you have a rest about every two hours. Stop where you are able to get out of the car for some fresh air and something to eat and drink.

Question 9.30

You are driving on a motorway. The car ahead shows its hazard lights for a short time. This tells you that

Mark one answer

☒ the driver wants you to overtake

☒ the other car is going to change lanes

☒ traffic ahead is slowing or stopping suddenly

☒ there is a police speed check up ahead.

Answer

☒ **traffic ahead is slowing or stopping suddenly**

There may be an accident or queuing due to roadworks. Look well ahead, not just at the car in front, and you'll get an earlier warning of any hazard.

Question 9.31

You are driving on a motorway. You have to slow down quickly due to a hazard. You should

Mark one answer

☒ switch on your hazard lights

☒ switch on your headlights

☒ sound your horn

☒ flash your headlights

Answer

☒ **switch on your hazard lights**

The traffic behind you will be given an extra warning, in addition to your brake lights. Switch them off again as the queue forms behind you.

Question 9.32

Which vehicles are normally fitted with amber flashing beacons on the roof?

Mark two answers

☒ Doctor's car.

☒ Bomb disposal team.

☒ Blood transfusion team.

☒ Breakdown recovery vehicles.

☒ Coastguard.

☒ Maintenance vehicles.

Answers

☒ **Breakdown recovery vehicles.**

☒ **Maintenance vehicles.**

These vehicles are often carrying out tasks on the hard shoulder. If you see an amber beacon ahead, be prepared in case you have to give them more room by moving into the middle lane.

Question 9.33

You get a puncture on the motorway. You manage to get your vehicle onto the hard shoulder. You should

Mark one answer

☒ change the wheel yourself immediately

☒ use the emergency telephone and call for assistance

☒ try to wave down another vehicle for help

☒ only change the wheel if you have a passenger to help you.

Answer

☒ **use the emergency telephone and call for assistance**

Due to the danger from passing traffic you shouldn't attempt repairs on the hard shoulder, especially if you have to change an offside wheel.

The emergency telephones on a motorway are connected to the

Mark one answer

☒ ambulance service

☒ police control

☒ fire brigade

☒ breakdown service.

Answer

✖ **police control**

The controller will ask you

- the make and colour of your vehicle
- whether you are a member of an emergency breakdown service
- the number shown on the emergency telephone casing
- whether you are travelling alone.

How should you use the emergency telephone on a motorway?

Mark one answer

☒ Stay close to the carriageway.

☒ Face the oncoming traffic.

☒ Keep your back to the traffic.

☒ Keep your head in the kiosk.

Answer

✖ **Face the oncoming traffic.**

Traffic is passing you at speed. The draught from a large lorry could unsteady you, so be prepared. By facing the oncoming traffic you can spot this in advance, as well as other hazards approaching.

What should you use the hard shoulder of a motorway for?

Mark one answer

☒ Stopping in an emergency.

☒ Overtaking.

☒ Stopping when you are tired.

☒ Joining the motorway.

Answer

✖ **Stopping in an emergency.**

Don't use the hard shoulder for stopping other than for emergencies. Drive to the next exit or service station if you're able to do so safely.

Question 9.37

After a breakdown you need to rejoin the main carriageway of a motorway from the hard shoulder. You should

Mark one answer

- [ ] move out onto the carriageway then build up your speed
- [ ] move out onto the carriageway using your hazard lights
- [ ] gain speed on the hard shoulder before moving out onto the carriageway
- [ ] wait on the hard shoulder until someone flashes their headlights at you.

Answer

 gain speed on the hard shoulder before moving out onto the carriageway

Wait for a safe gap in the traffic before you move out. Indicate your intention but don't force your way onto the traffic

Question 9.38

A crawler lane on a motorway is found

Mark one answer

- [ ] on a steep gradient
- [ ] before a service area
- [ ] before a junction
- [ ] along the hard shoulder.

Answer

 on a steep gradient

There are likely to be slow moving large vehicles which might slow down the progress of other traffic. This extra lane is provided for these slow moving vehicles helping the faster moving traffic to flow. If the crawler lane is free then use it as you would a normal left hand lane.

Question 9.39

Your vehicle has broken down on a motorway. You are not able to stop on the hard shoulder. What should you do FIRST?

Mark one answer

- [ ] Switch on your hazard warning lights.
- [ ] Stop following traffic and ask for help.
- [ ] Attempt to repair your vehicle quickly.
- [ ] Place a warning triangle in the road.

Answer

Switch on your hazard warning lights.

Use your hazard warning lights to warn others.

DON'T TRY TO REPAIR THE VEHICLE.

You are travelling in the left-hand lane of a busy motorway. Signs indicate that your lane is closed 800 yards ahead. You should

Mark one answer

☒ signal right, then pull up and wait for someone to give way

☒ switch on your hazard warning lights and edge over to the lane on your right

☒ wait until you reach the obstruction, then move across to the right

☒ move over to the lane on your right as soon as it is safe to do so.

Answer

☒ **move over to the lane on your right as soon as it is safe to do so**

Always look well ahead and be aware of road signs. If you see that your lane will be closing move across to the next lane in good time. The road signs will have given plenty of warning. Don't

• wait until the last moment before trying to change lane

• expect someone to let you in

• stop.

Be aware that the traffic on the right may be moving very quickly.

When may you stop on a motorway?

Mark three answers

☒ If you have to read a map.

☒ When you are tired and need a rest.

☒ If red lights show above your lane.

☒ When told to by the police.

☒ If a child in the car feels ill.

☒ In an emergency or a breakdown.

Answers

☒ **If red lights show above your lane.**

☒ **When told to by the police.**

☒ **In an emergency or a breakdown.**

You may only stop on the carriageway of a motorway

• when told to do so by the police

• when flashing red lights show above the lane that you're in

• in a traffic jam

• in an emergency or breakdown.

You are allowed to stop on a motorway when you

Mark one answer

☒ need to walk and get fresh air

☒ wish to pick up hitch hikers

☒ are told to do so by flashing red lights

☒ need to use a mobile telephone.

Answer

☒ **are told to do so by flashing red lights**

If any of the other lines show a green arrow you may move into that line and continue if it is safe to do so. If there are red lights above every lane you must stop.

Question 9.43

You are driving on a motorway. There are red flashing lights above every lane. You must

Mark one answer

☒ pull onto the hard shoulder

☒ slow down and watch for further signals

☒ leave at the next exit

☒ stop and wait.

Answer

☒ **stop and wait**

Flashing red lights above every lane mean you must not go on any further. You'll also see a red cross illuminated. Stop and wait. Don't

* change lanes
* continue
* pull onto the hard shoulder (unless in an emergency).

Question 9.44

You are driving in the right hand lane on a motorway. You see these overhead signs. This means

Mark one answer

☒ move to the left and reduce your speed to 50 mph

☒ there are roadworks 50 metres (55 yards) ahead

☒ use the hard shoulder untill you've passed the hazard

☒ leave the motorway at the next exit.

Answer

☒ **move to the left and reduce your speed to 50 mph**

You must obey this sign. There might not be any visible signs of a problem ahead. However, there might be queuing traffic, fog or another hazard ahead.

The minimum safe time gap to keep between you and the vehicle in front in good conditions is at least

Mark one answer

- ☒ four seconds
- ☒ one second
- ☒ three seconds
- ☒ two seconds.

When driving through a contraflow system on a motorway you should

Mark one answer

- ☒ ensure that you do not exceed 30 mph, for safety
- ☒ keep a good distance from the vehicle ahead, for safety
- ☒ switch lanes to keep the traffic flowing
- ☒ drive close to the vehicle ahead to reduce queues.

You are intending to leave the motorway at the next exit. Before you reach the exit you should normally position your vehicle

Mark one answer

- ☒ in the middle lane
- ☒ in the left-hand lane
- ☒ on the hard shoulder
- ☒ in any lane.

Answer

** two seconds**

Driving too close to the vehicle in front can cause accidents, potentially involving many vehicles and causing serious injury. As you drive at higher speeds you must increase your separation distance from the car in front. One way to judge this is to use the 'Two-Second Rule.'

Pick an object some distance ahead, such as a lamp-post or a bridge. As the vehicle in front passes it begin to say

'Only a fool breaks the Two-Second Rule.'

If you pass the object before you finish saying it, you're too close. Drop back and try again.

Answer

** keep a good distance from the vehicle ahead, for safety**

There's likely to be a speed restriction in force. Keep to this. Don't

- switch lanes
- drive too close to other traffic.

There will be no permanent barrier between you and the traffic coming towards you. Be extra cautious.

Answer

** in the left hand lane**

You'll see the first sign one mile from the exit. If you're travelling at 60 miles an hour in the right hand-lane you'll only have about 50 seconds before you reach the countdown markers. There's another sign at the half-mile point. Think about what you need to do to be in the left-hand lane in good time. Don't cut across traffic at the last moment.

Question 9.48

What do these motorway signs show?

Mark one answer

☒ They are countdown markers to a bridge.

☒ They are distance markers to the next telephone.

☒ They are countdown markers to the next exit.

☒ They warn of a police control ahead.

Answer

 They are countdown markers to the next exit.

The exit from a motorway is indicated by countdown markers. These are positioned 100 yards apart, the first being 300 yards from the slip road. Try to get yourself into the left lane in good time.

Question 9.49

At night, when leaving a well-lit motorway service area, you should

Mark one answer

☒ drive for some time using only your sidelights

☒ give your eyes time to adjust to the darkness

☒ switch on your interior light until your eyes adjust

☒ close your eyes for a moment before leaving the slip road.

Answer

 give your eyes time to adjust to the darkness

You should have your eyesight checked regularly. If you can't see well at night it could be that your eyes are to blame. Night driving might show a need for a check with an optician.

Question 9.50

You are driving on a motorway. By mistake, you go past the exit that you wanted to take. You should

Mark one answer

☒ carefully reverse on the hard shoulder

☒ carry on to the next exit

☒ carefully reverse in the left-hand lane

☒ make a U-turn at the next gap in the central reservation.

Answer

 carry on to the next exit

Don't

• reverse anywhere

• make a U-turn.

This is highly dangerous, as high-speed traffic might not be able to take evasive action.

Question 9.51

On a motorway the reflective amber studs can be found between

Mark one answer

☒ the hard shoulder and the carriagway

☒ the acceleration lane and the carriageway

☒ the central reservation and the carriageway

☒ each pair of the lanes.

Answer

☒ **the central reservation and the carriageway**

On motorways reflective studs are fitted into the road to help you

* in the dark

* in conditions of poor visibility.

The reflective studs are coloured. These will help you to know which lane you're in and where slip roads join or leave the motorway.

Question 9.52

What colour are the reflective studs between the lanes on a motorway?

Mark one answer

☒ Green

☒ Amber.

☒ White.

☒ Red.

Answer

☒ **White.**

These are especially useful in bad weather, when visibility is restricted. The light from your headlights is reflected back highlighting the markings between the lanes.

Question 9.53

You are driving on a three-lane motorway. There are red reflective studs on your left and white ones to your right. Where are you?

Mark one answer

☒ In the right-hand lane.

☒ In the middle lane.

☒ On the hard shoulder.

☒ In the left-hand lane.

Answer

☒ **In the left-hand lane.**

The colours of the reflective studs on the motorway and their locations are

Red

* between the hard shoulder and the carriageway.

White

* lane markings.

Amber

* between the edge of the carriageway and the central reserve.

Green

* along slip road exits and entrances.

Bright Green/Yellow

* roadworks and contraflow systems.

Question 9.54

What colour are the reflective studs between a motorway and its slip road?

Mark one answer

 Amber.

 White.

 Green.

 Red.

Answer

 Green.

These will help you when driving in conditions of poor visibility or in the dark.

Question 9.55

You are travelling on a motorway. What colour are the reflective studs on the left of the carriageway?

Mark one answer

 Green.

 Red.

 White.

 Amber.

Answer

 Red.

When you have passed your practical test ask your Approved Driving Instructor (ADI) about lessons on the motorway. Good professional instruction will help you to become confident and safe on the motorway.

This section looks at rules of the road.

The questions will ask you about

- speed limits
- lane discipline
- parking
- lighting.

Question 10.1

You are riding slowly in a town centre. Before turning left you should glance over your left shoulder to

Mark one answer

- [ ] check for cyclists
- [ ] help keep your balance
- [ ] look for traffic signs
- [ ] check for pot holes.

Answer

 check for cyclists

When riding slowly you must remember cyclists. They can travel quickly and fit through surprisingly narrow spaces. Before you turn left in slow moving traffic it's important to check that a cyclist isn't trying to overtake on your left.

Question 10.2

You may drive on a footpath

Mark one answer

- [ ] to overtake slow-moving traffic
- [ ] when the pavement is very wide
- [ ] if no pedestrians are near
- [ ] to get into a property.

Answer

 to get into a property

When you're crossing the pavement watch out for pedestrians and cyclists in both directions.

Question 10.3

What is the meaning of this sign?

Mark one answer

- [ ] Local speed limit applies.
- [ ] No waiting on the carriageway.
- [ ] National speed limit applies.
- [ ] No entry to vehicular traffic.

Answer

 National speed limit applies.

This sign doesn't tell you the speed limit in figures. You should know the speed limit for the type of road that you're on. Study your copy of *The Highway Code*.

Question 10.4

What is the national speed limit on a single carriageway road for cars and motorcycles?

Mark one answer

- ☒ 70 mph.
- ☒ 60 mph.
- ☒ 50 mph.
- ☒ 30 mph.

Answer

☒ **60 mph.**

Exceeding the speed limit is dangerous and can result in you receiving penalty points on your licence. It isn't worth it. Know the speed limit of the road that you're driving on by observing the road signs.

Question 10.5

What is the national speed limit for cars and motorcycles on a dual carriageway?

Mark one answer

- ☒ 30 mph.
- ☒ 50 mph.
- ☒ 60 mph.
- ☒ 70 mph.

Answer

☒ **70 mph.**

Ensure that you know the speed limit for the road that you're driving on.

The speed limit on a dual carriageway or motorway is 70 mph for cars and motorcycles, unless there are signs to indicate otherwise.

The speed limits for different vehicles are listed in *The Highway Code.*

Question 10.6

A single carriageway road has this sign. What is the maximum permitted speed for a car towing a trailer?

Mark one answer

- ☒ 30 mph.
- ☒ 40 mph.
- ☒ 50 mph.
- ☒ 60 mph.

Answer

☒ **50 mph.**

When towing trailers, speed limits are also lower on dual carriageways and motorways. On these roads vehicles towing a trailer are restricted to 60 mph.

You are driving along a road that has no traffic signs. There are street lights. What is the speed limit?

Mark one answer

 20 mph.

 30 mph.

 40 mph.

 60 mph.

Answer

✗ 30 mph.

If you aren't sure of the speed limit it can be indicated by the presence of street lights. If there is street lighting the speed limit will be 30 mph unless otherwise indicated.

There are no speed limit signs on the road. How is a 30 mph limit indicated?

Mark one answer

 By hazard warning lines.

 By street lighting.

 By pedestrian islands.

 By double or single yellow lines.

Answer

✗ By street lighting.

This usually indicates a 30 mph speed limit when there are no other signs to show other limits.

Where you see street lights but no speed limit signs the limit is usually

Mark one answer

 30 mph.

 40 mph.

 50 mph.

 60 mph

Answer

✗ 30 mph.

If you are travelling faster than the limit, slow down before you reach the sign. Check your mirror and ease off the accelerator.

You see this sign ahead of you. It means

Answer

❌ **do not exceed 30 mph after passing it**

Adjust your speed in good time. Don't

- brake sharply
- wait until you're beyond the limit sign before slowing down.

Mark one answer

❌ start to slow down to 30 mph after passing it

❌ you are leaving the 30 mph speed limit area

❌ do not exceed 30 mph after passing it

❌ the minimum speed limit ahead is 30 mph.

If you see a 30 mph limit ahead it means

Answer

❌ **that you must not exceed this speed**

Because the sign is round it gives you an order. You must obey it.

In a built-up area there are many hazards that call for reduced speed, such as

- pedestrians
- cyclists
- junctions
- busy traffic situations.

Mark one answer

❌ that the restriction applies only during the working day

❌ that you must not exceed this speed

❌ that it is a guide and you are allowed to drive 10% faster

❌ that you must keep your speed up to 30 mph.

Question 10.12

What does a speed limit sign like this mean?

Answer

  You must not exceed the speed shown.

Speed limit signs are there for a reason. There may be a large number of side roads. The lower speed limit makes emerging from these safer.

Mark one answer

- [ ] It is safe to drive at the speed shown.
- [ ] The speed shown is the advised maximum.
- [ ] The speed shown allows for various road and weather conditions.
- [ ] You must not exceed the speed shown.

Question 10.13

You are towing a small caravan on a dual carriageway. You must not exceed

Answer

✗ **60 mph**

Due to the increased weight and width of the combined vehicles you should plan well ahead. Be extra careful in wet or windy weather. Strong winds might cause the caravan to snake from side to side. The speed limit is reduced for vehicles towing trailers to lessen the risk of this.

Mark one answer

- [ ] 50 mph
- [ ] 40 mph
- [ ] 70 mph
- [ ] 60 mph

What does this sign mean?

Answer

❌ **End of minimum speed.**

A red slash through this sign indicates that the restriction has ended.

Mark one answer

☒ Minimum speed 30 mph.

☒ End of maximum speed.

☒ End of minimum speed.

☒ Maximum speed 30 mph.

You are driving along a street with parked vehicles on the left-hand side. For which THREE reasons must you keep your speed down?

Answers

❌ **Vehicles may be pulling out.**

❌ **Drivers' doors may open.**

❌ **Children may run out from between the vehicles.**

Care must be taken where there are parked vehicles in a built-up area. Beware of

- vehicles pulling out, especially motorcycles that are small and difficult to see
- pedestrians, especially children, who may run out from between cars
- drivers opening vehicle doors

Mark three answers

☒ So that oncoming traffic can see you more clearly.

☒ You may set off car alarms.

☒ Vehicles may be pulling out.

☒ Drivers' doors may open.

☒ Children may run out from between the vehicles.

You meet an obstruction on your side of the road. You must

Answer

❌ **give way to oncoming traffic**

If you have to pass a parked vehicle on your side of the road take care. Give way to oncoming traffic if there isn't enough room for you both to continue safely.

Mark one answer

☒ drive on; it is your right of way

☒ give way to oncoming traffic

☒ wave oncoming vehicles through

☒ accelerate to get past first.

Question 10.17

There is a tractor ahead of you. You wish to overtake but you are NOT sure if it is safe to do so. You should

Mark one answer

☒ follow another overtaking vehicle through

☒ sound your horn to the slow vehicle to pull over

☒ speed through but flash your lights to oncoming traffic

☒ not overtake if you are in doubt.

Answer

☒ **not overtake if you are in doubt**

Always ask yourself if you really need to overtake. Can you see well down the road? If the answer is no, don't go.

Question 10.18

Which three of the following may take an unusual course at roundabouts ?

Mark three answers

☒ Horse riders.

☒ Milk floats.

☒ Delivery vans.

☒ Long vehicles.

☒ Estate cars.

☒ Cyclists.

Answers

☒ **Horse riders.**

☒ **Long vehicles.**

☒ **Cyclists.**

Long vehicles might have to take a slightly different position when approaching the roundabout or going around it. This is to stop the rear of the vehicle cutting in and mounting the kerb. Horse riders and cyclists might also stay in the left hand lane although they are turning right. Be aware of this and allow them room.

Question 10.19

You are leaving your vehicle parked on a road. When may you leave the engine running?

Mark one answer

☒ If you will be parked for less than five minutes.

☒ If the battery is flat.

☒ If there is a passenger in the vehicle.

☒ Not on any occasion.

Answer

☒ **Not on any occasion.**

When you leave your vehicle parked on a road

• switch off the engine

• make sure that there aren't any valuables visible

• shut all the windows

• lock the vehicle. Use an anti-theft device if you have one.

Question 10.20

In which FOUR places must you NOT park or wait?

Mark four answers

- ☒ On a dual carriageway.
- ☒ At a bus stop.
- ☒ On the slope of a hill.
- ☒ Opposite a traffic island.
- ☒ In front of someone else's drive.
- ☒ On the brow of a hill.

Answers

- ☒ **At a bus stop.**
- ☒ **Opposite a traffic island.**
- ☒ **In front of someone else's drive.**
- ☒ **On the brow of a hill.**

Care and thought should be taken when parking your own vehicle. Don't park

- on a footpath, pavement or cycle track
- near a school entrance
- on the approach to a zebra crossing (except in an authorised parking place)
- opposite another parked vehicle.

Question 10.21

What is the nearest you may park your vehicle to a junction?

Mark one answer

- ☒ 10 metres (33 feet).
- ☒ 12 metres (40 feet).
- ☒ 15 metres (50 feet).
- ☒ 20 metres (65 feet).

Answer

- ☒ **10 metres (33 feet).**

Don't park within 10 metres (33 feet) of a junction (unless in an authorized parking place) or

- where you would force other traffic to enter a tram lane
- where the kerb has been lowered to help wheelchair users
- in front of an entrance to a property
- where your vehicle might obstruct a tram.

Question 10.22

You are finding it difficult to find a parking place in a busy town. You can see there is space on the zigzag lines of a zebra crossing. Can you park there?

Mark one answer

- ☒ No, unless you stay with your car.
- ☒ Yes, in order to drop off a passenger.
- ☒ Yes, if you do not block people from crossing.
- ☒ No, not in any circumstances.

Answer

- ☒ **No, not in any circumstances.**

It's an offence to park there. You will be causing an obstruction by obscuring the view of both pedestrians and drivers.

Question 10.23

In which TWO places must you NOT park?

Mark two answers

☒ Near a school entrance.

☒ Near a police station.

☒ In a side road.

☒ At a bus stop.

☒ In a one-way street.

Answers

☒ **Near a school entrance.**

☒ **At a bus stop.**

It may be tempting to park where you shouldn't while you run a quick errand. Careless parking is a selfish act and could endanger other road users.

Question 10.24

In which THREE places must you NEVER park your vehicle?

Mark three answers

☒ Near the brow of a hill.

☒ At or near a bus stop.

☒ Where there is no pavement.

☒ Within 10 metres (33 feet) of a junction.

☒ On a 40 mph road.

Answers

☒ **Near the brow of a hill.**

☒ **At or near a bus stop.**

☒ **Within 10 metres (33 feet) of a junction.**

Other traffic will have to pull out to pass you. This might mean they have to use the other side of the road where there might be oncoming traffic.

Parking near a junction could restrict the view for emerging vehicles.

Question 10.25

On a clearway you must not stop

Mark one answer

☒ at any time

☒ when it is busy

☒ in the rush hour

☒ during daylight hours.

Answer

☒ **at any time**

Clearways are in place so that traffic can flow without the obstruction of parked vehicles. Just one parked vehicle will cause an obstruction for all other traffic. You should not even stop to pick up or set down passengers.

Question 10.26

You are driving on an urban clearway. You may stop only to

Mark one answer

☒ set down and pick up passengers

☒ use a mobile telephone

☒ ask for directions

☒ load or unload goods.

Answer

☒ **set down and pick up passengers**

These may be provided in built up areas and times of operation will be clearly signed. You should stop only for a time that is reasonable to pick up and set down passengers. You should consider that you are not causing an obstruction for other traffic before you stop.

Question 10.27

You want to park and you see this sign. On the days and times shown you should

Meter ZONE

Mon - Fri
8.30 am - 6.30 pm
Saturday
8.30 am - 1.30 pm

Mark one answer

☒ park in a bay and not pay

☒ park on yellow lines and pay

☒ park on yellow lines and not pay

☒ park in a bay and pay. ✗

Answer

☒ **park in a bay and pay**

Parking restrictions vary from town to town. Look at the signs carefully. Parking in the wrong place could cause an obstruction and you could be fined.

Question 10.28

What is the meaning of this sign?

Mark one answer

☒ No entry.

☒ Waiting restrictions. ✗

☒ National speed limit.

☒ School crossing patrol.

Answer

☒ **Waiting restrictions.**

Don't cause an obstruction by stopping or waiting where there are restrictions

You should know the meaning of road signs. Buy a copy of *Know Your Traffic Signs* (The Stationery Office) and study it.

Question 10.29

At which of these places are you **sometimes** allowed to park your vehicle?

Mark one answer

☒ On the nearside lane of a motorway.

☒ On a clearway.

☒ Where there is a single broken yellow line. ✗

☒ On the zigzag lines of a zebra crossing.

Answer

☒ **Where there is a single broken yellow line.**

You may be able to park where there are broken lines along the edge of the road. Check the signs at the side of the road for parking restrictions. Where there are double yellow lines you may not be able to park at all.

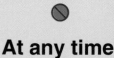

At any time

Question 10.30

What MUST you have to park in a disabled space?

Mark one answer

- ☒ An orange badge. ✗
- ☒ A wheelchair.
- ☒ An advanced driver certificate.
- ☒ A modified vehicle.

Answer

✖ **An orange badge.**

Don't park in a space reserved for disabled people unless you or your passenger are a disabled badge-holder. The badge must be displayed on your vehicle in the bottom left-hand corner of the windscreen.

Question 10.31

You are looking for somewhere to park your vehicle. The area is full EXCEPT for spaces marked 'disabled use'. You must

Mark one answer

- ☒ use these spaces when elsewhere is full
- ☒ stay with your vehicle when you park there
- ☒ use these spaces, disabled or not
- ☒ not park there unless permitted. ✗

Answer

✖ **not park there unless permitted**

Don't be selfish. Find somewhere else to park even if it means that you have to walk further. Leave the space free for those who can't do this.

Your vehicle is parked on the road at night. When must you use sidelights?

Mark one answer

☒ Where there are continuous white lines in the middle of the road.

☒ Where the speed limit exceeds 30 mph.

☒ Where you are facing oncoming traffic.

☒ Where you are near a bus stop.

Answer

❌ **Where the speed limit exceeds 30 mph.**

When parking at night, park in the direction of the traffic. This will enable other road users to see the reflectors on the rear of your vehicle.

Use your sidelights if the speed limit is over 30 mph or you're parking a vehicle over 1,525 kg (1.5 tons).

You park overnight on a road with a 40 mph speed limit. You should

Mark one answer

☒ park facing the traffic

☒ park with sidelights on

☒ park with dipped headlights on

☒ park near a street light.

Answer

❌ **park with sidelights on**

Make sure that other road users can see your vehicle. Park in the direction of the traffic flow so that your vehicle isn't mistaken for a moving oncoming car.

You can park on the right-hand side of a road at night

Mark one answer

☒ in a one-way street

☒ with your sidelights on

☒ more than 10 metres (32 feet) from a junction

☒ under a lamp-post

Answer

❌ **in a one way street**

Vehicles are fitted with red rear reflectors that show up when headlights shine on them. These are useful when cars are parked at night but will only reflect if the vehicles are parked in the same direction as the traffic passing alongside. Normally you should park on the left, but if you're in a one-way street the right-hand side is OK too.

Question 10.35

On a three-lane dual carriageway the right-hand lane can be used for

Mark one answer

- ☒ overtaking only, never turning right
- ☒ overtaking or turning right ✗
- ☒ fast-moving traffic only
- ☒ turning right only, never overtaking.

Answer

☒ overtaking or turning right

Use the left-hand lane at other times. When overtaking on a dual carriageway be on the lookout for vehicles ahead that are turning right. They're likely to be slowing or stopped. You need to see them in good time so that you can take appropriate action.

Question 10.36

You are driving at night with full beam headlights on. A vehicle is overtaking you. You should dip your lights

Mark one answer

- ☒ some time after the vehicle has passed you
- ☒ before the vehicle starts to pass you
- ☒ only if the other driver dips his headlights
- ☒ as soon as the vehicle passes you. ✗

Answer

☒ as soon as the vehicle passes you

Your lights on full beam could dazzle the driver in front. Make sure that your light beam falls short of the vehicle in front.

Question 10.37

You are riding on a busy dual carriageway. When changing lanes you should

Mark on answer

- ☒ rely totally on mirrors
- ☒ always increase your speed
- ☒ signal so others will give way
- ☒ use mirrors and shoulder checks. ✗

Answer

☒ use mirrors and shoulder checks

Before you change lanes you need to see if there's a safe gap to move across into. You have areas behind and to the side which are not covered by the mirrors. As well as using your mirrors you need to make a shoulder check to see if any vehicle is in this blind area before changing direction.

Question 10.38

You are driving on a two-lane dual carriageway. For which TWO of the following would you use the right-hand lane?

Mark two answers

☒ Turning right.

☒ Normal driving.

☒ Driving at the minimum allowed speed.

☒ Constant high-speed driving.

☒ Overtaking slower traffic.

☒ Mending punctures.

Answers

☒ **Turning right.**

☒ **Overtaking slower traffic.**

If you overtake on a dual carriageway move back into the left lane as soon as it's safe. Don't cut in across the path of the vehicle you've just passed.

Question 10.39

You are driving in the right lane of a dual carriageway. You see signs showing that the right lane is closed 800 yards ahead. You should

Mark one answer

☒ keep in that lane until you reach the queue

☒ move to the left immediately

☒ wait and see which lane is moving faster

☒ move to the left in good time. ✗

Answer

☒ **move to the left in good time**

Keep a lookout for traffic signs. If you're directed to change lanes do so in good time. Don't

• push your way into traffic in another lane

• leave changing lanes until the last moment.

Question 10.40

You are entering an area of roadworks. There is a temporary speed limit displayed. You must

Mark one answer

☒ not exceed the speed limit ✗

☒ obey the limit only during rush hour

☒ accept the speed limit as advisable

☒ obey the limit except for overnight.

Answer

☒ **not exceed the speed limit**

Where there are extra hazards, such as roadworks it's often necessary to slow traffic down by imposing a temporary speed limit. These speed limits aren't advisory – they must be adhered to.

Question 10.41

While driving, you approach roadworks. You see a temporary maximum speed limit sign. You must

Mark one answer

☒ comply with the sign during the working day

☒ comply with the sign at all times ✗

☒ comply with the sign when the lanes are narrow

☒ comply with the sign during the hours of darkness.

Answer

☒ **comply with the sign at all times**

The sign has been put there to allow traffic to deal with the hazard at a low speed. Reduce the risk and don't exceed the limit.

Question 10.42

You may drive a motor car in this bus lane

Mark one answer

☒ outside its operation hours ✗

☒ to get to the front of a traffic queue

☒ at no times at all

☒ to overtake slow moving traffic.

Answer

☒ **outside its operation hours**

Make full use of bus lanes if it's permitted. This can often be at times other than rush hours. Check the sign. Times will differ from place to place.

Question 10.43

As a car driver which THREE lanes must you NOT use?

Mark three answers

☒ Crawler lane.

☒ Bus lane at the times shown. ✗

☒ Overtaking lane.

☒ Acceleration lane.

☒ Cycle lane. ✗

☒ Tram lane. ✗

Answers

☒ **Bus lane at the times shown.**

☒ **Cycle lane.**

☒ **Tram lane.**

Look out for signs or road markings that tell you which lane to use. Some lanes can only be used by certain road users. These might be to allow the traffic to flow, or to protect vulnerable road users.

You are driving on a road that has a cycle lane. The lane is marked by a broken white line. This means that

Mark two answers

☒ you must not drive in the lane unless it is unavoidable ✗

☒ the lane cannot be used for parking your vehicle ✗

☒ you can drive in the lane at any time

☒ the lane must be used by motorcyclists in heavy traffic.

Answers

☒ **you must not drive in the lane unless it is unavoidable**

☒ **the lane cannot be used for parking your vehicle**

Where sign or road markings show lanes are for cyclists only, leave them free.

You are driving along a road that has a cycle lane. The lane is marked by an unbroken white line. This means that during its period of operation

Mark one answer

☒ the lane may be used for parking your car

☒ you may drive in that lane at any time

☒ the lane may be used when necessary

☒ you must not drive in that lane. ✗

Answer

☒ **you must not drive in that lane**

Leave the lane free for cyclists. At other times, when the lane is not in operation you should still be aware that there still might be cyclists about. Give them room and don't pass too closely.

A cycle lane is marked by an unbroken white line. You must not drive or park in it

Mark one answer

☒ at any time

☒ during the rush hour

☒ if a cyclist is using it

☒ during its period of operation. ✗

Answer

☒ **during its period of operation**

The cycle lanes are there for a reason. Keep them free and allow the cyclists to use them. Parking in the lane will force cyclists into the path of traffic on the main carriageway. This could be hazardous for both the cyclist and other road users.

Question 10.47

As a motorcycle rider which TWO lanes must you NOT use?

Mark two answers

 Crawler lane.

☒ Overtaking lane.

☒ Acceleration lane.

☒ Cycle lane. ✗

☒ Tram lane. ✗

Answers

☒ **Cycle lane.**

☒ **Tram lane.**

In some towns motorcycles are permitted to use bus lanes. Check the signs carefully.

Question 10.48

You are approaching a busy junction. There are several lanes with road markings. At the last moment you realise that you are in the wrong lane. You should

Mark one answer

☒ continue in that lane ✗

☒ force your way across

☒ stop until the area has cleared

☒ use clear arm signals to cut across.

Answer

 continue in that lane

There are times where road markings can be obscured by queueing traffic, or you might be unsure of your correct lane. Don't cut across lanes or bully other drivers to let you in. Follow the lane you're in and find somewhere safe to turn around if you need to.

Question 10.49

Where may you overtake on a one-way street?

Mark one answer

☒ Only on the left-hand side.

☒ Overtaking is not allowed.

☒ Only on the right-hand side.

☒ Either on the right or the left. ✗

Answer

 Either on the right or the left.

You can overtake other traffic on either side when travelling in a one-way street. Make full use of your mirrors and ensure that it's clear all around before you attempt to overtake. Look for signs and road markings and use the most suitable lane for your destination.

Question 10.50

You are going along a single-track road with passing places only on the right. The driver behind wishes to overtake. You should

Mark one answer

☒ speed up to get away from the following driver

☒ switch on your hazard warning lights

☒ wait opposite a passing place on your right ✗

☒ drive into a passing place on your right.

Question 10.51

You are on a road that is only wide enough for one vehicle. There is a car coming towards you. Which TWO of these would be correct?

Mark two answers

☒ Pull into a passing place on your right.

☒ Force the other driver to reverse.

☒ Pull into a passing place if your vehicle is wider.

☒ Pull into a passing place on your left. ✗

☒ Wait opposite a passing place on your right. ✗

☒ Wait opposite a passing place on your left.

Question 10.52

Signals are normally given by direction indicators and

Mark one answer

☒ brake lights ✗

☒ side lights

☒ fog lights

☒ interior lights

Answer

✖ **wait opposite a passing place on your right**

Some roads are only wide enough for one vehicle. Often this type of road has special passing places where the road is widened for a short distance.

If there's a car coming toward you pull into a passing place on your left or stop opposite one on your right. Don't

* force other vehicles to reverse

* pull into the passing place on the right.

Answers

✖ **Pull into a passing place on your left.**

✖ **Wait opposite a passing place on your right.**

If you meet another vehicle in a narrow road and the passing place is on the right, pull up opposite it. This will allow the oncoming vehicle to pull into it and pass you safely.

Answer

✖ **brake lights**

Your brake lights will give an indication to traffic behind that you're slowing down. Good anticipation will allow you time to check your mirrors before slowing.

If you're intending to change direction you should use your direction indicators before you brake.

Question 10.53

When going straight ahead at a roundabout you should

Mark one answer

☒ indicate left before leaving the ✗ roundabout

☒ not indicate at any time

☒ indicate right when approaching the roundabout

☒ indicate left when approaching the roundabout

Answer

☒ **indicate left before leaving the roundabout**

When you want to go ahead at a roundabout indicate left just after you pass the exit before the one you wish to take. Don't

- signal right on approach
- signal left on approach.

Question 10.54

Which vehicle might have to use a different course to normal at roundabouts?

Mark one answer

☒ Sports car.

☒ Van.

☒ Estate car.

☒ Long vehicle. ✗

Answer

☒ **Long vehicle.**

A long vehicle may have to straddle lanes either on or approaching a roundabout so that the rear wheels don't cut in over the kerb. Stay well back and give it room.

Question 10.55

You are going straight ahead at a roundabout. How should you signal?

Mark one answer

☒ Signal right on the approach and then left to leave the roundabout.

☒ Signal left as you leave the roundabout.

☒ Signal left on the approach to the roundabout and keep the signal on until you leave.

☒ Signal left just after you pass the exit ✗ before the one you will take.

Answer

☒ **Signal left just after you pass the exit before the one you will take.**

To go straight ahead at a roundabout you should normally approach in the left-hand lane. Where there are road markings, use the lane indicated.

Ensure that you signal correctly and in good time. Other road users need to know your intentions.

Question 10.56

You are turning right at a large roundabout. Just before you leave the roundabout you should

Mark one answer

☒ take a 'lifesaver' glance over your left shoulder ✗

☒ take a 'lifesaver' glance over your right shoulder

☒ put on your right indicator

☒ cancel the left indicator.

Answer

☒ **take a 'lifesaver' glance over your left shoulder**

You must be aware of what's happening behind and alongside you. A final, quick rearward glance will give you the chance to react if it isn't safe to make the manoeuvre.

Question 10.57

You may make a U-turn

Mark one answer

☒ when it is safe on a wide road ✗

☒ on a motorway, when it is safe

☒ in a wide one-way street

☒ by mounting both pavements carefully.

Answer

☒ **when it is safe on a wide road**

This manoeuvre should only be used when there's no traffic approaching in either direction. Make sure that you have the time and space to complete it.

Question 10.58

At a crossroads there are no signs or road markings. Two vehicles approach. Which has priority?

Mark one answer

☒ Neither vehicle. ✗

☒ The vehicle travelling the fastest.

☒ The vehicle on the widest road.

☒ Vehicles approaching from the right.

Answer

☒ **Neither vehicle.**

At a crossroads where there are no GIVE WAY signs or road markings BE VERY CAREFUL. No vehicle has priority, even if the size of the roads are different.

Question 10.59

At a crossroads with no road markings who has priority?

Mark one answer

☒ Traffic from the left.

☒ Traffic from the right.

☒ Nobody. ✗

☒ Traffic from ahead.

Answer

☒ **Nobody.**

Never assume that you have priority at a junction where there are no road signs or markings. This applies even in spite of the size of the road you're emerging from. Respond in a safe and responsible manner. Anticipate and adjust your speed – don't take risks.

Question 10.60

Who has priority at an unmarked crossroads?

Mark one answer

- [ ] The driver of the larger vehicle.
- [x] No one. ✗
- [ ] The driver who is going faster.
- [ ] The driver on the wider road.

Answer

- [x] **No one.**

Practise good observation in all directions before you emerge or make a turn.

Question 10.61

When filtering through slow moving or stationary traffic you should

Mark three answers

- [x] watch for hidden vehicles emerging from side roads ✗
- [ ] continually use your horn as a warning
- [x] look for vehicles changing course suddenly ✗
- [ ] always ride with your hazard lights on
- [ ] stand up on the footrests for a good view ahead
- [x] look for pedestrians walking between vehicles. ✗

Answers

- [x] **watch for hidden vehicles emerging from side roads**
- [x] **look for vehicles changing course suddenly**
- [x] **look for pedestrians walking between vehicles**

Other road users may not expect or look for motorcycles filtering through slow moving or stationary traffic. The view all around will be reduced by the vehicles and you will need to watch for

- pedestrians walking between the vehicles
- vehicles suddenly changing direction
- vehicles pulling out of side roads.

You are intending to turn right at a junction. An oncoming driver is also turning right. It will normally be safer to

Mark one answer

☒ keep the other vehicle to your RIGHT and turn behind it (offside to offside) ✗

☒ keep the other vehicle to your LEFT and turn in front of it (nearside to nearside)

☒ carry on and turn at the next junction instead

☒ hold back and wait for the other driver to turn first.

You are both turning right at these crossroads. It is safer to keep the car to your right so you can

Mark one answer

☒ see approaching traffic ✗

☒ keep close to the kerb

☒ keep clear of following traffic

☒ make oncoming vehicles stop.

The dual carriageway you are turning right onto has a narrow central reserve. You should

Mark one answer

☒ proceed to central reserve and wait

☒ wait until the road is clear in both directions ✗

☒ stop in first lane so that other vehicles give way

☒ emerge slightly to show your intentions.

Answer

☒ **keep the other vehicle to your RIGHT and turn behind it (offside to offside)**

At some junctions the layout may make it difficult to turn this way. Be prepared to pass nearside to nearside, but take extra care. Your view ahead will be obscured by the vehicle turning in front of you.

Answer

☒ **see approaching traffic**

When turning right at this crossroads you should keep the oncoming car on your right. This will give you a clear view of the road ahead and any oncoming traffic.

Answer

☒ **wait until the road is clear in both directions**

If you treat this carriageway as two seperate roads you could cause an obstruction to traffic in both directions.

Question 10.65

The car ahead of you is waiting to turn right. The driver should only turn

Mark one answer

- [ ] when the green filter arrow appears
- [ ] when the light changes to red
- [ ] after approaching traffic has cleared ✗
- [ ] when the light changes to amber

Answer

✗ **after approaching traffic has cleared**

Keep back so that you allow yourself a good, all round, view of the road. If you intend to continue ahead, be patient and allow the vehicle time to turn safely.

Question 10.66

While driving, you intend to turn left into a minor road. On the approach you should

Mark one answer

- [ ] keep just left of the middle of the road
- [ ] keep in the middle of the road
- [ ] swing out wide just before turning
- [ ] keep well to the left of the road ✗

Answer

✗ **keep well to the left of the road**

Don't swing out into the centre of the road in order to make the turn. This could endanger oncoming traffic and mislead other road users of your intentions.

You may only enter a box junction when

Answer

❌ **your exit road is clear**

Box junctions are marked on the road to prevent the road becoming blocked.

Don't enter the box unless your exit road is clear. You may only wait in the box if your exit road is clear but oncoming traffic is preventing you from completing the turn.

Mark one answer

❌ there are less than two vehicles in front of you

❌ the traffic lights show green

❌ your exit road is clear ✗

❌ you need to turn left.

You may wait in a yellow box junction when

Answer

❌ **oncoming traffic is preventing you from turning right**

The purpose of this road marking is to keep the centre of the junction clear of queuing traffic when the lights change priority. Don't stop in it if you aren't turning right.

Mark one answer

❌ oncoming traffic is preventing you from turning right ✗

❌ you are in a queue of traffic turning left

❌ you are in a queue of traffic to go ahead

❌ you are on a roundabout.

You want to turn right at a box junction. You should

Answer

❌ **wait in the box junction if your exit is clear**

As the lights change priority the oncoming traffic will stop, allowing you to proceed.

Mark one answer

❌ wait in the box junction if your exit is clear ✗

❌ wait before the junction until it is clear of all traffic

❌ drive on: you cannot turn right at a box junction

❌ drive slowly into the box junction when signalled by oncoming traffic.

Question 10.70

On which THREE occasions MUST you stop your vehicle?

Mark three answers

- [ ] When involved in an accident. ✗
- [ ] At a red traffic light. ✗
- [ ] When signalled to do so by a police officer. ✗
- [ ] At a junction with double broken white lines.
- [ ] At a pelican crossing when the amber light is flashing and no pedestrians are crossing.

Answers

✗ **When involved in an accident.**
✗ **At a red traffic light.**
✗ **When signalled to do so by a police officer.**

Don't stop or hold up traffic unnecessarily. However you MUST stop when signalled to do so by

- a police officer
- a school crossing patrol
- a red traffic light

or when you have had an accident.

Question 10.71

You MUST stop when signalled to do so by which THREE of these?

Mark three answers

- [ ] A police officer. ✗
- [ ] A pedestrian.
- [ ] A school crossing patrol. ✗
- [ ] A bus driver.
- [ ] A red traffic light. ✗

Answers

✗ **A police officer.**
✗ **A school crossing patrol.**
✗ **A red traffic light.**

Looking well ahead and 'reading' the road will help you to anticipate hazards. This will allow you to stop safely if asked to do so by a person or a road sign.

Question 10.72

At roadworks which of the following can control traffic flow?

Mark three answers

- [ ] A STOP–GO board. ✗
- [ ] Flashing amber lights.
- [ ] A policeman. ✗
- [ ] Flashing red lights.
- [ ] Temporary traffic lights. ✗

Answers

✗ **A STOP–GO board.**
✗ **A policeman.**
✗ **Temporary traffic lights.**

As you approach the warning signs you should be considering what actions you need to take. You might have to slow right down or stop. Obey any instructions you are given and don't try to beat any lights by driving up to them quickly.

You are waiting at a level crossing. The red warning lights continue to flash after a train has passed by. What should you do?

Mark one answer

☒ Get out and investigate.

☒ Telephone the signal operator.

☒ Continue to wait.

☒ Drive across carefully.

Answer

☒ **Continue to wait.**

At a level crossing flashing red lights mean you should stop. If the train passes but the lights keep flashing, wait. There may be another train coming.

You are driving over a level crossing. The warning lights come on and a bell rings. What should you do?

Mark one answer

☒ Get everyone out of the vehicle immediately.

☒ Stop and reverse back to clear the crossing.

☒ Keep going and clear the crossing.

☒ Stop immediately and use your hazard warning lights.

Answer

☒ **Keep going and clear the crossing.**

Keep going – don't stop on the crossing. If the warning lights come on as you're approaching the crossing, stop. Don't try to dart across before the train comes.

You are waiting at a level crossing. A train has passed but the lights keep flashing. You must

Mark one answer

☒ carry on waiting

☒ phone the signal operator

☒ edge over the stop line and look for trains

☒ park your vehicle and investigate.

Answer

☒ **carry on waiting**

If the lights at a level crossing continue to flash after a train has passed continue to wait, as there might be another train coming. Time seems to pass slowly when you're held up in a queue. Be patient and wait until the lights stop flashing.

Question 10.76

You will see these markers when approaching

Mark one answer

 a concealed level crossing

the end of a motorway

a concealed 'road narrows' sign

the end of a dual carriageway.

Answer

 a concealed level crossing

There may be a bend before a level crossing, in which case you won't be able to see barriers or waiting traffic ahead. These signs give you an early warning that you may find these hazards just around the bend.

Question 10.77

Someone is waiting to cross at a zebra crossing. They are standing on the pavement. You should normally

Mark one answer

go on quickly before they step onto the crossing

stop before you reach the zigzag lines and let them cross

stop, let them cross, wait patiently

ignore them as they are still on the pavement.

Answer

 stop, let them cross, wait patiently

The pedestrian is showing an intention to cross. If you are looking well down the road you will give yourself enough time to slow down and stop correctly. Don't forget to check your mirrors before slowing down.

Question 10.78

At toucan crossings, apart from pedestrians you should be aware of

Mark one answer

emergency vehicles emerging

buses pulling out

trams crossing in front

cyclists riding across.

Answer

cyclists riding across

The use of cycles is being encouraged and more toucan crossings are being installed. These crossings enable pedestrians and cyclists to cross the path of other traffic. Watch out as cyclists will approach the crossing faster than a pedestrian.

Question 10.79

Who can use a toucan crossing?

Mark two answers

☒ Trains.

☒ Cyclists.

☒ Buses.

☒ Pedestrians.

☒ Trams.

Answers

☒ **Cyclists.**

☒ **Pedestrians.**

Toucan crossings are similar to pelican crossings. Cyclists share the crossing with pedestrians without the need to dismount. They're shown a green cycle when it's safe to cross.

Question 10.80

At a pelican crossing, what does a flashing amber light mean?

Mark one answer

☒ You must not move off until the lights stop flashing.

☒ You must give way to pedestrians still on the crossing.

☒ You can move off, even if pedestrians are still on the crossing.

☒ You must stop because the lights are about to change to red.

Answer

☒ **You must give way to pedestrians still on the crossing.**

If the road is clear then proceed. The green light will show after the flashing amber.

Question 10.81

You are waiting at a pelican crossing. The red light changes to flashing amber. This means you must

Mark one answer

☒ wait for pedestrians on the crossing to clear

☒ move off immediately without any hesitation

☒ wait for the green light before moving off

☒ get ready and go when the continuous amber light shows.

Answer

☒ **wait for pedestrians on the crossing to clear**

This light allows time for the pedestrians already on the crossing to get to the other side in their own time, without undue hurry. Don't rev your engine or start to move off while they are still crossing.

Question 10.82

You are on a busy main road and find that you are travelling in the wrong direction. What should you do?

Mark one answer

☒ Turn into a side road on the right and reverse into the main road.

☒ Make a U-turn in the main road.

☒ Make a 'three-point' turn in the main road.

☒ Turn round in a side road.

Answer

☒ **Turn round in a side road.**

Don't

- turn in a busy street
- reverse into a main road.

Find a quiet side road. Choose a place where you won't obstruct an entrance or exit, and look out for pedestrians and cyclists as well as other traffic.

Question 10.83

You should only make a 'U' turn on a

Mark one answer

☒ motorway

☒ one way street

☒ narrow road

☒ wide quiet road.

Answer

☒ **wide quiet road**

Consider that if the road is not wide enough you will need the time to complete the turn using both the forward and reverse gears. This could result in holding up traffic if the road is busy.

Question 10.84

You may remove your seat belt when carrying out a manoeuvre that involves

Mark one answer

☒ reversing

☒ a hill start

☒ an emergency stop

☒ driving slowly.

Answer

☒ **reversing**

Don't forget to click your seat belt back on when you've finished reversing.

Question 10.85

You must not reverse

Mark one answer

☒ for longer than necessary

☒ for more than a car's length

☒ into a side road

☒ in a built-up area.

Answer

☒ **for longer than necessary**

You may decide to turn your vehicle around by reversing into an opening or side road. When you reverse, always look behind and watch for pedestrians. Don't

- reverse for longer than is necessary
- reverse from a side road into a main road.

You are parked in a busy high street. What is the safest way to turn your vehicle around to go the opposite way?

Mark one answer

☒ Find a quiet side road to turn round in.

☒ Drive into a side road and reverse into the main road.

☒ Get someone to stop the traffic.

☒ Do a U-turn.

Answer

☒ **Find a quiet side road to turn round in.**

You should carry out the manoeuvre without causing a hazard to other vehicles.

When you are NOT sure that it is safe to reverse your vehicle you should

Mark one answer

☒ use your horn

☒ rev your engine

☒ get out and check

☒ reverse slowly.

Answer

☒ **get out and check.**

If you can't see all around your vehicle get out and have a look. You could also ask someone outside the vehicle to guide you. A small child could easily be hidden directly behind you. Don't take risks.

Question 10.88

When may you reverse from a side road into a main road?

Mark one answer

☒ Only if both roads are clear of traffic.

☒ Not at any time.

☒ At any time.

☒ Only if the main road is clear of traffic.

Answer

 Not at any time.

Don't reverse into a main road from a side road. The main road is likely to be busy and the traffic on it moving quickly. Cut down the risks by using a quiet side road to reverse into.

Question 10.89

You are reversing your vehicle into a side road. When would the greatest hazard to passing traffic occur?

Mark one answer

☒ After you've completed the manoeuvre.

☒ Just before you actually begin to manoeuvre.

☒ After you've entered the side road.

☒ When the front of your vehicle swings out.

Answer

 When the front of your vehicle swings out.

Always check road and traffic conditions in all directions. Act on what you see and wait if you need to.

This section looks at road and traffic signs.

The questions will ask you about

- road signs
- speed limits
- road markings
- regulations.

You MUST obey signs giving orders. These signs are mostly in

Answer

X **red circles**

Traffic signs can be divided into three classes – those giving orders, those warning and those informing. On the road each class of sign has a different shape.

Mark one answer

- ☒ green rectangles
- ☒ red triangles
- ☒ blue rectangles
- ☒ red circles.

Traffic signs giving orders are generally which shape?

Mark one answer

Answer

Road signs in the shape of a circle give orders. Those with a red circle are mostly prohibitive. The stop sign is octagonal to give it greater prominence. These signs must always be obeyed.

Question 11.3

Which type of sign tells you NOT to do something?

Mark one answer

Answer

Signs in the shape of a circle mean that you aren't allowed to do something. Study *Know Your Traffic Signs* to ensure that you understand the order you're shown.

Question 11.4

What does this sign mean?

Mark one answer

- ☒ Maximum speed limit with traffic calming.
- ☒ Minimum speed limit with traffic calming.
- ☒ '20 cars only' parking zone.
- ☒ Only 20 cars allowed at any one time.

Answer

☒ **Maximum speed limit with traffic calming.**

If you're driving in areas where there are likely to be pedestrians such as

- outside schools
- near parks
- residential areas
- shopping areas

be extra cautious and keep your speed down. Many local authorities have taken measures to slow traffic down by creating traffic calming measures such as speed humps. They're there for a reason: slow down.

Question 11.5

Which sign means no motor vehicles are allowed?

Mark one answer

Answer

Certain areas are set aside for pedestrians to walk free of traffic.

Question 11.6

Which of these signs means no motor vehicles?

Mark one answer

Answer

If you are driving a motor vehicle or riding a motorcycle you must not enter. This area has been especially designated for pedestrians.

What does this sign
mean?

Answer

❌ **End of 20 mph zone.**

Where you see this sign the 20 mph
restriction ends. Only increase your speed if
it's safe to do so. Check all around and well
down the road before increasing your speed.

Mark one answer

❌ New speed limit 20 mph.

❌ No vehicles over 30 tonnes.

❌ Minimum speed limit 30 mph.

❌ End of 20 mph zone.

This traffic sign means there is

Answer

❌ **a compulsory maximum speed limit**

In this picture the traffic is slow moving, this
could be due to road works or another
temporary obstruction. The sign gives you an
early warning of a speed restriction. If you
are travelling at a higher speed, slow down in
good time.

Mark one answer

❌ a compulsory maximum speed limit

❌ an advised maximum speed limit

❌ a compulsory minimum speed limit

❌ an advised separation distance.

What does this sign mean?

Mark one answer

☒ No overtaking.

☒ No motor vehicles.

☒ Clearway (no stopping).

☒ Cars and motorcycles only.

Answer

 No motor vehicles.

Traffic may be prohibited from certain roads. A sign will indicate which types of vehicles aren't allowed to use it. Make sure that you know which signs apply to the vehicle you're using.

What does this sign mean?

Mark one answer

☒ No parking.

☒ No road markings.

☒ No through road.

☒ No entry.

Answer

 No entry.

Not knowing the meaning of a road sign could lead you into a dangerous situation.

What does this sign mean?

Mark one answer

☒ Bend to the right.

☒ Road on the right closed.

☒ No traffic from the right.

☒ No right turn.

Answer

 No right turn.

The road on the right might be a no entry or the sign could be there to allow the traffic on the main road to flow by stopping cars queuing to turn right.

Which sign means 'no entry'?

Mark one answer

Answer

Look out for traffic signs as you drive. Disobeying or not seeing a sign could not only be dangerous, but also an offence; you could be fined.

At this junction, when the green signal is showing, you must

Mark one answer

- ☒ not go ahead
- ☒ turn right
- ☒ turn left
- ☒ not turn right.

Answer

 not turn right.

The road on the right is a one way road and is showing a no entry sign. Don't attempt to turn into it.

Question 11.14

What does this sign mean?

Mark one answer

 Route for trams only.

Route for buses only.

Parking for buses only.

Parking for trams only.

Answer

 Route for trams only.

Avoid blocking tram routes. Trams are fixed on their route and can't dodge around other vehicles and pedestrians. Modern trams travel quickly and are quiet so you might not hear them approaching.

Question 11.15

Which type of vehicle does this sign apply to?

4.4 m
14′-6″

Mark one answer

Wide vehicles.

Long vehicles.

High vehicles.

Heavy vehicles.

Answer

 High vehicles.

The triangular shapes at the top and bottom of the sign mean that the sign is showing you the restricted height.

Which sign means NO motor vehicles allowed?

Mark one answer

Answer

This sign is used to enable pedestrians to walk free from traffic. It's often found in shopping areas

What does this sign mean?

Mark one answer

☒ Do not overtake.

☒ Oncoming cars have priority.

☒ Two-way traffic.

☒ No right turn ahead.

Answer

☒ **Do not overtake.**

The 'no overtaking' sign is in the shape of a circle so you must obey this order. You may see it where there's a series of bends or the road is narrow.

What does this sign mean?

Mark one answer

☒ You have priority.

☒ No motor vehicles.

☒ Two-way traffic.

☒ No overtaking.

Answer

☒ **No overtaking.**

Road signs that show no overtaking will be placed in locations where passing the vehicle in front is dangerous. If you see this sign don't attempt to overtake. The sign is there for a reason and you must obey it.

Question 11.19

What does this sign mean?

Mark one answer

- ☒ Keep in one lane.
- ☒ Priority to traffic coming towards you.
- ☒ Do not overtake.
- ☒ Form two lanes.

Answer

☒ **Do not overtake.**

If you're behind a slow-moving vehicle be patient. Wait until the restriction no longer applies and you can overtake safely.

Question 11.20

Which sign means no overtaking?

Mark one answer

☒   ☒

☒   ☒

Answer

☒

This sign indicates that your view down the road is restricted, or there may be a junction ahead. For these reasons overtaking here would be dangerous. Don't take risks.

What does this sign mean?

Mark one answer

 Waiting restrictions apply.

Waiting permitted.

National speed limit applies.

Clearway (no stopping).

What does this sign mean?

URBAN CLEARWAY	
Monday to Friday	
am	pm
8.00 - 9.30	4.30 - 6.30

Mark one answer

You can park on the days and times shown.

No parking on the days and times shown.

No parking at all from Monday to Friday.

You can park at any time; the urban clearway ends.

Answer

 Waiting restrictions apply.

There will be a plate or additional sign to tell you when the restrictions apply.

Answer

 No parking on the days and times shown.

Before you leave your vehicle parked at the side of the road check that the space isn't restricted. Parking times vary from place to place, so always check the sign before securing and leaving your car.

Question 11.23

What does this sign mean?

Mark one answer

- ☒ End of restricted speed area.
- ☒ End of restricted parking area.
- ☒ End of clearway.
- ☒ End of cycle route.

Answer

☒ **End of restricted parking area.**

Even though there are no restrictions make sure that you park where you won't cause an obstruction or endanger other road users.

Question 11.24

Which sign means 'no stopping'?

Mark one answer

Answer

Stopping where you see this sign is likely to cause congestion. Allow the traffic to flow by obeying the signs.

Question 11.25
What does this sign mean?

Mark one answer

- ⊠ Roundabout.
- ⊠ Crossroads.
- ⊠ No stopping. ✗
- ⊠ No entry.

Answer

✗ **No stopping.**

This sign is in place to ensure a clear route for traffic. Don't stop except in an emergency.

Question 11.26
You see this sign ahead. It means

Mark one answer

- ⊠ national speed limit applies
- ⊠ waiting restrictions apply
- ⊠ no stopping ✗
- ⊠ no entry.

Answer

✗ **no stopping**

There are stretches of road where you aren't allowed to stop (unless in an emergency). These are called 'clearways'. You'll see this sign. Stopping where these restrictions apply may be dangerous and could cause an obstruction. Restrictions might apply for several miles and this may be indicated on the sign.

Question 11.27
What does this sign mean?

Mark one answer

- ⊠ Distance to parking place ahead. ✗
- ⊠ Distance to public telephone ahead.
- ⊠ Distance to public house ahead.
- ⊠ Distance to passing place ahead.

Answer

✗ **Distance to parking place ahead.**

If you intend to stop and rest note this early indication. This sign allows you time to ask any passengers if they need to stop for any reason.

Question 11.28

What does this sign mean?

Answer

☒ **Vehicles may park fully on the verge or footway.**

In order to keep roads free from parked cars there are some areas where you're allowed to park on the verge. Only do this where you see the sign. Parking on verges or kerbs in other areas could lead to a fine.

Mark one answer

☒ Vehicles may not park on the verge or footway.

☒ Vehicles may park on the left-hand side of the road only.

☒ Vehicles may park fully on the verge or footway. ✗

☒ Vehicles may park on the right-hand side of the road only.

Question 11.29

What does this traffic sign mean?

Answer

☒ **Give priority to oncoming traffic.**

Priority signs are normally shown where the road is narrow and there isn't enough room for two vehicles to pass, such as

- a narrow bridge
- at roadworks
- a width restriction.

Make sure that you know who has priority. Comply with the sign and don't force a right of way. Show courtesy and consideration to other road users.

Mark one answer

☒ No overtaking allowed.

☒ Give priority to oncoming traffic. ✗

☒ No U-turns allowed.

☒ One-way traffic only.

Question 11.30

What is the meaning of this traffic sign?

Mark one answer

☒ End of two-way road.

☒ Give priority to vehicles coming towards you. ✗

☒ You have priority over vehicles coming towards you.

☒ Bus lane ahead.

Answer

✗ You have priority over vehicles coming towards you.

Don't force a right of way. Show courtesy and consideration to other road users.

Question 11.31

Which sign means 'traffic has priority over oncoming vehicles?

Mark one answer

☒   ☒

☒ ✗   ☒

Answer

Even though you may have priority, give way if proceeding is likely to cause an accident, congestion or confrontation.

Question 11.32

What should you do when you see this sign?

Mark one answer

- [ ] Stop, ONLY if traffic is approaching.
- [ ] Stop, even if the road is clear. ✕
- [ ] Stop, ONLY if children are waiting to cross.
- [ ] Stop, ONLY if a red light is showing.

Answer

✕ **Stop, even if the road is clear.**

A stop sign is shown on an octagonal-shaped background. The sign will be at a junction where visibility is restricted or there's heavy traffic.

IT MUST BE OBEYED. YOU MUST STOP.

Practice good all-round observation before moving off.

Question 11.33

What does this sign mean?

Mark one answer

- [ ] No overtaking.
- [ ] You are entering a one-way street.
- [ ] Two-way traffic ahead.
- [ ] You have priority over vehicles from the opposite direction. ✕

Answer

✕ **You have priority over vehicles from the opposite direction.**

Don't force the issue. Slow down and give way to avoid confrontation or an accident.

Question 11.34

What shape is a STOP sign at a junction?

Mark one answer

Answer

The STOP sign is distinctive and the only sign of this shape. You must stop and make effective observation before proceeding.

Question 11.35

At a junction you see this sign partly covered by snow. What does it mean?

Mark one answer

☒ Cross roads.

☒ Give way.

☒ Stop.

☒ Turn right.

Answer

☒ **Stop.**

The STOP sign is the only sign this shape. This is to give it greater prominence. Although the snow has covered the wording you must still be able to recognise and obey this sign.

Question 11.36

Which shape of traffic sign means that you must stop?

Mark one answer

Answer

You won't have enough time to make effective observation without stopping. Stop, and don't emerge until you're sure that it's safe.

Question 11.37

Which shape is used for a GIVE WAY sign?

Mark one answer

Answer

Other warning signs are the same shape and colour, but the GIVE WAY sign points downwards. You must give way to traffic already on the major road.

Question 11.38

What does this sign mean?

Mark one answer

 Service area 30 miles ahead.

 Maximum speed 30 mph.

 Minimum speed 30 mph. ✗

 Lay-by 30 miles ahead.

Answer

 Minimum speed 30 mph.

This sign is shown where slow-moving vehicles would impede the flow of traffic. However, if you need to slow down to avoid a potential accident you should do so.

Question 11.39

Which of these signs means turn left ahead ?

Mark one answer

Answer

This sign gives a clear instruction. You should be looking out for signs as you drive. Prepare to negotiate a left hand turn.

Question 11.40

At a mini-roundabout you should

Answer

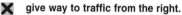 **give way to traffic from the right.**

Look out for other traffic as you approach. Vehicles entering the mini-roundabout from your left or ahead might prevent traffic on your right from proceeding. Watch for their signals and continue if it's safe to do so.

Mark one answer

 give way to traffic from the right ✗

 give way to traffic from the left

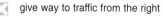 give way to traffic from the other way

stop even when empty.

Question 11.41

What does this sign mean?

Answer

 Mini roundabout.

Look out for any direction signs and judge whether you need to signal your intentions. Do this in good time so that other road users approaching the roundabout can assess the situation.

Mark one answer

Buses turning.

Ring road.

Mini roundabout. ✗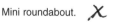

Keep right.

Question 11.42

What does this sign mean?

Mark one answer

- [ ] Give way to oncoming vehicles.
- [ ] Approaching traffic passes you on both sides.
- [ ] Turn off at the next available junction.
- [ ] Pass either side to get to the same destination. ✗

Answer

✗ **Pass either side to get to the same destination.**

These signs are often seen in one-way streets that have more than one lane. Use the route that's the most convenient and doesn't require a late change of direction.

Question 11.43

What does this sign mean?

Mark one answer

- [ ] Route for trams. ✗
- [ ] Give way to trams.
- [ ] Route for buses.
- [ ] Give way to buses.

Answer

✗ **Route for trams.**

Take extra care when you first encounter trams. Look out for road markings and signs that alert you to them. Modern trams are very quiet and you may not hear them approaching.

What does a circular traffic sign with a blue background do?

Mark one answer

☒ Give warning of a motorway ahead.

☒ Give directions to a car park.

☒ Give motorway information.

☒ Give an instruction. ✗

Answer

✗ **Give an instruction.**

Signs with blue circles give a positive instruction. They will often be seen in towns or urban areas. For example

mini-roundabout

pass either side.

Which of these signs means that you are entering a one-way street?

Mark one answer

Answer

✗

If the road has two lanes you can use either lane and overtake on either side. Use the lane that's more convenient for your destination.

Question 11.46

Where would you see a contraflow bus and cycle lane?

Mark one answer

☒ On a dual carriageway.

☒ On a roundabout.

☒ On an urban motorway.

☒ On a one-way street. ✗

Answer

✗ **On a one-way street.**

'Contraflow' means that the bus or cycle lane is going in the opposite direction to the other lanes in the road. Don't drive in or straddle these lanes.

Question 11.47

What does this sign mean?

Mark one answer

☒ Bus station on the right.

☒ Contraflow bus lane. ✗

☒ With-flow bus lane.

☒ Give way to buses.

Answer

✗ **Contraflow bus lane.**

There will also be markings on the road surface to indicate the bus lane. Don't use this lane for parking or overtaking.

Question 11.48

What does this sign mean?

Mark one answer

☒ With-flow bus and cycle lane. ✗

☒ Contraflow bus and cycle lane.

☒ No buses and cycles allowed.

☒ No waiting for buses and cycles.

Answer

✗ **With-flow bus and cycle lane.**

In this case buses and cycles may travel in this lane in the same direction as other traffic. There may be times shown on the sign to indicate when the lane is in use.

What does a sign with a brown background show?

Mark one answer

- Tourist directions.
- Primary roads.
- Motorway routes.
- Minor routes.

Answer

✖ **Tourist directions.**

Signs with a brown background give directions to places of interest. They will often be seen on the motorway directing you along the easiest route.

This sign means

Mark one answer

- tourist attraction
- beware of trains
- level crossing
- beware of trams.

Answer

✖ **tourist attraction**

These signs indicate places of interest and are designed to guide you by the easiest route. If you are a tourist you're likely to be unfamiliar with the area, so these signs are particularly useful.

What are triangular signs for?

Mark one answer

- To give warnings.
- To give information.
- To give orders.
- To give directions.

Answer

✖ **To give warnings.**

This type of sign will tell you about the road ahead and what to expect. Get into the habit of checking each sign that you pass. They will warn you of the hazards ahead.

Question 11.52

What does this sign mean?

Mark one answer

- [ ] Turn left ahead.
- [ ] T-junction. ✗
- [ ] No through road.
- [ ] Give way.

Answer

✗ **T-junction.**

Look well down the road and check the road signs as you drive. You'll then be able to anticipate any junction hazards.

Question 11.53

What does this sign mean?

Mark one answer

- [ ] Multi-exit roundabout.
- [ ] Risk of ice. ✗
- [ ] Six roads converge.
- [ ] Place of historical interest.

Answer

✗ **Risk of ice.**

It will take up to ten times longer to stop when it's icy. Consider this and drive carefully. Don't brake or steer harshly as your tyres could lose their grip on the road.

Question 11.54

What does this sign mean?

Mark one answer

- [ ] Crossroads. ✗
- [ ] Level crossing with gate.
- [ ] Level crossing without gate.
- [ ] Ahead only.

Answer

✗ **Crossroads.**

The priority through the junction is shown by the broader line. However, be aware of the danger when other traffic is crossing a major road.

What does this sign mean?

Mark one answer

☒ Ring road.

☒ Mini-roundabout.

☒ Restriction ends.

☒ Roundabout. ✗

Answer

☒ **Roundabout.**

Prepare yourself for approaching hazards by checking signs as you drive.

Decide which exit you wish to take. Prepare to position your vehicle correctly as you approach the roundabout.

Which FOUR of these would be indicated by a triangular road sign?

Mark four answers

☒ Road narrows. ✗

☒ Ahead only.

☒ Low bridge. ✗

☒ Minimum speed.

☒ Children crossing. ✗

☒ T-junction. ✗

Answers

☒ **Road narrows.**

☒ **Low bridge.**

☒ **Children crossing.**

☒ **T-junction.**

Make use of the warning sign and be prepared for the hazard ahead.

What does this sign mean?

Mark one answer

☒ Cyclists must dismount.

☒ Bicycles are not allowed.

☒ You are approaching a cycle route. ✗

☒ Walking is not allowed.

Answer

☒ **You are approaching a cycle route.**

Where there's a cycle route a sign will show a bicycle in a red warning triangle. Watch out for children on bicycles and cyclists rejoining the main road.

Question 11.58

Which sign means that pedestrians may be walking along the road?

Mark one answer

Answer

Be extra cautious especially if there is a bend in the road and you're unable to see well ahead. When you pass, leave plenty of room. Consider that you might have to use the right hand side of the road, so look well ahead down the road, as well as in your mirrors, before you pull out.

Question 11.59

Which of these signs warn you of a pedestrian crossing?

Mark one answer

Answer

Look well ahead and check the pavements and surrounding areas for pedestrians. Keep an eye on those who are walking towards the crossing. Check your mirrors for traffic behind, in case you have to slow down or stop.

Question 11.60

What does this sign mean?

Mark one answer

- [ ] No footpath ahead.
- [x] Pedestrians only ahead.
- [ ] Pedestrian crossing ahead.
- [ ] School crossing ahead.

Answer

❌ **Pedestrian crossing ahead.**

There are many signs relating to pedestrians. Study *The Highway Code* and *Know Your Traffic Signs*. Some of the signs look similar but give different warnings. Make a mental note as you drive so that you're prepared for any potential hazard.

Question 11.61

What does this sign mean?

Mark one answer

- [ ] School crossing patrol.
- [ ] No pedestrians allowed.
- [ ] Pedestrian zone – no vehicles.
- [x] Pedestrian crossing ahead.

Answer

❌ **Pedestrian crossing ahead.**

Look well ahead and be ready to stop for any pedestrians crossing the road. Also check the pavements for anyone who looks like they might step off into the road.

Question 11.62

Which of these signs means there is a double bend ahead?

Mark one answer

- [ ]
- [ ]
- [ ]
- [ ]

Answer

❌

Triangular signs give you a warning of hazards ahead. They're there to give you time to adjust your speed and drive accordingly.

Question 11.63

What does this sign mean?

Mark one answer

- [ ] Wait at the barriers.
- [ ] Wait at the crossroads.
- [ ] Give way to trams. ✗
- [ ] Give way to farm vehicles.

Answer

✗ **Give way to trams.**

Obey the 'GIVE WAY' signs. Trams are unable to steer around you or change their specific route.

Question 11.64

What does this sign mean?

Mark one answer

- [ ] Humpback bridge.
- [ ] Humps in the road. ✗
- [ ] Entrance to tunnel.
- [ ] Steep hill upwards.

Answer

✗ **Humps in the road.**

These have been put in place to slow the traffic down. They're usually found in residential areas. Slow down and drive at an appropriate speed.

What does this sign mean?

Mark one answer

☒ Low bridge ahead.

☒ Tunnel ahead.   ✗

☒ Ancient monument ahead.

☒ Accident black spot ahead.

Answer

✗ **Tunnel ahead.**

Be prepared to switch on your headlights, if required. Reduce your speed. Your eyes might need to adjust to the sudden darkness.

What does this sign mean?

Mark one answer

☒ Two-way traffic ahead.

☒ Two-way traffic crossing a one-way ✗
street.

☒ Two-way traffic over a bridge.

☒ Two-way traffic crosses a two-way road.

Answer

✗ **Two-way traffic crossing a one-way street.**

Be prepared for traffic approaching from junctions on either side of you.

Try to avoid unnecessary changing of lanes just before the junction.

Which sign means 'two-way traffic crosses a one-way road'?

Mark one answer

Answer

✗

Traffic could be joining the road you're in from either direction. Unless you need to turn, don't change lanes as you approach the junction.

Which of these signs means the end of a dual carriageway?

Mark one answer

 ✕

Answer

If you're travelling in the right-hand lane, prepare and move over into the left-hand lane as soon as it's safe to do so.

What does this sign mean?

Mark one answer

 End of dual carriageway. ✕

 Tall bridge.

 Road narrows.

 End of narrow bridge.

Answer

 End of dual carriageway.

Don't leave moving into the left-hand lane until the last moment. Early planning will prevent you having to rely on other traffic letting you in.

What does this sign mean?

Mark one answer

☒ Two-way traffic ahead across a one-way street.

☒ Traffic approaching you has priority.

☒ Two-way traffic straight ahead. ✗

☒ Motorway contraflow system ahead.

Answer

✗ **Two-way traffic straight ahead.**

This sign may be at the end of a dual carriageway or a one-way street. The sign is there to warn you of oncoming traffic.

What does this sign mean?

Mark one answer

☒ Crosswinds. ✗

☒ Road noise.

☒ Airport.

☒ Adverse camber.

Answer

✗ **Crosswinds.**

Where weather conditions are often bad, signs will give you a warning. A sign with a picture of a wind-sock will indicate there may be strong crosswinds. This sign is often found on exposed roads.

What does this traffic sign mean?

Mark one answer

☒ Slippery road ahead.

☒ Tyres liable to punctures ahead.

☒ Danger ahead. ✗

☒ Service area ahead.

Answer

✗ **Danger ahead.**

A sign showing an exclamation mark (!) will alert you to the likelihood of danger ahead. Be ready for any situation that requires you to reduce your speed.

Question 11.73

You are about to overtake when you see this sign. You should

Hidden dip

Mark one answer

☒ overtake the other driver as quickly as possible

☒ move to the right to get a better view

☒ switch your headlights on before overtaking

☒ hold back until you can see clearly ahead ✗

Answer

✖ **hold back until you can see clearly ahead**

You won't be able to see any hazards that might be out of sight in the dip.

Imagine there might be

• cyclists

• horse riders

• parked vehicles

• pedestrians.

There might be oncoming traffic to deal with, too.

Question 11.74

What does this sign mean?

Mark one answer

☒ Level crossing with gate or barrier. ✗

☒ Gated road ahead.

☒ Level crossing without gate or barrier. ✗

☒ Cattle grid ahead.

Answer

✖ **Level crossing with gate or barrier.**

Some crossings have gates but no attendant or signals. You should

• stop

• look both ways

• listen and make sure that there is no train approaching.

If there is a telephone contact the signal operator to make sure that it's safe to cross.

What does this sign mean?

Mark one answer

☒ No trams ahead.

☒ Oncoming trams.

☒ Trams crossing ahead. ✗

☒ Trams only.

Answer

☒ **Trams crossing ahead.**

This is a warning sign. Watch out for trams. If you are not used to driving in a town where there are trams be especially careful at junctions. Watch out for road signs.

What does this sign mean?

Mark one answer

☒ Adverse camber.

☒ Steep hill downwards. ✗

☒ Uneven road.

☒ Steep hill upwards.

Answer

☒ **Steep hill downwards.**

This warning sign will give you an early indication. Prepare to alter your speed and gear. Looking at the sign from left to right, will show you whether it's up or downhill.

What does this sign mean?

Mark one answer

☒ Quayside or river bank. ✗

☒ Steep hill downwards.

☒ Slippery road.

☒ Road liable to flooding.

Answer

☒ **Quayside or river bank.**

Be aware that the road surface in this location is likely to be wet and slippery.

Question 11.78

What does this sign mean?

Mark one answer

- [ ] Uneven road surface.
- [ ] Bridge over the road.
- [ ] Road ahead ends.
- [ ] Water across the road.

Answer

 Water across the road.

This sign is found where a shallow stream crosses the road. Heavy rainfall could increase the flow of water. If the water looks too deep or the stream has swelled over a large distance, stop and find another route.

Question 11.79

What does this sign mean?

Mark one answer

- [ ] Humpback bridge.
- [ ] Traffic calming hump.
- [ ] Low bridge.
- [ ] Uneven road.

Answer

 Humpback bridge.

Slow right down. Driving over a humpback bridge too fast could cause your wheels to leave the road surface and result in a loss of control.

Question 11.80

What does this sign mean?

Mark one answer

- [ ] Turn left for parking area.
- [ ] No through road on the left. ✗
- [ ] No entry for traffic turning left.
- [ ] Turn left for ferry terminal.

Answer

❌ **No through road on the left.**

Signs are there to help you to drive and to help you to avoid making late decisions. If you intend to take a left turn this sign shows you that you can't get through to another route.

What does this sign mean?

Answer

❌ **No through road.**

You will not be able to find a through route to another road. Only use this road for access.

Mark one answer

☒ T-junction.

☒ No through road. ✗

☒ Telephone box ahead.

☒ Toilet ahead.

Which sign means 'no through road'?

Mark one answer

☒   ☒

☒ ✗   ☒

Answer

❌

This sign is found at the entrance to the road.

Which of the following signs informs you that you are coming to a No Through Road ?

Mark one answer

☒   ☒

☒ ✗   ☒

Answer

❌

This sign is found at the entrance to the road.

Question 11.84

What does this sign mean?

Mark one answer

☒ Direction to park and ride car park. ✗

☒ No parking for buses or coaches.

☒ Directions to bus and coach park.

☒ Parking area for cars and coaches.

Answer

✗ **Direction to park and ride car park.**

To ease the congestion in centres, some cities and towns provide a park and ride scheme. This allows you to park in a designated area and ride by bus into the centre. This is usually cheaper and easier than car parking in the centre.

Question 11.85

You are driving through a tunnel and you see this sign. What does it mean?

Mark one answer

☒ Direction to emergency pedestrian exit. ✗

☒ Beware of pedestrians, no footpath ahead.

☒ No access for pedestrians.

☒ Beware of pedestrians crossing ahead.

Answer

✗ **Direction to emergency pedestrian exit.**

If you find yourself having to evacuate a tunnel, do so as quickly as you can. Follow the signs, these will direct you to the nearest exit point. If there are several people, don't panic but try to leave in an calm and orderly manner.

Question 11.86
Which is the sign for a ring road?

Mark one answer

Answer

Ring roads are designed to relieve congestion in towns and cities.

Question 11.87
What does this sign mean?

Mark one answer

☒ Route for lorries.

☒ Ring road.

☒ Rest area.

☒ Roundabout.

Answer

☒ **Ring road.**

Signs are also designed to give you advice. Ring road signs direct traffic around major towns and cities. Ring roads help the traffic to flow and ease congestion in town centres.

Question 11.88
What does this sign mean?

Mark one answer

☒ Railway station.

☒ Route for cyclists.

☒ Ring road.

☒ Scenic route.

Answer

☒ **Ring road.**

These routes help through traffic to avoid town centres. This relieves congestion in the town and helps through traffic to flow.

Question 11.89

What does this sign mean?

Mark one answer

☒ Hilly road.

☒ Humps in road.

☒ Holiday route. ✗

☒ Hospital route.

Answer

☒ **Holiday route.**

In some areas where the volume of traffic increases during the summer months signs show a route that diverts traffic away from town centres. This helps the traffic to flow, decreasing queues.

Question 11.90

What does this sign mean?

Mark one answer

☒ The right-hand lane ahead is narrow.

☒ Right-hand lane for buses only.

☒ No turning to the right.

☒ The right-hand lane is closed. ✗

Answer

☒ **The right-hand lane is closed.**

Temporary signs may tell you about roadworks or lane restrictions. Look well ahead. If you have to change lanes do so in good time.

Question 11.91

What does this sign mean?

Mark one answer

- ☒ Change to the left lane.
- ☒ Leave at the next exit.
- ☒ Contraflow system. ✗
- ☒ One-way street.

Question 11.92

To avoid an accident when entering a contraflow system, you should

Mark three answers

- ☒ reduce speed in good time ✗
- ☒ switch lanes anytime to make progress
- ☒ choose an appropriate lane early ✗
- ☒ keep the correct separation distance ✗
- ☒ increase speed to pass through quickly
- ☒ follow other motorists closely to avoid long queues

Answer

- ✗ **Contraflow system.**

If you use the right-hand lane, you'll be travelling with no permanent barrier between your vehicle and the traffic coming towards you. Observe speed limits and keep a good distance from the car ahead.

Answers

- ✗ **reduce speed in good time**
- ✗ **choose an appropriate lane early**
- ✗ **keep the correct separation distance**

In a contraflow system you will be travelling close to oncoming traffic and sometimes in narrow lanes. You should

- obey the temporary signs governing speed limits
- get into the correct lane in good time
- keep a safe separation distance from the vehicle ahead.

Question 11.93

You are travelling uphill when you see this sign. Who does it apply to?

Mark one answer

- ☒ Large goods vehicles only.
- ☒ Any slow moving vehicles. ✕
- ☒ Left turning vehicles.
- ☒ Vehicles coming to a halt.

Answer

✗ **Any slow moving vehicles.**

This allows the slower vehicles to move into a lane on the extreme left. Faster moving traffic can pass without having to slow down which could cause congestion or bunching. If the lane is free, then you should treat it as a normal left hand lane.

Question 11.94

What does this sign mean?

Mark one answer

- ☒ Leave motorway at next exit.
- ☒ Lane for heavy and slow vehicles. ✕
- ☒ All lorries use the hard shoulder.
- ☒ Rest area for lorries.

Answer

✗ **Lane for heavy and slow vehicles.**

Where there's a long, steep, uphill gradient on a motorway there may be a crawler lane. This type of lane helps the traffic to flow by diverting the slower heavy vehicles into an extra lane on the left.

Which exit from this roundabout leads onto a dual carriageway?

Mark one answer

☒ 1st.

☒ 3rd.

☒ 4th.

☒ 2nd.

Answer

☒ **2nd.**

The exits from the roundabout are shown as pointers. Look at the sign as you approach and be sure of your intentions. Approach at the appropriate speed and in the correct gear; you may not have to come to a stop if the road is clear to proceed.

You see this traffic light ahead. Which light(s) will come on next?

Mark one answer

☒ Red alone.

☒ Red and amber together.

☒ Green and amber together.

☒ Green alone.

Answer

☒ **Red alone.**

At junctions controlled by traffic lights you must stop behind the white line until the lights change to green. Don't

• move forward when the red and amber lights are showing together

• proceed when the light is green if your exit road is blocked.

If you're approaching traffic lights that are visible from a distance and the light has been green for some time it's likely to change. Try to anticipate this. Be ready to slow down and stop.

Question 11.97

You are approaching a red traffic light. The signal will change from red to

Mark one answer

- [x] red and amber, then green
- [ ] green, then amber
- [ ] amber, then green
- [ ] green and amber, then green.

Answer

✖ red and amber, then green

If you know which light is going to show next you can plan your approach accordingly. This will prevent excessive braking or hesitation at the junction.

Question 11.98

A red traffic light means

Mark one answer

- [ ] you should stop unless turning left
- [ ] stop, if you are able to brake safely
- [x] you must stop and wait behind the stop 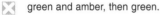 line
- [ ] proceed with caution.

Answer

✖ you must stop and wait behind the stop line

Learn the sequence of traffic lights.

RED means stop and wait behind the stop line.

RED-AND-AMBER also means stop. Don't go until the green light shows.

GREEN means you may go if your way is clear. Don't proceed if your exit road is blocked, and don't block the junction. Look out for pedestrians.

AMBER means stop at the stop line. You may go if the amber light appears after you've crossed the stop line or you're so close to it that to pull up might cause an accident.

Question 11.99

At traffic lights, amber on its own means

Mark one answer

- ⊠ prepare to go
- ⊠ go if the way is clear
- ⊠ go if no pedestrians are crossing
- ⊠ stop at the stop line. ✗

Answer

❌ **stop at the stop line**

If the lights have been on green for a while they're likely to change to red as you approach. Anticipate this so that you're able to stop in time.

Question 11.100

A red traffic light means

Mark one answer

- ⊠ you must stop behind the white stop line ✗
- ⊠ you may drive straight on if there is no other traffic
- ⊠ you may turn left if it is safe to do so
- ⊠ you must slow down and prepare to stop if traffic has started to cross.

Answer

❌ **you must stop behind the white stop line**

The white line is positioned so that pedestrians have room to cross in front of waiting vehicles. If pedestrians are crossing make sure your handbrake is on.

Question 11.101

You are approaching traffic lights. Red and amber are showing. This means

Answer

 wait for the green light before you pass the lights

Other traffic might still be clearing the junction. Don't take risks.

Mark one answer

 pass the lights if the road is clear

 there is a fault with the lights – take care

 wait for the green light before you pass the lights

 the lights are about to change to red.

Question 11.102

You are at a junction controlled by traffic lights. When should you NOT proceed at green?

Answer

 When your exit from the junction is blocked.

As you approach the lights look into the road you wish to take. Only proceed if your exit road is clear. If the road is blocked hold back, even if you have to wait for the next green signal.

Mark one answer

 When pedestrians are waiting to cross.

 When your exit from the junction is blocked.

 When you think the lights may be about to change.

 When you intend to turn right.

Question 11.103

You are in the left-hand lane at traffic lights. You are waiting to turn left. At which of these traffic lights must you NOT move on?

Mark one answer

Answer

At some junctions there may be a separate signal for each lane. These are called 'filter' lights. They're designed to help traffic flow at major junctions. Make sure that you're in the correct lane and proceed if the green light shows.

Question 11.104

What does this sign mean?

Mark one answer

☒ Traffic lights out of order. ✗

☒ Amber signal out of order.

☒ Temporary traffic lights ahead.

☒ New traffic lights ahead.

Answer

☒ **Traffic lights out of order.**

Where traffic lights are out of order you might see this sign. Proceed with caution as nobody has priority at the junction.

Question 11.105

You see this sign at a crossroads. You should

Answer

 drive on with great care

Only do so if the road is clear, treat the road if it was an unmarked junction, that is, no one has priority.

Mark one answer

- ☒ maintain the same speed
- ☒ drive on with great care ✗
- ☒ find another route
- ☒ telephone the police.

Question 11.106

When traffic lights are out of order, who has priority?

Mark one answer

- ☒ Traffic going straight on.
- ☒ Traffic turning right.
- ☒ Nobody. ✗
- ☒ Traffic turning left.

Answer

 Nobody.

Treat the junction as an unmarked cross-roads. Deal with the situation with caution.

These flashing red lights mean STOP. In which THREE of the following places could you find them?

Mark three answers

- ☒ Pelican crossings.
- ☒ Lifting bridges.
- ☒ Zebra crossings.
- ☒ Level crossings.
- ☒ Motorway exits.
- ☒ Fire stations.

Answers

- ☒ **Lifting bridges.**
- ☒ **Level crossings.**
- ☒ **Fire stations.**

Don't take risks by trying to beat the lights, even if it's clear. You must stop.

What do these zigzag lines at pedestrian crossings mean?

Mark one answer

- ☒ No parking at any time.
- ☒ Parking allowed only for a short time.
- ☒ Slow down to 20 mph.
- ☒ Sounding horns is not allowed.

Answer

- ☒ **No parking at any time.**

The approach to hazards may be marked with signs on the road surface. The approach to a pedestrian crossing is marked with zigzag lines.

Don't

- park on them
- overtake the leading vehicle when approaching the crossing.

Parking here will block the view for pedestrians and the approaching traffic.

Question 11.109

You are approaching a zebra crossing where pedestrians are waiting. Which arm signal might you give?

Mark one answer

Answer

A 'slowing down' signal will indicate your intentions to oncoming and following vehicles. Be aware that pedestrians might start to cross as soon as they see this signal.

Question 11.110

The white line along the side of the road

Mark one answer

- [ ] shows the edge of the carriageway
- [ ] shows the approach to a hazard
- [ ] means no parking
- [ ] means no overtaking.

Answer

 shows the edge of the carriageway

This if found at the edge of the road other than at junctions. This can be especially useful when visibility is restricted.

The white line painted in the centre of the road means

Answer

☒ **do not cross the line unless the road ahead is clear**

A long white line with short gaps is a warning line so if you wish to overtake or need to turn, consider the risks.

Mark one answer

☒ the area is hazardous and you must not overtake

☒ you should give priority to oncoming vehicles

☒ do not cross the line unless the road ahead is clear

☒ the area is a national speed limit zone.

When may you cross a double solid white line in the middle of the road?

Mark one answer

☒ To pass traffic that is queuing back at a junction.

☒ To pass a car signalling to turn left ahead.

☒ To pass a road maintenance vehicle travelling at 10 mph or less.

☒ To pass a vehicle that is towing a trailer.

Answer

☒ **To pass a road maintenance vehicle travelling at 10 mph or less.**

Only overtake such a vehicle if you're sure that you can complete the manoeuvre safely. Keep well back before you overtake so that you have a clear view of the road. Double solid white lines indicate that there are hazards, such as bends in the road or junctions, so be extra cautious.

Question 11.113

A white line like this along the centre of the road is a

Mark one answer

- ☒ bus lane marking
- ☒ hazard warning
- ☒ 'give way' marking
- ☒ lane marking.

Answer

 hazard warning

Make a note of hazard lines as you drive. Look well ahead and around so that you're prepared for any potential dangers.

Question 11.114

You see this white arrow on the road ahead. It means

Mark one answer

- ☒ entrance on the left
- ☒ all vehicles turn left
- ☒ keep left of the hatched markings
- ☒ road bending to the left.

Answer

 keep left of the hatched markings

Don't attempt to overtake here, there might be unseen hazards over the brow of the hill, keep to the left.

What does this road marking mean?

Mark one answer

☒ Do not cross the line.

☒ No stopping allowed.

☒ You are approaching a hazard. ✗

☒ No overtaking allowed.

Answer

✗ **You are approaching a hazard.**

Road markings will warn you of a hazard ahead. A single broken line, with long markings and short gaps, along the centre of the road is a hazard warning line. Don't cross it unless you can see that the road is clear WELL ahead.

This marking appears on the road just before a

Mark one answer

☒ no entry sign

☒ give way sign ✗

☒ stop sign

☒ no through road sign.

Answer

✗ **give way sign**

You must give way to the traffic on the main road. This road marking might not be used at junctions where there is relatively little traffic. The give way rules still apply.

Question 11.117

Where would you see this road marking?

Answer

✖ **On road humps.**

Due to the dark colour of the road, changes in surface aren't easily seen. White triangles painted on the road surface give you an indication of where there are road humps.

Mark one answer

☒ At traffic lights.

☒ On road humps. ✖

☒ Near a level crossing.

☒ At a box junction.

Question 11.118

Which is a hazard warning line?

Mark one answer

☒

☒ ✖

 ✖

☒

☒

Answer

✖

Look out for places where the single broken line on the road surface gets longer. This will mean there's a hazard ahead.

At this junction there is a stop sign with a solid white line on the road surface. Why is there a stop sign here?

Mark one answer

☒ Speed on the major road is de-restricted.

☒ It is a busy junction.

☒ Visibility along the major road is restricted. ✗

☒ There are hazard warning lines in the centre of the road.

Answer

☒ **Visibility along the major road is restricted.**

If your view is restricted at a road junction you must stop. There may also be a stop sign. Don't emerge until you're sure there's no traffic approaching.

IF YOU DON'T KNOW, DON'T GO.

You see this line across the road at the entrance to a roundabout. What does it mean?

Mark one answer

☒ Give way to traffic from the right. ✗

☒ Traffic from the left has right of way.

☒ You have right of way.

☒ Stop at the line.

Answer

☒ **Give way to traffic from the right.**

Slow down as you approach, checking the traffic as you do so. If you need to stop and give way, stay behind the broken line until it is safe to emerge onto the roundabout.

Question 11.121

Where would you find this road marking?

Mark one answer

- [ ] At a railway crossing.
- [x] At a junction. ✗
- [ ] On a motorway.
- [ ] On a pedestrian crossing.

Answer

✖ **At a junction.**

This marking indicates the direction in which the traffic should flow.

Question 11.122

How will a police officer in a patrol vehicle get you to stop?

Mark one answer

- [x] Flash the headlights, indicate left and point to the left. ✗
- [ ] Wait until you stop, then approach you.
- [ ] Use the siren, overtake, cut in front and stop.
- [ ] Pull alongside you, use the siren and wave you to stop.

Answer

✖ **Flash the headlights, indicate left and point to the left.**

You must obey signals given by the police. If a police officer in a patrol vehicle wants you to stop he or she will indicate this without causing danger to you or other traffic.

Question 11.123

There is a police car following you. The police officer flashes the headlights and points to the left. What should you do?

Mark one answer

- [ ] Turn at the next left.
- [x] Pull up on the left. ✗
- [ ] Stop immediately.
- [ ] Move over to the left.

Answer

✖ **Pull up on the left.**

You must pull up on the left, as soon as it's safe to do so, and switch off your engine.

You approach a junction. The traffic lights are not working. A police officer gives this signal. You should

Mark one answer

- ☒ turn left only
- ☒ turn right only
- ☒ stop level with the officer's arm
- ☒ stop at the stop line

Answer

☒ **stop at the stop line**

If a police officer or traffic wardens are directing traffic you must obey them. They will use the arm signals shown in *The Highway Code*. Learn what these mean and act accordingly.

The driver of the car in front is giving this arm signal. What does it mean?

Mark one answer

- ☒ The driver is slowing down.
- ☒ The driver intends to turn right.
- ☒ The driver wishes to overtake.
- ☒ The driver intends to turn left.

Answer

☒ **The driver intends to turn left.**

There might be an occasion where another driver uses a hand signal. This may be because the vehicle's indicators are obscured by other traffic. In order for such signals to be effective all drivers should know the meaning of them.

Be aware that the 'left turn' signal might look similar to the 'slowing down' signal

Question 11.126

The driver of this car is giving a hand signal. What is he about to do?

Answer

❌ **Turn to the left.**

This could be used where there is a complicated junction and you wish to make your intentions clear.

For hand signals to be effective all road users should know their meaning.

Mark one answer

☒ Turn to the left.

☒ Turn to the right.

☒ Go straight ahead.

☒ Let pedestrians cross.

Question 11.127

Which arm signal tells a following vehicle that you intend to turn left?

Mark one answer

Answer

❌

There may be occasions when you need to give an arm signal. For example

• where other road users can't see your indicators

• in bright sunshine, when your indicator may be difficult to see

• to reinforce a signal at a complex road layout.

Make sure that they're clear, correct and decisive.

How should you give an arm signal to turn left?

Answer

Mark one answer

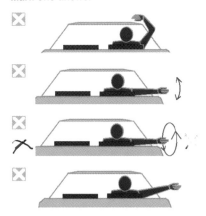

There may be occasions where other road users are unable to see your indicator, such as in bright sun light, or at a busy complicated junction. In these cases a hand signal will help others to understand your intentions.

You are signalling to turn right in busy traffic. How would you confirm your intention safely?

Answer

✖ **Put your arm out.**

Mark one answer

- ✖ Put your arm out.
- ✖ Sound the horn.
- ✖ Flash your headlamp.
- ✖ Position over the centre line.

In some situations you may feel your indicators cannot be seen by other road users. If you feel you need to make your intention more clearly seen give the arm signal shown in the highway code.

How should you give an arm signal to turn left?

Answer

✖

Mark one answer

Arm signals are very effective during daylight, especially when you're wearing bright clothing.

Practise giving arm signals when you're learning. You need to be able to keep full control of your machine with one hand off the handlebars.

Question 11.131

Your indicators are difficult to see due to bright sunshine. When using them you should

Mark one answer

- [ ] also give an arm signal
- [ ] sound your horn
- [ ] flash your headlamp
- [ ] keep both hands on the handlebars.

Answer

 also give an arm signal

Arm signals are effective when you aren't sure that your indicators can be seen by other road users. Make sure that your signal is decisive, and return your hand to the handlebars before you turn.

Question 11.132

You are giving an arm signal ready to turn left. Why should you NOT continue with the arm signal while you turn?

Mark one answer

- [ ] Because you might hit a pedestrian on the corner.
- [ ] Because you will have less steering control.
- [ ] Because you will need to keep the clutch applied.
- [ ] Because other motorists will think that you are stopping on the corner.

Answer

 Because you will have less steering control.

Don't maintain an arm signal when turning. You should have full control of your machine at all times.

Question 11.133

You want to turn right at a junction but you think that your indicators cannot be seen clearly. What should you do?

Mark one answer

- [ ] Get out and check if your indicators can be seen.
- [ ] Stay in the left-hand lane.
- [ ] Keep well over to the right.
- [ ] Give an arm signal as well as an indicator signal.

Answer

 Give an arm signal as well as an indicator signal.

If you think that your indicators can't be seen clearly due to other vehicles obscuring them, make sure that your signal is seen by using an arm signal too.

Question 11.134

When may you sound the horn on your vehicle?

Mark one answer

- ☒ To give you right of way.
- ☒ To attract a friend's attention.
- ☒ To warn other drivers of your presence.
- ☒ To make slower drivers move over.

Answer

☒ **To warn other drivers of your presence.**

Don't use the horn aggressively. You must not sound it

- between 11.30 pm and 7 am
- when your vehicle's stationary

unless a moving vehicle poses a danger.

Question 11.135

You must not use your horn when your vehicle is stationary

Mark one answer

- ☒ unless a moving vehicle may cause you danger
- ☒ at any time whatsoever
- ☒ unless it is used only briefly
- ☒ except for signalling that you have just arrived

Answer

☒ **unless a moving vehicle may cause you danger**

Do this only if you think that there is a risk of an accident. Don't use as for attracting the attention of others for social reasons.

Question 11.136

When motorists flash their headlights at you it means

Mark one answer

- ☒ that there is a radar speed trap ahead
- ☒ that they are giving way to you
- ☒ that they are warning you of their presence
- ☒ that there is something wrong with your vehicle.

Answer

☒ **that they are warning you of their presence**

If other drivers flash their headlights this isn't a signal to show priority. The flashing of headlights has the same meaning as sounding the horn – it's a warning of their presence.

Question 11.137

Why should you make sure that you have cancelled your indicators after turning?

Mark one answer

- ☒ To avoid flattening the battery.
- ☒ To avoid misleading other road users.
- ☒ To avoid dazzling other road users.
- ☒ To avoid damage to the indicator relay.

Answer

☒ **To avoid misleading other road users.**

If you haven't taken a sharp turn your indicators might not turn off automatically. Be aware of this if you've used them for slight deviations, such as passing parked vehicles.

Question 11.138

You are waiting at a T-junction. A vehicle is coming from the right with the left signal flashing. What should you do?

Mark one answer

☒ Move out and accelerate hard.

☒ Wait until the vehicle starts to turn in.

☒ Pull out before the vehicle reaches the junction.

☒ Move out slowly.

Answer

✖ **Wait until the vehicle starts to turn in.**

Try to anticipate the actions of other road users. Their signals might be misleading.

When you're waiting at a junction don't emerge if you'll impede the progress of other traffic. Pulling out safely calls for accurate judgement.

Question 11.139

When may you use hazard warning lights when driving?

Mark one answer

☒ Instead of sounding the horn in a built-up area between 11.30 pm and 7 am.

☒ On a motorway or unrestricted dual carriageway, to warn of a hazard ahead.

☒ On rural routes, after a warning sign of animals.

☒ On the approach to toucan crossings, where cyclists are waiting to cross.

Answer

✖ **On a motorway or unrestricted dual carriageway to warn of a hazard ahead.**

Where there's queuing traffic ahead and you have to slow down and maybe stop, showing your hazard warning lights will alert the traffic behind to the situation. Don't forget to switch them off as the queue forms behind you.

Question 11.140

Where would you see these road markings?

Mark one answer

- ☒ At a level crossing.
- ☒ On a motorway slip road.
- ☒ At a pedestrian crossing.
- ☒ On a single-track road.

Answer

☒ **On a motorway slip road.**

You must not enter into the area marked except in an emergency.

Question 11.141

When may you NOT overtake on the left?

Mark one answer

- ☒ On a free-flowing motorway or dual carriageway.
- ☒ When the traffic is moving slowly in queues.
- ☒ On a one-way street.
- ☒ When the car in front is signalling to turn right.

Answer

☒ **On a free-flowing motorway or dual carriageway.**

You may only overtake on the left

- when traffic is moving slowly in queues
- when a vehicle ahead is positioned to turn right and there's room to pass on the left
- in a one-way street.

Don't overtake on the left if the traffic on a dual carriageway is flowing freely. Other road users won't anticipate your action.

Question 11.142

You are driving on a motorway. There is a slow-moving vehicle ahead. On the back you see this sign. You should

Mark one answer

- ☒ pass on the right
- ☒ pass on the left
- ☒ leave at the next exit
- ☒ drive no further.

Answer

☒ **pass on the left**

You'll have to change lanes in order to pass the vehicle. Use your mirror and signal. If it's safe to do so move over into the lane on your left. Look well down the road so that you can spot such hazards early, leaving you time to complete the manoeuvre safely.

Question 11.143

What does this motorway sign mean?

Mark one answer

- [ ] Change to the lane on your left.
- [ ] Leave the motorway at the next exit.
- [ ] Change to the opposite carriageway.
- [ ] Pull up on the hard shoulder.

Question 11.144

What does this motorway sign mean?

Mark one answer

- [ ] Temporary minimum speed 50 mph.
- [ ] No services for 50 miles.
- [ ] Obstruction 50 metres (165 feet) ahead.
- [ ] Temporary maximum speed 50 mph.

Answer

 Change to the lane on your left.

On the motorway, signs might show temporary warnings. This allows for different traffic or weather conditions and might indicate

- lane closures
- speed limits
- weather warnings.

Answer

✖ **Temporary maximum speed 50 mph.**

Look out for signs above your lane or on the central reserve. These will give you important information or warnings about the road ahead.

Due to the high speeds of motorway traffic these signs may light up some distance from any hazard. Don't ignore the signs just because the road looks clear to you.

What does this sign mean?

Mark one answer

- Through traffic to use left lane.
- Right-hand lane T-junction only.
- Right-hand lane closed ahead.
- 11 tonne weight limit.

Answer

 Right-hand lane closed ahead.

Move over as soon as you see the sign and it's safe to do so. Don't stay in the lane, which is closed ahead, until the last moment to beat a queue of traffic.

On a motorway this sign means

Mark one answer

- move over onto the hard shoulder
- pass a temporary obstruction on the left
- leave the motorway at the next exit
- move to the lane on your left.

Answer

 move to the lane on your left

If signs instruct you to change lanes do so in good time.

What does '25' mean on this motorway sign?

Mark one answer

- The distance to the nearest town.
- The route number of the road.
- The number of the next junction.
- The speed limit on the slip road.

Answer

✖ **The number of the next junction.**

Before you set out on your journey use a road map to plan your route. You should give yourself enough time to get into the correct lane for the exit that you wish to take. Uncertainty at road junctions can lead to danger.

Question 11.148

You are driving on a motorway. Red flashing lights appear above your lane. What should you do?

Mark one answer

 Continue in that lane and await further information.

☒ Go no further in that lane.

☒ Drive onto the hard shoulder.

☒ Stop and wait for an instruction to proceed.

Answer

✖ **Go no further in that lane.**

If flashing red lights appear above, and all lanes are shown as blocked, STOP even if others don't.

Question 11.149

The right-hand lane of a three-lane motorway is

Mark one answer

 for lorries only

☒ an overtaking lane

☒ the right-turn lane

☒ an acceleration lane.

Answer

✖ **an overtaking lane**

Motorways today can become very busy. If a vehicle in the right-hand lane is preventing traffic to the rear from overtaking, or is travelling at a slower speed than those on the nearside, bunching can occur. This means that drivers will begin to travel too close to the vehicle in front of them. If you aren't overtaking, use the left-hand lane.

Question 11.150

Where can you find reflective amber studs on a motorway?

Mark one answer

 Separating the slip road from the motorway.

☒ On the left-hand edge of the road.

☒ On the right-hand edge of the road.

☒ Separating the lanes.

Answer

✖ **On the right-hand edge of the road.**

At night or in poor visibility reflective studs on the road will help you to judge your position on the carriageway.

Question 11.151

Where on a motorway would you find green reflective studs?

Mark one answer

☒ Separating driving lanes.

☒ Between the hard shoulder and the carriageway.

☒ At slip road entrances and exits.

☒ Between the carriageway and the central reservation.

Answer

❌ **At slip road entrances and exits.**

Knowing the colours of the reflective studs on the road will help you in foggy conditions or when visibility is poor.

Question 11.152

You are travelling along a motorway. You see this sign. You should

Mark one answer

☒ leave the motorway at the next exit

☒ turn left immediately

☒ change lane

☒ move onto the hard shoulder.

Answer

❌ **leave the motorway at the next exit**

You'll see this sign if the motorway is closed ahead. When you see it prepare to get into the nearside lane so that you can take the exit safely. Don't leave it to the last moment.

Question 11.153

You see these signs overhead on the motorway. They mean

Mark one answer

☒ leave the motorway at the next exit

☒ all vehicles use the hard shoulder

☒ sharp bend to the left ahead

☒ stop, all lanes ahead closed.

Answer

❌ **leave the motorway at the next exit**

There has been an incident ahead and the motorway is closed. You must obey the sign. Make sure that you prepare to leave as soon as you see the warning sign. Don't leave it until the last moment by cutting across other traffic.

Question 11.154

What does this sign mean?

Mark one answer

☒ No motor vehicles.

☒ End of motorway.

☒ No through road.

☒ End of bus lane.

Answer

☒ **End of motorway.**

When you leave the motorway make sure that you check your speedometer. You may be going faster than you realise. Slow down using the slip road. Look out for speed limit signs.

Question 11.155

Which of these signs means that the national speed limit applies?

Mark one answer

Answer

You should know the speed limit for the road that you're travelling on and the vehicle that you're driving. Study your copy of *The Highway Code*, where the limits are clearly shown.

Question 11.156

What is the maximum speed on a single carriageway road?

Mark one answer

☒ 50 mph.

☒ 60 mph.

☒ 40 mph.

☒ 70 mph.

Answer

 ☒ **60 mph.**

If you're travelling on a dual carriageway that's reduced to a single lane cut your speed gradually so that you aren't exceeding the limit as you enter. There might not be a sign to remind you of the limit, so learn the speed limits.

SECTION 12 DOCUMENTS

This section looks at the documents needed for drivers and their vehicles.

The questions will ask you about

- licences

- insurance

- MOT test certificates.

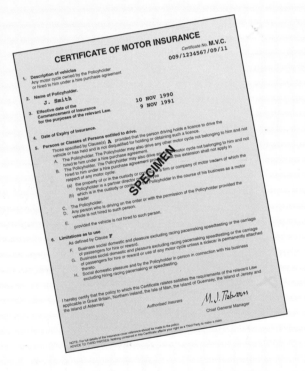

Question 12.1

To drive on the road learners MUST

Mark one answer

- [ ] have NO penalty points on their licence
- [ ] have taken professional instruction
- [ ] have a signed, valid provisional licence
- [ ] apply for a driving test within 12 months.

Answer

✖ **have a signed, valid provisional licence**

Before you drive on the road you must have a signed provisional licence in the category of vehicle that you're driving. As soon as you've received your licence, sign it. It isn't valid until you've done so.

Question 12.2

Your driving licence must be signed by

Mark one answer

- [ ] a police officer
- [ ] a driving instructor
- [ ] your next of kin
- [ ] you.

Answer

✖ **you**

Do this as soon as you receive it through the post. Don't drive until you've signed it.

Question 12.3

How long is a provisional motorcycle licence valid for?

Mark one answer

- [ ] One year.
- [ ] Two years.
- [ ] Three years.
- [ ] Five years.

Answer

✖ **Two years.**

A provisional motorcycle licence is valid for two years only. You must take and pass the theory and practical tests within two years or you'll have to wait a year before you can apply for another licence. This doesn't apply if you have a full car or moped licence.

In Northern Ireland provisional licences are valid for ten years.

Question 12.4

You have passed compulsory basic training (CBT). You want a direct access test. You must

Mark four answers

- [ ] be aged 21 or over
- [ ] not exceed 60 mph
- [ ] have an approved instructor with you
- [ ] remain in radio contact while learning
- [ ] only learn in daylight hours
- [ ] wear fluorescent or reflective clothing.

Answers

✖ **be aged 21 or over**
✖ **have an approved instructor with you**
✖ **remain in radio contact while learning**
✖ **wear fluorescent or reflective clothing**

If you wish to learn to ride a motorcycle via the direct access route you must be at least 21 years old. When practising on the road you must

- have L plates fitted (D plates in Wales)
- be accompanied by an approved instructor in radio contact
- wear fluorescent or reflective safety clothing.

You want a licence to ride a large motorcycle via **direct access.** You will

Mark one answer

☒ not require L plates if you have passed a car test

☒ require L plates only when learning on your own machine

☒ require L plates while learning with a qualified instructor

☒ not require L plates if you have passed a moped test.

Answer

☒ **require L plates while learning with a qualified instructor**

While training through the direct access scheme you must be accompanied by an instructor on another motorcycle and in radio contact. You will have to display L plates on your motorcycle and follow all normal learner restrictions.

You are a learner motorcyclist. The law states that you can carry a passenger when

Mark one answer

☒ the motorcycle is no larger than 125cc

☒ your pillion passenger is a full licence-holder

☒ you have passed your test for a full licence

☒ you have had three years' experience of riding.

Answer

☒ **you have passed your test for a full licence**

When you're a learner motorcyclist you must comply with certain legal restrictions. The law states that you must

• display L plates (or D plates in Wales) to the front and rear on your machine

• not carry pillion passengers

• not use the motorway.

NI

What should you bring with you when taking your motorcycle test?

Mark three answers

☒ A service record book.

☒ An insurance certificate.

☒ A signed driving licence.

☒ An MOT certificate.

☒ A CBT certificate.

☒ Signed photo identity.

Answers

☒ **A CBT certificate.**

☒ **A signed driving licence.**

☒ **Signed photo identity.**

When you attend a motorcycle test your examiner will ask to see

• your driving licence

• your CBT certificate (except in Northern Ireland).

Question 12.8

Before taking a motorcycle test you need a

Mark one answer

- [ ] full moped licence
- [ ] full car licence
- [ ] Compulsory Basic Training (CBT) certificate
- [ ] motorcycle pass certificate.

Answer

☒ Compulsory Basic Training (CBT) certificate

You can find out about a CBT course by asking your motorcycle dealer or by telephoning 0115 901 2595.

In Northern Ireland the CBT scheme doesn't operate so all reference to CBT isn't applicable.

Question 12.9

Compulsory Basic Training (CBT) can only be carried out by

Mark one answer

- [ ] any Approved Driving Instructor (ADI)
- [ ] any road safety officer
- [ ] any DSA-approved training body
- [ ] any motorcycle main dealer.

Answer

☒ any DSA-approved training body

DSA approves bodies to provide training in a safe environment. Frequent checks are made to ensure a high standard of instruction. Taking a CBT course will provide you with the right start to your motorcycling life.

Question 12.10

After passing your motorcycle test you must exchange the pass certificate for a full motorcycle licence within

Mark one answer

- [ ] six months
- [ ] one year
- [ ] two years
- [ ] five years.

Answer

☒ two years

When you pass your practical motorcycle test you'll be issued with a pass certificate (form D.10 – DL8 in Northern Ireland). You must exchange the certificate for a full licence within two years of passing your test. If you don't

- the certificate will lapse
- you'll have to retake your test if you wish to resume full motorcycle licence entitlement.

For which TWO of these must you show your motor insurance certificate?

Mark two answers

- [ ] When you are taking your driving test.
- [ ] When buying or selling a vehicle.
- [ ] When a police officer asks you for it.
- [ ] When you are taxing your vehicle.
- [ ] When having an MOT inspection.

Answers

- [x] **When a police officer asks you for it.**
- [x] **When you are taxing your vehicle.**

When you take out motor insurance you'll be issued with a Certificate of Insurance. This contains details explaining who and what is insured. You'll have to produce your Certificate of Insurance when you're paying your vehicle excise duty (road tax).

If a police officer asks for your Certificate of Insurance and you don't have it with you, you may produce it at a police station within seven days (five days in Northern Ireland).

Vehicle excise duty is often called 'Road Tax' or 'The Tax Disc'. You must

Mark one answer

- [ ] keep it with your registration document
- [ ] display it clearly on your vehicle
- [ ] keep it concealed safely in your vehicle
- [ ] carry it on you at all times.

Answer

- [x] **display it clearly on your vehicle**

It should be displayed on the left hand bottom of the windscreen. This allows it to be easily seen from the kerbside. It must be current, and you can't transfer the disc from vehicle to vehicle.

For which TWO of these must you show your motorcycle insurance certificate?

Mark two answers

- [ ] When you are taking your motorcycle test.
- [ ] When buying or selling a machine.
- [ ] When a police officer asks you for it.
- [ ] When you are taxing your machine.
- [ ] When having an MOT inspection.

Answers

- [x] **When a police officer asks you for it.**
- [x] **When you are taxing your machine.**

You don't have to carry it with you at all times. However, it must be valid and available to present at a police station (within 7 days) if requested.

Question 12.14

A police officer asks to see your driving documents. You do not have them with you. You may produce them at a police station within

Mark one answer

☒ five days

☒ seven days

☒ 14 days

☒ 21 days.

Answer

 seven days

You don't have to carry your documents with you. If a police officer asks to see them and you don't have them with you, you may produce them at a police station within seven days (five days in Northern Ireland).

Question 12.15

Before riding anyone else's motorcycle you should make sure that

Mark one answer

☒ the machine owner has third party insurance cover

☒ your own machine has insurance cover

☒ the machine is insured for your use

☒ the owner has the insurance documents with them.

Answer

 the machine is insured for your use

If you borrow a motorcycle you must make sure that you're insured. Find out yourself. Don't take anyone else's word for it.

Question 12.16

Before driving anyone else's motor vehicle you should make sure that

Mark one answer

☒ the vehicle owner has third party insurance cover

☒ your own vehicle has insurance cover

☒ the vehicle is insured for your use

☒ the owner has left the insurance documents in the vehicle.

Answer

 the vehicle is insured for your use

Don't take someone else's word on the matter. New drivers are considered a high risk and this is reflected in high insurance costs. If you're careful and don't have an accident the cost of your insurance will come down, although other factors, such as your occupation and where you live, are taken into account.

Question 12.17

What is the legal minimum insurance cover you must have to drive on public roads?

Mark one answer

☒ Third party, fire and theft.

☒ Fully comprehensive.

☒ Third party only.

☒ Personal injury cover.

Answer

☒ **Third party only.**

The minimum insurance requirement by law is third party cover. This covers others involved in an accident but not damage to your vehicle. Basic third party insurance won't cover theft or fire damage. Check with your insurance company for advice on the best cover for you. Make sure that you read the policy carefully.

Question 12.18

Your car has third party insurance. What does this cover?

Mark three answers

☒ Damage to your own car.

☒ Damage to your car by fire.

☒ Injury to another person.

☒ Damage to someone else's property.

☒ Damage to other vehicles.

☒ Injury to yourself.

Answers

☒ **Injury to another person.**

☒ **Damage to someone else's property.**

☒ **Damage to other vehicles.**

Third party insurance doesn't cover damage to your own vehicle or injury to yourself. If you have an accident and you damage your vehicle you might have to carry out the repairs at your own expense.

Question 12.19

The cost of your insurance will be reduced if

Mark one answer

☒ your car is large and powerful

☒ you are using the car for work purposes

☒ you have penalty points on your licence

☒ you are over 25 years old.

Answer

☒ **you are over 25 years old**

Provided you haven't had previous accidents or committed any driving offences, your insurance should be less costly as you get beyond the age of 25. This is because statistics show that most accidents are caused by or involve young and/or inexperienced drivers.

Question 12.20

NI

Motor cars and motorcycles must FIRST have an MOT test certificate when they are

Mark one answer

☒ one year old

☒ three years old

☒ five years old

☒ seven years old.

Answer

☒ **three years old**

The vehicle you drive must be in good condition and roadworthy. If it's over three years old it must have a valid MOT test certificate.

In Northern Ireland a vehicle first needs an MOT test certificate when it's four years old.

Question 12.21

An MOT certificate is normally valid for

Mark one answer

☒ three years after the date it was issued

☒ 10,000 miles

☒ one year after the date it was issued

☒ 30,000 miles.

Answer

☒ **one year after the date it was issued**

Make a note of the date that your vehicle is due for an MOT. Some garages remind you, but not all of them.

Question 12.22

Your car needs an MOT certificate. If you drive without one this could invalidate your

Mark one answer

☒ vehicle service record

☒ insurance

☒ road tax disc

☒ vehicle registration document.

Answer

☒ **insurance**

You are driving a vehicle which is illegal and could be unsafe. As there is a higher risk of an accident your insurance company would not cover you for any damage incurred.

Question 12.23

When is it legal to drive a car over three years old without an MOT certificate?

Mark one answer

☒ Up to seven days after the old certificate has run out.

☒ When driving to an MOT centre to arrange an appointment.

☒ Just after buying a second-hand car with no MOT.

☒ When driving to an appointment at an MOT centre.

Answer

☒ **When driving to an appointment at an MOT centre.**

If a vehicle's over three years old it must have a valid MOT certificate if you want to use it on the road. The only time a vehicle's exempt is when it's being driven to an appointment at an MOT testing station.

In Northern Ireland the time limit before an MOT test is needed is four years.

Question 12.24

Your vehicle needs a current MOT certificate. You do not have one. Until you do have one you will not be able to renew your

Mark one answer

☒ driving licence

☒ vehicle insurance

☒ road tax disc

☒ vehicle registration document.

Answer

☒ **road tax disc**

You'll have to produce your MOT certificate when you renew your road tax disc (road fund licence).

Question 12.25

Which of these vehicles is not required to have an MOT certificate?

Mark two answers

☒ Police vehicle.

☒ Small trailer.

☒ Ambulance.

☒ Caravan.

Answers

☒ **Small trailer.**

☒ **Caravan.**

Despite not needing an MOT certificate, you should ensure that your trailer is in good order and properly serviced. Tyres, wheel nuts, lights and indicators should be checked regularly.

Question 12.26

Which THREE of the following do you need before you can drive legally?

Mark three answers

☒ A valid signed driving licence.

☒ A valid tax disc displayed on your vehicle.

☒ Proof of your identity.

☒ A current MOT certificate if the car is over three years old (or four years in Northern Ireland).

☒ Fully comprehensive insurance.

☒ A vehicle handbook.

Answers

☒ **A valid signed driving licence.**

☒ **A valid tax disc displayed on your vehicle.**

☒ **A current MOT certificate if the car is over three years old (or four years in Northern Ireland).**

Make sure that your vehicle's not only safe but legal.

Question 12.27

CBT completion certificates (DL196) are valid for

Mark one answer

- ☒ three years
- ☒ two years
- ☒ indefinitely
- ☒ five years.

Answer

☒ **three years**

In order to complete the CBT course you'll have to demonstrate that you can ride confidently and safely in a variety of road and traffic conditions. Your certificate will enable you to apply for your tests. If you don't pass your tests within its three-year life you'll have to complete the CBT course again.

Question 12.28

If you DO NOT pass your motorcycle tests within two years your provisional motorcycle entitlement will expire. You can reapply for motorcycle entitlement after a gap of

Mark one answer

- ☒ three years
- ☒ six months
- ☒ one year
- ☒ two years.

Answer

☒ **one year**

Provisional motorcycle entitlement on a provisional licence is valid for two years. If you don't pass your motorcycle test within that time the motorcycle entitlement will lapse. You can only apply for renewal of motorcycle entitlement after a period of one year.

This provision doesn't apply in Northern Ireland

Question 12.29

When you buy a motorcycle you will need a vehicle registration document from

Mark one answer

- ☒ any MOT testing station
- ☒ the person selling the motorcycle
- ☒ your local council offices
- ☒ your local trading standards officer.

Answer

☒ **the person selling the motorcycle**

You must fill in your details and send it to the Driver and Vehicle Licensing Authority (DVLA) at the address given on the document.

Which THREE pieces of information are found on a vehicle registration document?

Mark three answers

- [ ] Registered keeper.
- [ ] Make of the vehicle.
- [ ] Service history details.
- [ ] Date of the MOT.
- [ ] Type of insurance cover.
- [ ] Engine size.

Answers

- ☒ **Registered keeper.**
- ☒ **Make of the vehicle.**
- ☒ **Engine size.**

Every vehicle used on the road has a registration document. This is issued by the Driver Vehicle Licensing Agency (DVLA) or the Driver and Vehicle Licensing Northern Ireland (DVLNI) and it keeps a record of the change of ownership. The document states

- date of first registration
- registration number
- previous keeper
- registered keeper
- make of vehicle
- engine size and chassis number
- year of manufacture
- colour.

You have a duty to contact the licensing authority when

Mark three answers

- [ ] you go abroad on holiday
- [ ] you change your vehicle
- [ ] you change your name
- [ ] your job status is changed
- [ ] your permanent address changes
- [ ] your job involves travelling abroad.

Answers

- ☒ **you change your vehicle**
- ☒ **you change your name**
- ☒ **your permanent address changes**

The licencing authority need to keep their records up to date. You will receive a reminder when your road tax is due and they will need your current address for this purpose. Every vehicle in the country is registered, so it's possible to trace it's history.

Question 12.32

You must notify the licensing authority when

Mark three answers

- [x] you change your vehicle
- [x] your health affects your driving
- [x] your eyesight does not meet a set standard
- [ ] you intend lending your vehicle
- [ ] your vehicle requires an MOT certificate.

Answers

- ✖ **you change your vehicle**
- ✖ **your health affects your driving**
- ✖ **your eyesight does not meet a set standard**

The Driver and Vehicle Licencing Agency (DVLA) hold the records of all vehicles and drivers in Great Britain. They need to know of any change in circumstances so that they can keep their records up to date. Your health might affect your ability to drive safely. This should not be underestimated as you and others on the road could be at risk.

Question 12.33

You have just bought a second-hand vehicle. When should you tell the licensing authority of change of ownership?

Mark one answer

- [ ] Immediately.
- [ ] After 28 days.
- [ ] When an MOT is due.
- [ ] Only when you insure it.

Answer

- ✖ **Immediately.**

As soon as you can, fill out the registration document of the vehicle and send it off. The requirements will be written on the document. It is an offence not to notify the licensing agency.

Question 12.34

To supervise a learner driver you must

Mark two answers

- [ ] have held a full licence for at least 3 years
- [ ] be at least 21
- [ ] be an approved driving instructor
- [ ] hold an advanced driving certificate.

Answers

- ✖ **have held a full licence for at least 3 years**
- ✖ **be at least 21**

Don't just take someone's word that they are qualified to supervise you. The person who sits alongside you while you are learning should be a responsible adult.

SECTION 13 ACCIDENTS

This section looks at what to do in the event of an accident.

The questions will ask you about

- First Aid

- warning devices

- reporting procedures

- safety regulations.

Question 13.1

Which of these items should you carry in your vehicle for use in the event of an accident?

Mark three answers
- ☒ Road map.
- ☒ Bottle of water.
- ☒ Jump leads.
- ☒ Fire extinguisher.
- ☒ First Aid kit.
- ☒ Warning triangle.

Answers
- ☒ **Fire extinguisher.**
- ☒ **First Aid kit.**
- ☒ **Warning triangle.**

This equipment could be invaluable and a small price to pay if it helps prevent or lessen injury.

Question 13.2

At the scene of an accident you must

Mark one answer
- ☒ not put yourself at risk
- ☒ go to those casualties who are screaming
- ☒ pull everybody out of their vehicles
- ☒ leave vehicle engines switched on.

Answer
- ☒ **not put yourself at risk**

It's important that those at the scene of an accident do not create a further risk to themselves or other road users. If the accident has occurred on a motorway traffic will be approaching at speed. Consider this when trying to help casualties or warn other drivers.

Question 13.3

You are the first to arrive at the scene of an accident. Which FOUR of these should you do?

Mark four answers
- ☒ Leave as soon as another motorist arrives.
- ☒ Switch off the vehicle engine(s).
- ☒ Move uninjured people away from the vehicle(s).
- ☒ Call the emergency services.
- ☒ Warn other traffic.

Answers
- ☒ **Switch off the vehicle engine(s).**
- ☒ **Move uninjured people away from the vehicle(s).**
- ☒ **Call the emergency services.**
- ☒ **Warn other traffic.**

If you're involved in, or arrive at, the scene of an accident there are certain actions you should take. It's important to know what to do and also what NOT to do. You could save someone's life, or endanger it.

An accident has just happened. An injured person is lying in the busy road. What is the first thing you should do to help?

Mark one answer

☒ Treat the person for shock.

☒ Warn other traffic.

☒ Place them in the recovery position.

☒ Make sure the injured person is kept warm.

Answer

☒ **Warn other traffic.**

You could do this by

- displaying an advanced warning signal, if you have one
- switching on hazard warning lights or other lights
- any other means that does not put you at risk

You are the first person to arrive at an accident where people are badly injured. Which THREE should you do?

Mark three answers

☒ Switch on your own hazard warning lights.

☒ Make sure that someone telephones for an ambulance.

☒ Try and get people who are injured to drink something.

☒ Move the people who are injured clear of their vehicles.

☒ Get people who are not injured clear of the scene.

Answers

☒ **Switch on your own hazard warning lights.**

☒ **Make sure that someone telephones for an ambulance.**

☒ **Get people who are not injured clear of the scene.**

If you're the first to arrive at the scene of an accident further collisions and fire are the first concerns. Switching off vehicle engines will reduce the risk of fire.

Your hazard warning lights will let approaching traffic know that there's a need for caution.

Don't assume someone else has called the emergency services. Do it yourself.

You are at the scene of an accident and there are several bystanders. Which TWO of the following should you do first?

Mark two answers

☒ Always pull people who are hurt out of their vehicles.

☒ Ask the bystanders to check the casualties for signs of bleeding.

☒ Make sure that the emergency services have been called for.

☒ Keep the bystanders clear as they do not know first aid.

☒ Clear a parking area for ambulance and fire service crews.

Answers

☒ **Ask the bystanders to check the casualties for signs of bleeding.**

☒ **Make sure that the emergency services have been called for.**

Encourage the bystanders to help. Do this calmly and decisively, they may be very willing to help, but don't know what to do.

Question 13.7

You arrive at the scene of a motorcycle accident. The rider is injured. When should the helmet be removed?

Mark one answer

- Only when it is essential.
- Always straight away.
- Only when the motorcyclist asks.
- Always, unless they are in shock.

Answer

❌ **Only when it is essential.**

If a motorcyclist has been injured in an accident it's important not to remove their helmet unless it is necessary to keep them alive.

Question 13.8

You arrive at a serious motorcycle accident. The motorcyclist is unconscious and bleeding. Your main priorities should be to

Mark three answers

- try to stop the bleeding
- make a list of witnesses
- check the casualty's breathing
- take the numbers of the vehicles involved
- sweep up any loose debris
- check the casualty's airways.

Answers

❌ **try to stop the bleeding**
❌ **check the casualty's breathing**
❌ **check the casualty's airways**

At a road accident the danger of further collisions and fire need to be dealt with first. Injuries should be dealt with in the order

- Airway
- Breathing
- Circulation and bleeding.

Question 13.9

You arrive at an accident. A motorcyclist is unconscious. Your first priority is the casualty's

Mark one answer

- breathing
- bleeding
- broken bones
- bruising.

Answer

❌ **breathing**

At the scene of an accident you must first make sure there is no danger from further collisions or fire before dealing with any casualties.

The first priority when dealing with an unconscious person is to make sure they can breathe. This may involve clearing their airway if they're having difficulty or some obstruction is obvious.

An accident has just happened. An injured person is lying in the road. What is the first thing you should do to help?.

Mark one answer

☒ Treat the person for shock.

☒ Place them in the recovery position.

☒ Warn other traffic.

☒ Make sure the injured person is kept warm.

Answer

☒ **Warn other traffic.**

It's important to keep calm and try to deal with the situation without panicking. You could use your hazard warning lights to alert the other road users. If you have a warning triangle, place it approximately 45 metres (149 feet) from the hazard. Give the traffic enough time to slow down or stop if necessary.

At an accident a casualty is unconscious. Which three of the following should you check urgently?

Mark three answers

☒ Circulation.

☒ Airway.

☒ Shock.

☒ Breathing.

☒ Broken bones.

Answers

☒ **Circulation.**

☒ **Airway.**

☒ **Breathing.**

An unconscious casualty may have difficulty breathing. Check that their tongue has not fallen back, blocking their airway. Do this by tilting the head back slightly.

In first aid what does ABC stand for?

Mark three answers

☒ Airway.

☒ Bleeding.

☒ Conscious.

☒ Breathing.

☒ Circulation.

☒ Alert.

Answers

☒ **Airway.**

☒ **Breathing.**

☒ **Circulation.**

To check if a casualty is breathing put your face close to their mouth. Look, listen and feel for any sign of breathing.

Question 13.13

You arrive at the scene of an accident. It has just happened and someone is unconscious. Which of the following should be given urgent priority to help them?

Mark three answers

- [ ] Clear the airway and keep it open.
- [ ] Try to get them to drink water.
- [ ] Check that they are breathing.
- [ ] Look for any witnesses.
- [ ] Stop any heavy bleeding.
- [ ] Take the numbers of vehicles involved.

Answers

- ☒ Clear the airway and keep it open
- ☒ Check that they are breathing.
- ☒ Stop any heavy bleeding.

Stay with the casualty and send someone to ring for an ambulance.

Question 13.14

Which of the following safety checks is in the correct order?

Mark one answer

- [ ] Breathing – Circulation – Airway.
- [ ] Airway – Breathing – Circulation.
- [ ] Circulation – Breathing – Airway.
- [ ] Breathing – Airway – Circulation.

Answer

- ☒ Airway – Breathing – Circulation.

Remembering this important order of safety checks is easy as ABC.

Question 13.15

At an accident someone is unconscious. Your main priorities should be to

Mark three answers

- [ ] sweep up the broken glass
- [ ] take the names of witnesses
- [ ] count the number of vehicles involved
- [ ] check the airway is clear
- [ ] make sure they are breathing
- [ ] stop any heavy bleeding.

Answers

- ☒ check the airway is clear
- ☒ make sure they are breathing
- ☒ stop any heavy bleeding

Remember this procedure by saying **ABC.**
Airway – **B**reathing – **C**irculation

You have stopped at the scene of an accident to give help. Which THREE things should you do?

Mark three answers

☒ Keep injured people warm and comfortable.

☒ Keep injured people calm by talking to them reassuringly.

☒ Keep injured people on the move by walking them around.

☒ Give injured people a warm drink.

☒ Make sure that injured people are not left alone.

Answers

☒ **Keep injured people warm and comfortable.**

☒ **Keep injured people calm by talking to them reassuringly.**

☒ **Make sure that injured people are not left alone.**

If you stop at the scene of an accident to give help and there are casualties don't

- move injured people, unless further danger is threatened
- give the injured anything to drink.

You arrive at the scene of an accident. It has just happened and someone is injured. Which of the following should be given urgent priority?

Mark three answers

☒ Stop any severe bleeding.

☒ Get them a warm drink.

☒ Check that their breathing is OK.

☒ Take numbers of vehicles involved.

☒ Look for witnesses.

☒ Clear their airway and keep it open.

Answers

☒ **Stop any severe bleeding.**

☒ **Check that their breathing is OK.**

☒ **Clear their airway and keep it open.**

When you have done this, call the emergency services, they are the experts.

If you feel you are not capable of carrying out first aid, then consider doing some training. It could save a life.

At an accident a casualty has stopped breathing. You should

Mark two answers

☒ remove anything that is blocking the mouth

☒ keep the head tilted forwards as far as possible

☒ raise the legs to help with circulation

☒ try to give the casualty something to drink

☒ keep the head tilted back as far as possible.

Answers

☒ **remove anything that is blocking the mouth**

☒ **keep the head tilted back as far as possible**

These actions will ensure that the casualty has clear airways and in the correct position if mouth to mouth ventilation is required.

Question 13.19

You arrive at the scene of a motorcycle accident. The rider is conscious but in shock. You should make sure that

Mark one answer

- [ ] the rider's helmet is removed
- [ ] the rider is moved to the side of the road
- [ ] the rider's helmet is not removed
- [ ] the rider is put in the recovery position.

Answer

✖ the rider's helmet is not removed.

At the scene of a motorcycle accident where a rider or passenger is injured

- don't remove the helmet – it could cause further injury
- offer reassurance and comfort until the emergency services arrive.

Question 13.20

You are at the scene of an accident. Someone is suffering from shock. You should

Mark four answers

- [ ] reassure them constantly
- [ ] offer them a cigarette
- [ ] keep them warm
- [ ] avoid moving them if possible
- [ ] loosen any tight clothing
- [ ] give them a warm drink.

Answers

✖ reassure them constantly
✖ keep them warm
✖ avoid moving them if possible
✖ loosen any tight clothing

The effects of trauma may not be immediately obvious. Prompt treatment can help to minimise the effects of shock.

- lay the casualty down
- loosen tight clothing
- call an ambulance
- check their breathing and pulse.

Question 13.21

Which of the following should you not do at the scene of an accident?

Mark one answer

- [ ] Warn other traffic by switching on your hazard warning lights.
- [ ] Call the emergency services immediately.
- [ ] Offer someone a cigarette to calm them down.
- [ ] Ask drivers to switch off their engines.

Answer

✖ Offer someone a cigarette to calm them down.

Keeping casualties or witnesses calm is important, but never offer a cigarette because of the risk of fire. Check for any signs of shock, such as,

- sweating
- clammy skin,
- giddiness
- rapid or shallow breathing
- a weak pulse.

When treating someone for shock you should

Mark two answers

☒ reassure them ✗

☒ loosen tight clothes ✗

☒ walk them around

☒ give them a hot drink

☒ offer them an alcoholic drink.

Answers

✗ **reassure them**

✗ **loosen tight clothes**

Keep talking to the casualty to keep them calm, don't leave them alone.

There has been an accident. The driver is suffering from shock. You should

Mark two answers

☒ give them a drink

☒ reassure them ✗

☒ not leave them alone ✗

☒ offer them a cigarette

☒ ask who caused the accident.

Answers

✗ **reassure them**

✗ **not leave them alone**

They could have an injury that is not immediately obvious. Loosen any tight clothing and check that their breathing is not rapid or slow.

You are at the scene of an accident. Someone is suffering from shock. You should

Mark three answers

☒ offer them a cigarette

☒ offer them a warm drink

☒ keep them warm ✗

☒ loosen any tight clothing ✗

☒ reassure them constantly. ✗

Answers

✗ **keep them warm**

✗ **loosen any tight clothing**

✗ **reassure them constantly**

People who seem to be unhurt may be suffering from shock. So try to reassure everyone involved at the scene and keep everybody calm.

Question 13.25

You have to treat someone for shock at the scene of an accident. You should

Mark one answer

- [ ] reassure them constantly
- [ ] walk them around to calm them down
- [ ] give them something cold to drink
- [ ] cool them down as soon as possible.

Answer

✗ reassure them constantly

You should lay the casualty down, loosen any tight clothing, whilst reassuring them. If possible, get someone else to call an ambulance to avoid leaving the casualty alone.

Question 13.26

You arrive at the scene of a motorcycle accident. No other vehicle is involved. The rider is unconscious, lying in the middle of the road. The first thing you should do is

Mark one answer

- [ ] move the rider out of the road
- [ ] warn other traffic
- [ ] clear the road of debris
- [ ] give the rider reassurance.

Answer

✗ warn other traffic

The motorcyclist is in an extremely vulnerable position, exposed to further danger from traffic. The traffic needs to slow right down and be aware of the hazard in good time.

Question 13.27

At an accident a small child is not breathing. When giving mouth to mouth you should blow

Mark one answer

- [ ] sharply
- [ ] gently
- [ ] heavily
- [ ] rapidly.

Answers

✗ gently

With a small child breathe gently into the nose and mouth until you see the chest rise. Give five breaths, allowing two seconds for the lungs to inflate.

Question 13.28

To start mouth to mouth on a casualty you should

Mark three answers

- [ ] tilt the head forward
- [ ] clear the airway ✗
- [ ] turn them on their side
- [ ] tilt their head back ✗
- [ ] pinch the nostrils together ✗
- [ ] put their arms across their chest.

Answers

- ✗ **clear the airway**
- ✗ **tilt their head back**
- ✗ **pinch the nostrils together**

Use your finger to check for and move any obvious obstruction in the mouth. It's important to ensure that the air ways are clear.

Question 13.29

You are giving mouth to mouth to a casualty. They are still not breathing on their own. You should

Mark one answer

- [ ] give up if you think they are dead
- [ ] only keep trying for up to two minutes
- [ ] carry on until an ambulance arrives ✗
- [ ] only keep trying for up to four minutes.

Answer

- ✗ **carry on until an ambulance arrives**

Make sure that someone has called the emergency services. They have the expertise and equipment to deal with the situation.

Question 13.30

When you are giving mouth to mouth you should only stop when

Mark one answer

- [ ] you think the casualty is dead
- [ ] the casualty can breathe without help ✗
- [ ] the casualty has turned blue
- [ ] you think the ambulance is coming.

Answer

- ✗ **the casualty can breathe without help**

Don't give up. Look for signs of recovery and check the casualty's pulse. When the casualty starts to breathe place them in the recovery position.

Question 13.31

You arrive at the scene of an accident. There has been an engine fire and someones hands and arms have been burnt. You should **NOT**

Mark one answer

- [ ] douse the burn thoroughly with cool liquid
- [ ] lay the casualty down
- [X] remove anything sticking to the burn ✕
- [ ] remove smouldering clothing.

Answer

 remove anything sticking to the burn

This could cause further damage and infection to the wound. Your first priorities are to cool the burn and check the patient for shock.

Question 13.32

You arrive at an accident where someone is suffering from severe burns. You should

Mark one answer

- [ ] apply lotions to the injury
- [ ] burst any blisters
- [ ] remove anything stuck to the burns
- [X] douse the burns with cool liquid. ✕

Answer

 douse the burns with cool liquid

Try to find fluid that is clean, cold and non-toxic. It's coolness will stop the burn and relieve the pain. Keep the wound doused for at least ten minutes. If blisters appear don't attempt to burst them as this could lead to infection.

Question 13.33

You arrive at an accident where someone is suffering from severe burns. You should

Mark one answer

- [ ] burst any blisters
- [X] douse the burns thoroughly with cool liquid ✕
- [ ] apply lotions to the injury
- [ ] remove anything sticking to the burns.

Answer

 douse the burns thoroughly with cool liquid

Do this for about ten minutes making sure that the casualty is comfortable. If any clothing is stuck to the wound, don't try to remove it.

You arrive at the scene of an accident. A pedestrian has a severe bleeding wound on their leg, although it is not broken. What should you do?.

Mark two answers

- Dab the wound to stop bleeding.
- Keep both legs flat on the ground..
- Apply firm pressure to the wound. ✗
- Raise the leg to lessen bleeding. ✗
- Fetch them a warm drink.

Answers

- ✗ **Apply firm pressure to the wound.**
- ✗ **Raise the leg to lessen bleeding.**

As soon as you can, apply a pad to the wound with a bandage or a clean length of cloth. Raising the leg will lessen the flow of blood. Be aware that any restriction of blood circulation for more than a short period of time may result in long-term injury.

You arrive at the scene of an accident A passenger is bleeding badly from an arm wound What should you do?

Mark one answer

- Apply pressure over the wound and keep the arm down.
- Dab the wound.
- Get them a drink.
- Apply pressure over the wound and ✗ raise the arm.

Answer

- ✗ **Apply pressure over the wound and raise the arm.**

If possible, lay the casualty down. Raising the arm above the level of the heart will stem the flow of blood.

You arrive at the scene of an accident. A pedestrian is bleeding heavily from a leg wound but the leg is not broken. What should you do?

Mark one answer

- Dab the wound to stop the bleeding.
- Keep both legs flat on the ground.
- Apply firm pressure to the wound. ✗
- Fetch them a warm drink.

Answer

- ✗ **Apply firm pressure to the wound.**

Lift the casualty's leg so that the wound is higher than their heart. This should reduce the flow of blood.

Question 13.37

At an accident a casualty is unconscious but still breathing. You should only move them if

Mark one answer

- [ ] an ambulance is on its way
- [ ] bystanders advise you to
- [ ] there is further danger
- [ ] bystanders will help you to.

Answer

✖ there is further danger

Moving them could cause further injury. So it's important that this is only done if there is obvious danger to the casualty.

Question 13.38

At an accident you suspect a casualty has back injuries. The area is safe. You should

Mark one answer

- [ ] offer them a drink
- [ ] not move them
- [ ] raise their legs
- [ ] offer them a cigarette.

Answer

✖ not move them

Talk to the casualty and keep them calm. If you attempt to move them it could cause further injury. Call an ambulance at the first instance.

Question 13.39

At an accident it is important to look after the casualty. When the area is safe, you should

Mark one answer

- [ ] get them out of the vehicle
- [ ] give them a drink
- [ ] give them something to eat
- [ ] keep them in the vehicle.

Answer

✖ keep them in the vehicle

Don't move casualties who are trapped in vehicles unless they are in danger.

You have an accident and your pillion passenger is injured. You must NOT

Mark one answer

 reassure them

keep them in the same position

remove their helmet

keep them warm.

Answer

 remove their helmet

Removing a motorcycle helmet could cause further injury. If the rider's conscious reassure them while waiting for the emergency services.

A tanker is involved in an accident. Which sign would show if the tanker is carrying dangerous goods?

Mark one answer

LONG VEHICLE

Answer

There will be an orange label on the side and rear of the lorry. Look at this carefully and report what it says when you phone the emergency services.

Question 13.42

While driving a warning light on your vehicle's instrument panel comes on. You should

Mark one answer

☒ continue if the engine sounds alright

☒ hope that it is just a temporary electrical fault

☒ deal with the problem when there is more time

☒ check out the problem quickly and safely.

Answer

☒ **check out the problem quickly and safely**

An illuminated warning light could mean that your car is unsafe to drive. Don't take risks. If you aren't sure about the problem get a qualified mechanic to check it.

Question 13.43

For which TWO should you use hazard warning lights?

Mark two answers

☒ When you slow down quickly on a motorway because of a hazard ahead.

☒ When you have broken down.

☒ When you wish to stop on double yellow lines.

☒ When you need to park on the pavement.

Answers

☒ **When you slow down quickly on a motorway because of a hazard ahead.**

☒ **When you have broken down.**

Hazard warning lights are fitted to all modern cars and some motorcycles. They should be used to warn other road users of a hazard ahead.

Question 13.44

For which THREE should you use your hazard warning lights?

Mark three answers

☒ When you are parking in a restricted area.

☒ When you are temporarily obstructing traffic.

☒ To warn following traffic of a hazard ahead.

☒ When you have broken down.

Answers

☒ **When you are temporarily obstructing traffic.**

☒ **To warn following traffic of a hazard ahead.**

☒ **When you have broken down.**

Use them on the motorway when you have to slow down suddenly because of a queue of traffic ahead. This is to warn following traffic that you're slowing suddenly and rapidly.

When are you allowed to use hazard warning lights?

Mark one answer

☒ When stopped and temporarily obstructing traffic. ✗

☒ When driving during darkness without headlights.

☒ When parked for shopping on double yellow lines.

☒ When travelling slowly because you are lost.

Answer

✗ **When stopped and temporarily obstructing traffic.**

Don't use hazard lights

- to excuse yourself for illegal, dangerous or inconsiderate parking

- when you're moving slowly because you're lost

- when you're moving slowly due to bad weather.

When should you switch on your hazard warning lights?

Mark one answer

☒ When you cannot avoid causing an obstruction. ✗

☒ When you are driving slowly due to bad weather.

☒ When you are towing a broken down vehicle.

☒ When you are parked on double yellow lines.

Answer

✗ **When you cannot avoid causing an obstruction.**

This doesn't mean parking to shop or use a bank machine. If you need to stop for these reasons do so in an authorised parking place.

You have broken down on a two-way road. You have a warning triangle. You should place the warning triangle at least how far from your vehicle?

Mark one answer

☒ 5 metres (16 feet).

☒ 25 metres (80 feet).

☒ 45 metres (149 feet). ✗

☒ 100 metres (330 feet).

Answer

✗ **45 metres (149 feet).**

Carry an advance warning triangle in your vehicle. They fold flat and don't take up much room. Use it to warn other road users if your vehicle has broken down or there's been an accident. Place your warning triangle

- at least 45 metres (149 feet) from your vehicle on a straight, level road.

Question 13.48

You are in an accident on an 'A' class road. You have a warning triangle with you. At what distance before the obstruction should you place the warning triangle?

Mark one answer

☒ 100 metres (330 feet).

☒ 45 metres (149 feet). ✗

☒ 25 metres (80 feet).

☒ 150 metres (492 feet).

Answer

✖ **45 metres (149 feet).**

If there's a bend or hump in the road place the triangle so that approaching traffic slows down before the bend. You must give traffic enough time to react to the warning.

Use your hazard warning lights as well as a warning triangle, especially in the dark.

Question 13.49

Your motorcycle has broken down on a motorway. How will you know the direction of the nearest emergency telephone?

Mark one answer

☒ By walking with the flow of traffic.

☒ By following an arrow on a marker post. ✗

☒ By walking against the flow of traffic.

☒ By remembering where the last phone was.

Answer

✖ **By following an arrow on a marker post.**

If you break down on a motorway you should

• pull onto the hard shoulder and stop as far over to the left as you can

• switch on hazard lights (if you they are fitted)

• make your way to the nearest emergency telephone.

Marker posts spaced every 100 meters will direct you to the nearest telephone.

Question 13.50

You have broken down on an ordinary road. You have a warning triangle. It should be displayed

Mark one answer

☒ on the roof of your vehicle

☒ at least 150 metres (492 feet) behind your vehicle

☒ at least 45 metres (149 feet) ✗ behind your vehicle

☒ just behind your vehicle.

Answer

✖ **at least 45 metres (149 feet) behind your vehicle**

If you need to display a warning triangle make sure that it can be seen clearly by other road users. Place it on the same side of the road and clear of any obstruction.

Your vehicle is broken down on a straight road. You have a warning triangle. Where should you place it?

Mark one answer

☒ Securely on the roof of your car.

☒ 45 metres (47 yards) from your vehicle.

☒ 10 metres (11 yards) from your vehicle.

☒ Directly at the rear of your vehicle.

Answer

☒ **45 metres (47 yards) from your vehicle.**

Place it so that it can be seen by other road users but does not cause an obstruction.

You are advised to buy and carry one of these in your vehicle.

The police may ask you to produce which three of these documents following an accident?.

Mark three answers

☒ Vehicle registration document.

☒ Driving licence.

☒ Theory test certificate.

☒ Insurance certificate.

☒ MOT test certificate.

☒ Road tax disc.

Answers

☒ **Driving licence.**

☒ **Insurance certificate.**

☒ **MOT test certificate.**

The first thing you must do is stop. It is an offence not to do so.

Question 13.53

You are involved in a road accident with another driver. Your vehicle is damaged. Which FOUR of the following should you find out?

Mark four answers

☒ Whether the driver owns the other vehicle involved.

☒ The other driver's name, address and telephone number.

☒ The car make and registration number of the other vehicle.

☒ The occupation of the other driver.

☒ The details of the other driver's vehicle insurance.

☒ Whether the other driver is licensed to drive.

Answers

☒ **Whether the driver owns the other vehicle involved.**

☒ **The other driver's name, address and telephone number.**

☒ **The car make and registration number of the other vehicle.**

☒ **The details of the other driver's vehicle insurance.**

Try to keep calm and don't rush the proceedings. Take your time. You might be a little shaken by the incident, but try to ensure that you have all the details before you leave the scene.

Question 13.54

You have an accident while driving and someone is injured. You do not produce your insurance certificate at the time. You must report it to the police as soon as possible, or in any case within

Mark one answer

☒ 24 hours

☒ 48 hours

☒ five days

☒ seven days.

Answer

☒ **24 hours**

You must also give

• your name and address
• your vehicle owner's address
• the registration number of the vehicle

to the police, or anyone with reasonable grounds for wanting them.

In Northern Ireland accidents have to be reported to the police 'forthwith'.

Question 13.55

At a railway level crossing the red light signal continues to flash after a train has gone by. What should you do?

Mark one answer

☒ Phone the signal operator.

☒ Alert drivers behind you.

☒ Wait.

☒ Proceed with caution.

Answer

☒ **Wait.**

Don't

• proceed
• phone the signal operator immediately
• zigzag between the gates.

There may be another train coming.

Question 13.56

You break down on a level crossing. The lights have not yet begun to flash. Which THREE things should you do?

Mark three answers

☒ Telephone the signal operator.

☒ Leave your vehicle and get everyone clear.

☒ Walk down the track and signal the next train.

☒ Move the vehicle if a signal operator tells you to.

☒ Tell drivers behind what has happened.

Answers

✖ **Telephone the signal operator.**

✖ **Leave your vehicle and get everyone clear.**

✖ **Move the vehicle if a signal operator tells you to.**

Keep calm. Don't

• walk up the track to warn approaching trains

• try to restart the engine

• try to move the vehicle unless told to do so by the signal operator.

Question 13.57

You have stalled in the middle of a level crossing and cannot restart the engine. The warning bell starts to ring. You should

Mark one answer

☒ get out and clear of the crossing

☒ run down the track to warn the signalman

☒ carry on trying to restart the engine

☒ push the vehicle clear of the crossing.

Answer

✖ **get out and clear of the crossing**

Try not to panic, and stay calm, especially if you have passengers on board. If you can't restart your engine before the warning bells ring then leave the vehicle.

Question 13.58

Your vehicle has broken down on an automatic railway level crossing. What should you do FIRST?

Mark one answer

☒ Get everyone out of the vehicle and clear of the crossing.

☒ Phone the signal operator so that trains can be stopped.

☒ Walk along the track to give warning to any approaching trains.

☒ Try to push the vehicle clear of the crossing as soon as possible.

Answer

✖ **Get everyone out of the vehicle and clear of the crossing.**

Ensure that everyone is WELL clear of the crossing. In the event of an accident debris could be scattered in several directions.

Question 13.59

Your tyre bursts while you are driving. Which TWO things should you do?

Mark two answers

- [ ] Pull on the handbrake.
- [ ] Brake as quickly as possible.
- [ ] Pull up slowly at the side of the road.
- [ ] Hold the steering wheel firmly to keep control.
- [ ] Continue on at a normal speed.

Answers

- ☒ **Pull up slowly at the side of the road.**
- ☒ **Hold the steering wheel firmly to keep control.**

A tyre bursting can lead to a loss of control, especially if you're travelling at high speed. The correct procedure can help to stop the vehicle safely.

Question 13.60

Which TWO things should you do when a front tyre bursts?

Mark two answers

- [ ] Apply the handbrake to stop the vehicle.
- [ ] Brake firmly and quickly.
- [ ] Let the vehicle roll to a stop.
- [ ] Hold the steering wheel lightly.
- [ ] Grip the steering wheel firmly.

Answers

- ☒ **Let the vehicle roll to a stop.**
- ☒ **Grip the steering wheel firmly.**

Try not to react by applying the brakes harshly. This could lead to further loss of steering control. Indicate your intention to pull up at the side of the road and roll to a stop.

Question 13.61

You are driving on the motorway and get a puncture. You should

Mark one answer

- [ ] pull onto the hard shoulder as safely as possible
- [ ] stop in the lane you are in and change the wheel
- [ ] pull into the central reserve as safely as possible
- [ ] stop in any lane but use emergency flashers.

Answer

- ☒ **pull onto the hard shoulder as safely as possible**

The vehicle might swerve and weave. Try not to brake and hold onto the steering wheel as it might shudder or pull to one side. Try to let your vehicle roll to a stop onto the safety of the hard shoulder.

Your vehicle has a puncture on a motorway. What should you do?

Mark one answer

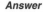 Drive slowly to the next service area to get assistance.

Pull up on the hard shoulder. Change the wheel as quickly as possible.

Pull up on the hard shoulder. Use the emergency phone to get assistance.

Switch on your hazard lights. Stop in your lane.

Answer

Pull up on the hard shoulder. Use the emergency phone to get assistance.

Pull up on the hard shoulder and make your way to the nearest emergency telephone and request assistance. It is dangerous to try and change an offside wheel, due to fast traffic passing very close to your vehicle.

You use the engine cut-out switch to

Mark one answer

stop the engine in an emergency

stop the engine for short stops

save wear on the ignition switch

start the engine if you lose the key.

Answer

stop the engine in an emergency

Most motorcycles are fitted with an engine cut-out switch. This is designed to stop the engine in an emergency and so reduce the risk of fire.

You see a car on the hard shoulder of a motorway with a HELP pennant displayed. This means the driver is most likely to be

Mark one answer

a disabled person

first Aid trained

a foreign visitor

a rescue patrol person.

Answer

a disabled person

The driver might not be able to walk the distance to the emergency telephone. Disabled persons can show this sign to alert police controls.

Question 13.65

On the motorway the hard shoulder should be used

Mark one answer

☒ to answer a mobile phone

☒ when an emergency arises

☒ for a short rest when tired

☒ to check a road atlas.

Answer

✖ **when an emergency arises**

Pull onto the hard shoulder and use the emergency telephone to report your problem. The telephone connects you to police control, who will put you through to an emergency breakdown service. Never cross the carriageway to use the telephone on the other side.

Question 13.66

What TWO safeguards could you take against fire risk to your vehicle?

Mark two answers

☒ Keep water levels above maximum.

☒ Carry a fire extinguisher.

☒ Avoid driving with a full tank of petrol.

☒ Use unleaded petrol.

☒ Check out any strong smell of petrol.

☒ Use low octane fuel.

Answers

✖ **Carry a fire extinguisher.**

✖ **Check out any strong smell of petrol.**

The fuel in your vehicle can be a dangerous fire hazard. Don't

- use a naked flame near the vehicle if you can smell fuel
- smoke when refuelling your vehicle.

Question 13.67

You have broken down on a motorway. When you use the emergency telephone you will be asked

Mark three answers

☒ for the number on the telephone that you are using

☒ for your driving licence details

☒ for the name of your vehicle insurance company

☒ for details of yourself and your vehicle

☒ whether you belong to a motoring organisation.

Answers

✖ **for the number on the telephone you are using**

✖ **for details of yourself and your vehicle**

✖ **whether you belong to a motoring organisation**

Have these details ready before you phone to save time. Be sure to give the correct information. For safety sake, always face the traffic when you speak on the telephone.

You are on the motorway. Luggage falls from your vehicle. What should you do?

Mark one answer

☒ Stop at the next emergency telephone and contact the police.

☒ Stop on the motorway and put on hazard lights whilst you pick it up.

☒ Reverse back up the motorway to pick it up.

☒ Pull up on the hard shoulder and wave traffic down.

Answer

❌ **Stop at the next emergency telephone and contact the police.**

- Pull over onto the hard shoulder near an emergency telephone
- phone for assistance.

Don't

- stop on the carriageway
- attempt to retrieve anything.

You are travelling on a motorway. A bag falls from your motorcycle. There are valuables in the bag. What should you do?

Mark one answer

☒ Go back carefully and collect the bag as quickly as possible.

☒ Stop wherever you are and pick up the bag, but only when there is a safe gap.

☒ Stop on the hard shoulder and use the emergency telephone to inform the police.

☒ Stop on the hard shoulder and then retrieve the bag yourself.

Answer

❌ **Stop on the hard shoulder and use the emergency telephone to inform the police.**

However important you think retrieving your property may be DON'T walk onto the motorway. Your bag might be creating a hazard but not as great a hazard as you would be.

You are travelling on a motorway. A suitcase falls from your vehicle. There are valuables in the suitcase. What should you do?

Mark one answer

☒ Reverse your vehicle carefully and collect the case as quickly as possible.

☒ Stop wherever you are and pick up the case but only when there is a safe gap.

☒ Stop on the hard shoulder and use the emergency telephone to inform the police.

☒ Stop on the hard shoulder and then retrieve the suitcase yourself.

Answer

❌ **Stop on the hard shoulder and use the emergency telephone to inform the police.**

Walking onto the carriageway is very dangerous. The traffic is travelling at high speeds and may not have the time or room to change lanes to avoid you. Your property is never as valuable as your life.

ACCIDENTS

Question 13.71

You are driving on a motorway. A large box falls onto the carriageway from a lorry ahead of you. The lorry does not stop. You should

Mark one answer

☒ drive to the next emergency telephone and inform the police

☒ catch up with the lorry and try to get the driver's attention

☒ stop close to the box and switch on your hazard warning lights until the police arrive

☒ pull over to the hard shoulder, then try and remove the box.

Answer

☒ **drive to the next emergency telephone and inform the police**

Lorry drivers are sometimes unaware of objects falling from their vehicles. If you see something fall off a lorry onto the motorway watch to see if the driver pulls over. If the lorry doesn't stop you should

• pull over onto the hard shoulder near an emergency telephone

• report the hazard to the police.

Question 13.72

You are driving on a motorway. When can you use hazard warning lights?

Mark two answers

☒ When a vehicle is following too closely.

☒ When you slow down quickly because of danger ahead.

☒ When you are towing another vehicle.

☒ When driving on the hard shoulder.

☒ When you have broken down, on the hard shoulder.

Answers

☒ **When you slow down quickly because of danger ahead.**

☒ **When you have broken down, on the hard shoulder.**

Hazard lights will warn the traffic travelling behind you that your vehicle is a potential hazard. Don't forget to turn them off again when you return to the carriageway or normal speed.

Question 13.73

You are riding on a motorway. The car in front switches on its hazard warning lights whilst moving. This means

Mark one answer

☒ they are going to take the next exit

☒ there is a hazard ahead

☒ there is a police car in the left lane

☒ they are trying to change lanes.

Answer

☒ **there is a hazard ahead**

Hazard lights should only be used when driving if you're on a

• motorway

• unrestricted dual carriageway

and you want to warn following traffic of a hazard ahead.

DSA THEORY TEST for car drivers and motorcyclists   393

SECTION 14 VEHICLE LOADING

This section looks at the safety of loads.

The questions will ask you about

- vehicle loading
- stability
- towing regulations.

Question 14.1

Overloading your vehicle can seriously affect the

Mark two answers

- [ ] gearbox
- [ ] steering
- [ ] handling
- [ ] battery life
- [ ] journey time.

Answers

- [x] **steering**
- [x] **handling**

Any load will have an affect on the handling of your vehicle, this becomes worse if you overload it. Any change in the centre of gravity or weight the vehicle is carrying will affect it's handling on bends.

Question 14.2

Who is responsible for making sure that a vehicle is not overloaded?

Mark one answer

- [ ] The driver or rider of the vehicle.
- [ ] The owner of the items being carried.
- [ ] The person who loaded the vehicle.
- [ ] The owner of the vehicle.

Answer

- [x] **The driver or rider of the vehicle.**

Your vehicle must not be overloaded. This will affect control and handling characteristics. If your vehicle is overloaded and it causes an accident you'll be responsible.

Question 14.3

On which **two** occasions should you inflate your tyres to **more** than the recommended normal pressure?

Mark two answers

- [ ] When the roads are slippery.
- [ ] When driving fast for a long distance.
- [ ] When the tyre tread is worn below 2mm.
- [ ] When carrying a heavy load.
- [ ] When the weather is cold.
- [ ] When the vehicle is fitted with anti-lock brakes.

Answers

- [x] **When driving fast for a long distance.**
- [x] **When carrying a heavy load.**

Check the vehicle hand book, this should give you guidance on the correct tyre pressure in these circumstances.

Travelling at speed for long distances can cause the tyres to become hot, which could damage the side walls.

When travelling for long periods at high speed you should normally

Mark one answer

☒ lessen your tyre pressures

☒ keep at your regular tyre pressures

☒ increase your tyre pressures before leaving

☒ increase tyre pressures on your return.

Answer

✖ increase your tyre pressures before leaving

You should check your vehicle thoroughly before you travel on a long journey. Use your vehicle handbook which will give you information about the model of vehicle you are driving.

Any load that is carried on a luggage rack MUST be

Mark one answer

☒ securely fastened when riding

☒ carried only when strictly necessary

☒ as light as possible

☒ covered with plastic sheeting.

Answer

✖ securely fastened when riding

Don't risk losing any luggage off your machine. It could fall into the path of following vehicles and cause danger. It's an offence to travel with an insecure load.

Any load that is carried on a roof rack MUST be

Mark one answer

☒ securely fastened when driving

☒ carried only when strictly necessary

☒ as light as possible

☒ covered with plastic sheeting.

Answer

✖ securely fastened when driving

If you wish to carry items on the roof there are roof boxes available from automotive supply stores. These will help to keep your luggage secure and dry.

Question 14.7

When your vehicle is loaded you MUST make sure that the load will

Mark one answer

☒ remain secure

☒ be easy to unload

☒ not be damaged

☒ not damage the vehicle.

Answer

 remain secure

If the load is insecure it could become loose and fall into the path of other traffic. This could cause injury and you would be responsible.

Question 14.8

You have a heavy load on your roof rack. What effect will it have when you are driving?

Mark one answer

☒ Make the fuel consumption less.

☒ Reduce the stopping distance.

☒ Make the steering lighter.

☒ Reduce stability.

Answer

✖ Reduce stability.

Be aware of this when you negotiate bends and corners. Your vehicle and/or load could become unstable, you could lose control.

Question 14.9

Which THREE are suitable restraints for a child under three years?

Mark three answers

☒ A child seat.

☒ An adult holding a child.

☒ An adult seat belt.

☒ A lap belt.

☒ A harness.

☒ A baby carrier.

Answers

✖ A child seat.

✖ A harness.

✖ A baby carrier.

The driver is responsible for ensuring that children under three wear suitable child restraints. If the child is in the front seat a restraint **must** be used. If the child is in the rear seat restraints **must** be used if available.

A harness or booster seat should be appropriate to the child's weight.

Your car is fitted with child safety door locks. When used this means that normally

Mark one answer

☒ the rear doors can only be opened from the outside

☒ the rear doors can only be opened from the inside

☒ all the doors can only be opened from the outside

☒ all the doors can only be opened from the inside.

Answer

✖ **the rear doors can only be opened from the outside**

Safety locks prevent the doors being opened accidentally. Children travelling in the back of the car might play with the door handle, opening the door accidentally.

What do child locks in a vehicle do?

Mark one answer

☒ Lock the seat belt buckles in place.

☒ Lock the rear windows in the up position.

☒ Stop children from opening rear doors.

☒ Stop the rear seats from tipping forward.

Answer

✖ **Stop children from opening rear doors.**

Child locks are fitted to most modern cars. They prevent the door being opened from the inside.

Your vehicle is fitted with child safety door locks. You should use these so that children inside the car cannot open

Mark one answer

☒ the right-hand doors

☒ the left-hand doors

☒ the rear doors

☒ any of the doors

Answer

✖ **the rear doors**

If you're travelling with children in the rear seats, fitting child safety locks is a sensible safety precaution. There will be times when children are eager to get out of the car as it comes to a stop, and child safety locks will prevent them doing so until you're sure it's safe for them to do so.

Question 14.13

You should load a trailer so that the weight is

Mark one answer

☒ mostly over the nearside wheel

☒ evenly distributed

☒ mainly at the front

☒ mostly at the rear.

Answer

☒ **evenly distributed**

If you tow a trailer you need to give some thought as to how you load it. The load should be

- secured so that it can't move about while you're travelling. Movement of the load might affect steering and cause danger to other road users.

- evenly distributed.

Question 14.14

You want to tow a trailer with your motorcycle Which one applies?

Mark one answer

☒ The motorcycle should be attached to a sidecar.

☒ The trailer should weigh more than the motorcycle.

☒ The trailer should be fitted with brakes.

☒ The trailer should not be more than 1 metre (3 feet 3 inches) wide.

Answer

☒ **The trailer should not be more than 1 metre (3 feet 3 inches) wide.**

To tow a trailer behind a motorcycle you must

- have a full motorcycle licence

- have a motorcycle with an engine larger than 125cc.

Motorcycle trailers must not exceed 1 metre (3 feet 3 inches) wide.

Question 14.15

You are planning to tow a caravan. Which of these will **mostly** help to aid the vehicle handling?

Mark one answer

☒ A jockey-wheel fitted to the towbar.

☒ Power steering fitted to the towing vehicle.

☒ Anti-lock brakes fitted to the towing vehicle.

☒ A stabiliser fitted to the towbar.

Answer

☒ **A stabiliser fitted to the towbar.**

It is highly recommended that you take a caravan manoeuvring course. The Camping and Caravanning Club provide a course for those wishing to tow trailers. They also publish literature and a really helpful video.

For more information tel: 01203 694995

You plan to carry a load on a trailer. You **must** make sure that the load is

Mark one answer

☒ properly secured

☒ not heavier than the trailer

☒ not overhanging the trailer

☒ covered with sheeting.

Answer

❌ **properly secured**

You will be responsible if your load falls from your vehicle. It could cause damage or injury. Check it before you start your journey and everytime you stop for a break.

Before towing a caravan you should ensure that heavy items in it are loaded

Mark one answer

☒ as high as possible, mainly over the axle(s)

☒ as low as possible, mainly over the axle(s)

☒ as low as possible, forward of the axle(s)

☒ as high as possible, forward of the axle(s).

Answer

❌ **as low as possible, mainly over the axle(s)**

Loading like this will help the caravan to be more stable

A trailer must stay securely hitched-up to the towing vehicle. What additional safety device can be fitted to the trailer braking system?

Mark one answer

☒ Stabiliser.

☒ Jockey wheel.

☒ Corner steadies.

☒ Breakaway cable.

Answer

❌ **Breakaway cable.**

In the event of a tow bar failure the cable pulls on the caravan brakes, snaps and allows the car to run free of the stopped caravan.

Question 14.19

If a trailer swerves or snakes when you are towing it you should

Mark one answer

- ☒ ease off the accelerator and reduce your speed
- ☒ let go of the steering wheel and let it correct itself
- ☒ brake hard and hold the pedal down
- ☒ increase your speed as quickly as possible.

Answer

❌ **ease off the accelerator and reduce your speed**

Strong winds or buffeting from large vehicles might cause a trailer or caravan to snake or swerve. If this happens ease off the accelerator. Don't

- brake harshly
- steer sharply
- increase speed.

Question 14.20

Are passengers allowed to ride in a caravan that is being towed?

Mark one answer

- ☒ Yes.
- ☒ No.
- ☒ Only if all the seats in the towing vehicle are full.
- ☒ Only if a stabilizer is fitted.

Answer

❌ **No.**

Riding in a towed caravan is highly dangerous. The safety of the entire unit is dependent on the stability of the trailer. Moving passengers would render the caravan unstable and could cause loss of control.

Question 14.21

You are towing a caravan along a motorway. The caravan begins to swerve from side to side. What should you do?

Mark one answer

- ☒ Ease off the accelerator slowly.
- ☒ Steer sharply from side to side.
- ☒ Do an emergency stop.
- ☒ Speed up a little.

Answer

❌ **Ease off the accelerator slowly.**

Try not to brake or steer heavily, this will only make matters worse and you could lose control altogether. Keep calm and regain control by easing off the accelerator.

Question 14.22

If a trailer swerves or snakes when you are towing it you should

Mark one answer

- [ ] ease off the throttle and reduce your speed
- [ ] let go of the handlebars and let it correct itself
- [ ] brake hard and hold the brake on
- [ ] increase your speed as quickly as possible.

Answer

✗ **ease off the throttle and reduce your speed**

Don't be tempted to use the steering to stop swerving or snaking. This won't help the situation. Ease off the throttle and reduce your speed.

Question 14.23

You are towing a trailer and experience snaking. How would you reduce it?

Mark one answer

- [ ] Ease off the accelerator slowly.
- [ ] Press the accelerator firmly.
- [ ] Steer sharply.
- [ ] Brake hard.

Answer

✗ **Ease off the accelerator slowly.**

Don't try to correct snaking or swerving by increasing your speed, braking or trying to steer against the trailer's swing.

Question 14.24

How can you stop a caravan snaking from side to side?

Mark one answer

- [ ] Turn the steering wheel slowly to each side.
- [ ] Accelerate to increase your speed.
- [ ] Stop as quickly as you can.
- [ ] Slow down very gradually.

Answer

✗ **Slow down very gradually.**

Keep calm and don't brake harshly or you could lose control completely.

Question 14.25

You are towing a small trailer on a busy three-lane motorway. All the lanes are open. You must

Mark two answers

- [ ] not exceed 60 mph
- [ ] not overtake
- [ ] have a stabilizer fitted
- [ ] use only the left and centre lanes.

Answers

- ☒ **not exceed 60 mph**
- ☒ **use only the left and centre lanes**

You should be aware of the speed limit for the vehicle that you're driving. Allow the faster-moving traffic to flow. Don't use the right-hand lane.

Question 14.26

You have a side-car fitted to your motorcycle. What effect will it have?

Mark one answer

- [ ] Reduce stability.
- [ ] Make steering lighter.
- [ ] Increase stopping distance.
- [ ] Increase fuel economy.

Answer

- ☒ **Increase stopping distance.**

If you want to fit a side-car to your motorcycle

- make sure that your machine is suitable to cope with the extra load
- make sure that the side-car is fixed correctly and properly aligned.

A side-car will affect the handling of your machine. Give yourself time to adjust to the different characteristics.

Question 14.27

When riding with a sidecar attached for the first time you should

Mark two answers

- [ ] keep your speed down
- [ ] be able to stop more quickly
- [ ] accelerate quickly round bends
- [ ] approach corners more carefully.

Answers

- ☒ **keep your speed down**
- ☒ **approach corners more carefully**

A motorcycle with a sidecar will feel very different to ride than a solo motorcycle. Until you get used to the outfit keep your speed down especially around corners and bends.

A trailer on a motorcycle must be no wider than

Mark one answer

- [ ] 1 metre (3 feet 3 inches)
- [ ] ½ metre (1 foot 4 inches)
- [ ] 1½ metres (4 feet 6 inches)
- [ ] 2 metres (6 feet 4 inches).

Answer

❌ **1 metre (3 feet 3 inches)**

When you're towing a trailer you must remember that you might not be able to filter through traffic. Don't 'forget' that the trailer is there.

Before fitting a side-car riders must

Mark one answer

- [ ] have the wheels of their bike balanced
- [ ] have their bike's engine tuned
- [ ] pass the extended bike test
- [ ] check that their bike is suitable.

Answer

❌ **check that their bike is suitable**

Make sure that the sidecar is fixed and is properly aligned. If your machine is registered on or after 1 August 1981 the sidecar must be fitted on the left side of the machine.

You want to tow a trailer behind your motorcycle. You should

Mark two answers

- [ ] display a 'long vehicle' sign
- [ ] fit a larger battery
- [ ] have a full motorcycle licence
- [ ] ensure that your engine is more than 125cc
- [ ] ensure that your machine has shaft drive.

Answers

❌ **have a full motorcycle licence**

❌ **ensure your engine is more than 125cc**

When you tow a trailer

- you must obey the speed limit restrictions that apply to all vehicles with trailers
- your stopping distance may be increased
- any load on the trailer must be secure
- the trailer must be fitted to the machine correctly.

Question 14.31

When may a learner motorcyclist carry a pillion passenger?

Mark one answer

☒ If the passenger holds a full licence.

☒ Not at any time.

☒ If the rider is undergoing training.

☒ If the passenger is over 21.

Answer

☒ **Not at any time.**

If you carry a pillion passenger the overall weight of riders and machine will be significantly increased compared to when riding alone.

You should have experience riding solo before carrying a passenger.

Question 14.32

Which THREE must a learner motorcyclist under 21 NOT do?

Mark three answers

☒ Ride a motorcycle with an engine capacity greater than 125cc.

☒ Pull a trailer.

☒ Carry a pillion passenger.

☒ Ride faster than 30 mph.

☒ Use the right-hand lane on dual carriageways.

Answers

☒ **Ride a motorcycle with an engine capacity greater than 125cc.**

☒ **Pull a trailer.**

☒ **Carry a pillion passenger.**

If you're a learner motorcyclist under 21 you must not ride a motorcycle on the road with an engine capacity over 125cc.

Question 14.33

Pillion passengers MUST

Mark one answer

☒ have a provisional motorcycle licence

☒ be lighter than the rider

☒ wear a helmet

☒ wear reflective or fluorescent clothing.

Answer

☒ **wear a helmet**

Pillion passengers must

- sit astride the machine facing forward on a proper passenger seat
- wear a safety helmet, which is correctly fastened.

Question 14.34

Pillion passengers should

Mark one answer

☒ give the rider directions

☒ lean with the rider when going round bends and corners

☒ check the road behind for the rider

☒ give hand signals for the rider.

Answer

☒ **lean with the rider when going round bends and corners**

Pillion passengers should also keep both feet on the pillion footrests provided.

Question 14.35

When carrying extra weight on a motorcycle, you may need to make adjustments to the

Mark three answers

☒ headlight

☒ gears

☒ suspension

☒ tyres

☒ footrests.

Answers

☒ **headlight**

☒ **suspension**

☒ **tyres**

Extra weight can affect a motorcycles feel and balance. To help you can adjust the

• suspension

• tyre pressures.

You may find extra weight on the back affects the headlamp aim and this can be adjusted to compensate.

Question 14.36

To carry a pillion passenger your bike should have which TWO?

Mark two answers

☒ Rear footrests.

☒ An engine of 250cc or over.

☒ A top box.

☒ A grab handle.

☒ A proper passenger seat.

Answers

☒ **Rear footrests.**

☒ **A proper passenger seat.**

Pillion passengers should be instructed not to

• give hand signals

• lean away from the rider when cornering

• fidget or move around

• put their feet down to try and support the machine as you stop

• wear long, loose items that might get caught in the rear wheel or drive chain.

Question 14.37

To obtain the full category 'A' licence through the accelerated or direct access scheme, your motorcycle must be

Mark one answer

☒ solo with maximum power 25kw (33 bhp)

☒ solo with maximum power of 11kw (14.6 bhp)

☒ fitted with a sidecar and have minimum power of 35kw (46.6 bhp)

☒ solo with minimum power of 35 kw (46.6 bhp)

Answer

☒ **solo with minimum power of 35 kw (46.6 bhp)**

If you want to ride in countries who are members of the European Community you must have a valid driving licence. You will also want to find out what specific rules apply to any country you may be visiting concerning insurance, visas and other motoring regulations.

Conclusion

This book has been produced to help
you to prepare for and pass your
theory test. If you've spent sufficient
time and effort you won't find the
theory question paper difficult.

Passing the theory test is the first
stage in becoming a safe driver or
rider. Use the knowledge you've
learned and put it into practice on the
road. You'll never know all the
answers. Throughout your driving life
there will always be more to learn.

The aim of DSA is to improve road
safety throughout the UK. By
improving skills and knowledge we
can ensure 'Safe driving for life'. This
will save lives – one of them could be
yours.

Service standards for theory test candidates

DSA and DVTA are committed to providing the following standards of service for test candidates.

- Theory tests will be available during weekdays, evenings and on Saturdays. A test appointment should be available for 95% of test candidates within two weeks.

- Test notification will be issued within five working days of receipt of a correctly completed application form and appropriate fee.

- 95% of telephone calls will be answered within ten seconds.

- More time may be needed to make arrangements for candidates with special needs, but a test should be available for 95% of such candidates within four weeks.

- A refund of test fees will be issued within three weeks of a valid claim with the supporting information.

- All letters, including complaints, will be answered within 15 working days.

- All candidates should be able to obtain a test booking within two months of their preferred date and time at the centre of their choice.

- No more than 0.5% of tests will be cancelled by DriveSafe Ltd (acting on behalf of DSA and DVTA).

Complaints guide for theory test candidates

DSA and DVTA aim to give their customers the best possible service. Please tell us

- when we've done well

- when you aren't satisfied.

Your comments can help us to improve the service we offer. If you have any questions about your theory test please contact 0870 01 01 372, or fax 0870 01 04 372.

If you have any complaints about how your theory test was carried out, or any part of our customer service, please take up the matter with a member of staff if the circumstances allow. You may complete a form, available at theory test centres. Alternatively, you can write to the Head of Central Services at the following address

Head of Central Services
Driving Theory Test
PO Box 445
Coventry CV1 2ZZ

Tel: 0870 01 01 372

Fax: 0870 01 04 372

If you're dissatisfied with the reply you can write to the Managing Director at the same address.

If you're still not satisfied you can take up your complaint with

The Chief Executive
Driving Standards Agency
Stanley House
Talbot Street
Nottingham NG1 5GU

In Northern Ireland

The Chief Executive
Driver and Vehicle Licensing Agency
Balmoral Road
Belfast BT12 6QL

None of this removes your right to take your complaint to your Member of Parliament, who may decide on your case personally with the Chief Executive, the Minister, or the Parliamentary Commissioner for Administration (the Ombudsman).

Before doing this you should seek legal advice.

Compensation code for theory test candidates

DSA will normally refund the test fee, or give a free re-booking, in the following cases

- if we cancel your test

- if you cancel and give us at least three clear working days' notice

- if you keep the test appointment but the test doesn't take place, or isn't finished, for a reason that isn't your fault.

We'll also repay the expenses that you incurred on the day of the test because we cancelled your test at short notice. We'll consider reasonable claims for

- travelling to and from the test centre

- any pay or earnings you lost after tax (usually for half a day).

Please write to the office where you booked your test and send a receipt showing the travel costs and/or an employer's letter, which shows the earnings you lost.

DVTA has a different compensation code. If you think that you're entitled to compensation apply to the centre where you booked your test.

This compensation code doesn't affect your existing legal rights.

Theory test centres in Great Britain and Northern Ireland

England

Avon	Bristol		
Bedfordshire	Luton		
Berkshire	Reading	Slough	
Buckinghamshire	Milton Keynes		
Cambridgeshire	Cambridge	Peterborough	
Cheshire	Chester	Runcorn	
Cleveland	Middlesbrough		
Cornwall	Penzance	Truro	
County Durham	Durham		
Cumbria	Barrow	Carlisle	Workington
Derbyshire	Chesterfield	Derby	
Devon	Barnstaple	Exeter	Plymouth
	Torquay		
Dorset	Bournemouth	Weymouth	
East Sussex	Brighton	Eastbourne	Hastings
East Yorkshire	Hull		
Essex	Basildon	Chelmsford	Colchester
	Harlow	Southend-on-Sea	
Gloucestershire	Cheltenham	Gloucester	
Greater Manchester	Manchester	Oldham	Salford
	Stockport	Wigan	
Hampshire	Aldershot	Basingstoke	Fareham
	Portsmouth	Southampton	
Hereford and Worcester	Hereford	Worcester	
Hertfordshire	Stevenage	Watford	

Isle of Wight	Newport		
Kent	Canterbury	Gillingham	
Lancashire	Blackpool	Bolton	Preston
	Southport		
Leicestershire	Leicester		
Lincoln	Boston	Grantham	Lincoln
London – Greater	Bexley	Croydon	Ilford
	Kingston	Uxbridge	Wood Green
London – Inner	Vauxhall		
Merseyside	Birkenhead	Liverpool	St Helens
Norfolk	King's Lynn	Norwich	
North Lincolnshire	Scunthorpe		
North Yorkshire	Harrogate	Scarborough	York
North-East Lincolnshire	Grimsby		
Northamptonshire	Northampton		
Northumberland	Berwick-upon-Tweed		Morpeth
Nottinghamshire	Mansfield	Nottingham	
Oxfordshire	Oxford		
Shropshire	Shrewsbury		
Somerset	Bath	Taunton	Yeovil
South Yorkshire	Doncaster	Sheffield	
Staffordshire	Stoke-on-Trent		
Suffolk	Bury St Edmunds	Ipswich	Lowestoft
Surrey	Guildford	Staines	
Tyne and Wear	Newcastle	Sunderland	

Warwickshire	Stratford-upon-Avon		
West Midlands	Birmingham	Coventry	Dudley
	Redditch	Solihull	Sutton Coldfield
	Wolverhampton		
West Sussex	Crawley	Worthing	
West Yorkshire	Bradford	Leeds	
HuddersfieldWiltshire	Salisbury	Swindon	

Scotland

Borders	Galashiels		
Central	Stirling		
Dumfries and Galloway	Dumfries	Stranraer	
Fife	Dunfermline		
Grampian	Aberdeen	Elgin	Huntly
Highland	Fort William	Gairloch	Helmsdale
	Inverness	Isle of Arran	Isle of Islay
	Kyle of Lochalsh	Portree	Tongue
	Ullapool	Wick	
Lothian	Edinburgh		
Orkney	Kirkwall		
Shetland	Lerwick		
Strathclyde	Ayr	Glasgow Central	
	Glasgow North-West		Greenock
	Motherwell	Oban	Salen
	Tarbet		
Tayside	Dundee	Pitlochry	
Western Isles	Barra	Benbecula	Stornoway

Wales

Clwyd	Rhyl	
Dyfed	Aberystwyth	Haverford West
Gwent	Newport	
Gwyned	Bangor	
Mid Glamorgan	Merthyr Tydfil	
Powys	Builth Wells	
South Glamorgan	Cardiff	
West Glamorgan	Swansea	

Northern Ireland

Ballymena

Belfast

Londonderry

Newry

Omagh

Portadown

*Essential reading from the **Driving Standards Agency***

Prepare for the driving tests wi

The DSA Compulsory Basic Training Manual for Motorcyclists

Providing instruction on machine handling, road awareness and basic maintenance. This fully illustrated manual is written in an easy to follow style and is the definitive manual for trainers and trainees alike.

88 PAGES ILLUSTRATED IN FULL COLOUR
ISBN 0 11 552013 9
PAPERBACK £6.99

The Driving Manual

Covering everything that the driver needs to know about good driving techniques for today's challenging driving conditions.

336 PAGES ILLUSTRATED IN FULL COLOUR
ISBN 0 11 551782 0
PAPERBACK £12.99

The Motorcycling Manual

The authoritative guide to motorcycling, containing new graphics and photos. An essential reference book for motorcyclists who are keen to improve their machine handling and safety skills.

176 PAGES ILLUSTRATED IN FULL COLOUR
ISBN 0 11 551781 2
PAPERBACK £9.99

Test Yourself Papers for the Driving Theory Test

Five practice papers for the theory test, with questions taken from the official question bank and the correct answers supplied for further reference and revision.

ISBN 0 11 551984 X
£4.99 (INCL VAT)

e official guidance ...

Know Your Traffic Signs

The best-selling booklet which aims to illustrate and explain the vast majority of traffic signs which any road user is likely to encounter.
100 pages illustrated in colour

ISBN 0 11 551612 3
£2.50

The Driving Test

Advice on the practical test - from the official syllabus, preparation, test requirements, skills to be acquired and faults to avoid.

ISBN 0 11 551778 2
£4.99

New ways to take your test
Preview the theory test by telephone, online and on CD-ROM

The Audio Mock Theory Test

Devised to simulate the real theory test, this telephone service gives results - with 4 papers to choose from, each containing 35 questions.

Call 0930 2-3-4-5-6-7

(Calls cost 50p per minute; each paper takes approx 30 minutes to complete; callers must be 18 or over)

cyberdrive – the new web site for learner drivers

Visit our new online site for everything you need to know to help you to pass your theory and practical tests, and to help you to advance your driving skills. Including the new online mock theory test - which simulates the real test and gives immediate results.

http://www.cyberdrive.co.uk

Driving Skills: Theory Test and Beyond on CD-Rom – See overleaf for details.

Order Form

Please send me the following titles:

Title	ISBN	Quantity	Price
The DSA Compulsory Basic Training Manual for Motorcyclists	ISBN 0 11 552013 9	....	£6.99
The Driving Manual	ISBN 0 11 551782 0	....	£12.99
The Motorcycling Manual	ISBN 0 11 551781 2	....	£9.99
Test Yourself Papers for the Driving Theory Test	ISBN 0 11 551984 X	....	£4.99 inc. VAT
Know Your Traffic Signs	ISBN 0 11 551612 3	....	£2.50
The Driving Test	ISBN 0 11 551778 2	....	£4.99
Driving Skills - Theory Test and Beyond CD-ROM Version II	ISBN 0 11 312062 1	....	£24.95 inc. VAT
Making A Pass (Video)	ISBN 0 11 551877 0	....	£14.99

PLEASE COMPLETE IN BLOCK CAPITALS

Name ....

Address ....

....

.... Postcode 992

☐ I enclose a cheque for £.................. payable to: *'The Stationery Office'*

☐ Please charge to my account with The Stationery Office: Account no:

....

☐ Please debit my Access/Visa/Amex/Connect Acc No.

Signature... Expiry date ....

☐ Please tick if you do not wish to receive further details on titles from The Stationery Office.
Prices are correct at time of going to press but may be subject to change without notice. A full listing of terms and conditions of sale can be obtained on request from The Stationery Office Publications Centre, 51 Nine Elms Lane, London SW8 5DR.

The Stationery Office

DS — DRIVING STANDARDS AGENCY

'Safe driving for life'

Printed in The United Kingdom for The Stationery Office J0056101 08/98 C100 63789